45.00

Media Psychology

Media Psychology

Edited by

Gayle Brewer

First published 2011 by
PALGRAVE MACMILLAN

Palgrave Macmillan in the UK is an imprint of Macmillan Publishers Limited,
registered in England, company number 785998, of Houndmills, Basingstoke,
Hampshire RG21 6XS.

Palgrave Macmillan in the US is a division of St Martin's Press LLC,
175 Fifth Avenue, New York, NY 10010.

Palgrave Macmillan is the global academic imprint of the above companies
and has companies and representatives throughout the world.

Palgrave® and Macmillan® are registered trademarks in the United States,
the United Kingdom, Europe and other countries.

ISBN 978–0–230–27920–9

This book is printed on paper suitable for recycling and made from fully
managed and sustained forest sources. Logging, pulping and manufacturing
processes are expected to conform to the environmental regulations of the
country of origin.

A catalogue record for this book is available from the British Library.

A catalog record for this book is available from the Library of Congress.

10 9 8 7 6 5 4 3 2 1
20 19 18 17 16 15 14 13 12 11

Printed in China

In memory, with love from your sweetheart

Contents

List of Figures and Tables

Figures

Tables

Preface

Media psychology represents one of the most diverse and rapidly evolving areas of psychological research. The content of the media and the potential impact of this on the consumer have also captured widespread public interest. Comprehensive texts are available (e.g. *The media & body image*, Wykes & Gunter (2005)) for readers interested in one particular subject area. However, for readers seeking a broader overview of media psychology, it is difficult to find a text that covers a range of subject areas.

Media Psychology has been designed to provide a detailed overview of 11 areas of media psychology. It is intended to support readers enrolled on psychology courses or those with a media focus such as media studies, journalism or communication studies. Prior knowledge of each area or the wider subject area is not assumed, making this text suitable for students at all levels and for readers with a general interest in the field.

Acknowledgments

The development of this book was inspired by the Psychology of the Media course delivered at the University of Central Lancashire, UK. I thank all colleagues and students that have contributed to the program, and the researchers providing such diverse and absorbing content.

I would like to thank the editorial and production team at Palgrave Macmillan (Neha Sharma, Jamie Joseph, Paul Stevens and the team at MPS) for their expertise and support throughout the development of the book and anonymous reviewers for their feedback and encouragement. The book is greatly enhanced by their dedication, knowledge, and understanding.

Supporting material has been provided by a number of organizations and I thank the United States Department of Health and Human Services, The Pew Research Center for the People and the Press and the Pew Internet and American Life Project for the inclusion of these tables and figures.

Finally, this book could not have been completed without the support of family and friends. In particular I would like to thank my parents and my nephews Charlie and Jack for their constant love and encouragement.

Notes on Contributors

Elizabeth Behm-Morawitz is currently an assistant professor in the Department of Communication at the University of Missouri, US. Her research investigates media effects, with a focus on race/ethnicity and gender. Dr Behm-Morawitz has addressed both the negative impacts of media stereotyping and the potential for media to produce pro-social outcomes.

Gayle Brewer is a senior lecturer (School of Psychology) at the University of Central Lancashire, UK. Dr Brewer has published in a wide range of academic journals and her work has attracted widespread public interest. Dr Brewer leads a module entitled "Psychology of the Media."

Jo Bryce is a senior lecturer within the School of Psychology at the University of Central Lancashire, UK. Dr Bryce has published a number of texts in her specialist subject area, including *Understanding Digital Games* in 2005. Dr Bryce is also a member of the Expert Research Panel of the UK Council on Child Internet Safety (UKCCIS).

Jon Cabiria is a media psychologist and founder of Teksylos, a consulting firm that connects the human factor to new and emerging technologies. In addition to his consulting practice, Dr Cabiria holds a faculty position at Walden University, US.

Petya Eckler is an assistant professor of Health Communication at the School of Journalism and Mass Communication at the University of Iowa, US. Dr Eckler's research interests include electronic word of mouth, social media, and international health communication, and she has worked in the areas of tobacco control, cancer, particularly breast cancer, and arthritis.

Barrie Gunter is currently Head of the Department of Media and Communication and Professor of Mass Communications at the University of Leicester, UK. Professor Gunter has written and co-authored over fifty books and produced more than 300 journal papers and articles, book chapters, and other publications. In 2005, he published a textbook entitled *The Media and Body Image*.

Linda Heath is Director of Peace Studies and a professor in the Department of Psychology, Loyola University, Chicago, US. She has conducted a wide range of studies investigating media reporting of crime, fear of crime, and criminal behavior. Professor Heath has also considered the role of relevant psychological constructs, including social comparison and perceived control.

Gregory G. Holyk is currently based at the Department of Politics, Washington and Lee University, US. His primary research interests focus on political science, mass media, and political attitudes. In particular, Professor Holyk has investigated media coverage of political issues, the formation of political attitudes, and attitudes on foreign policy.

James Houran is a partner with HVS Executive Search (New York) and is a recognized expert in workplace, media, and compatibility psychology. He has published over one hundred journal articles and is joint author of the Celebrity Worship Scale. Dr Houran's award-winning research has been featured on a range of international media forums.

Linda K. Kaye is a Ph.D. student at the University of Central Lancashire, UK. Her research interests center on the motivations, experiences, and outcomes of playing video games—more specifically, the influence of "flow" experiences in gaming for positive mood and psychological well-being.

Rense Lange holds a Doctorate in Psychology and a Masters degree in Computer Science from the University of Illinois at Urbana-Champaign. He is the CEO of Integrated Knowledge Systems, specializing in Computer Adaptive Testing (CAT), the application of natural language processing techniques to achievement testing, online dating, and marketing research. As a consultant to the Illinois State Board of Education, Dr Lange oversees the psychometrics of testing over 1.5 million elementary and high school students annually.

Lynn E. McCutcheon has written over 120 research articles and his research has appeared in a range of publications, including the *British Journal of Psychology*, *Journal of Sport Behavior*, and *The Skeptical Inquirer*. Professor McCutcheon is co-author of a book on celebrity worshippers and is the editor of the *North American Journal of Psychology*.

Erin O'Gara is a doctoral candidate at the University of Iowa, US. She received her Master of Science and Bachelor of Science degrees from Iowa State University. Erin's research interests include mass media and domestic violence, injury prevention, and health disparities. She also serves on the executive board of a local domestic violence shelter.

Sarita Robinson is currently based at the School of Psychology, University of Central Lancashire, UK. As well as teaching undergraduate research methods, Dr Robinson actively undertakes research in the fields of health and cognitive psychology.

Nancy Signorielli has authored four books, including *Mass Media Images and Impact on Health* and a *Sourcebook on Children and Television*. She has also published an edited book, two annotated bibliographies, and over ninety research articles. Professor Signorielli is based within the Department of Communication at the University of Delaware, US.

Jennifer Smith Maguire lectures in the Department of Media and Communication, University of Leicester, UK. A sociologist of culture and consumption, Dr Smith Maguire's research examines the cultural production of consumer fields, including the role of cultural intermediaries and lifestyle media in shaping the fitness market and the wine market.

David Ta is a Ph.D. student of Communication at the University of Missouri, US. His research interests are psychophysiology and the media. In particular, he is interested in the impacts media have on cognition and the body.

Gayle Brewer and Sarita Robinson

Introduction

In this modern age, the media is all around us. The influence of the media can reach us in the remotest areas of the world at any time of the night or day. Many forms of media are available—traditional newspapers through to online gaming, radio shows through to tweets on Twitter feeds—all of which can provide us with information, offer us entertainment, or give us a way to communicate. The media can also act as a mirror in which we can examine the best and the worst of human behavior.

Another interesting facet of the media is the rapid development in media technologies, which mean that the way in which we access the media changes. Our experiences of the media are very different in today's world where we can receive information broadcast worldwide on a hand-held device the size of a bar of chocolate compared to a hundred years ago where news was obtainable only via printed newspapers or word of mouth. Today the media plays a central role in our daily lives, and with the constant evolution of media technologies, the psychology of the media is not only an important area of human behavior to study but also a fascinating and dynamic topic.

Defining "media"

So what is media? Giving a universal definition of "media" is problematic to say the least and with the development of new technologies, which blur the line between a personal communication and media, these definitions have become even more difficult. For example, personal letters are considered not to be a form of media as they are a form of communication from one person to another. Television programs, on the other hand, can be considered to be a form of media as television programs broadcast to a large audience. However, with new media technologies the distinction between personal and public communication blurs, as new technologies can facilitate both personal and wider communication. The blurring of the boundaries is most evident in online social networking groups, such as Facebook or Twitter. For example, updating a Facebook status could be considered to be a form of personal communication. However, if your Facebook status is broadcast to many "friends," does it then become a form of media? And if it does become a form of media, where is the tipping point when your Facebook status stops being a personal communication and becomes a form of broadcasting media?

Even descriptions of specific genres within the media are problematic as media forms are evolving so quickly. For example, definitions of video games based on the early primitive versions of this media are wholly inappropriate if used to describe the modern-day version. In the game PONG, a very early version of table tennis developed by Atari, players used a simple input device to control a rectangular paddle, which could be moved only up and down to hit a small 2D ball across the screen. Today's video games are far removed from these early attempts with advanced graphics, which allow greater interactivity either with fellow game players in the same physical location or virtually with online gamers. Further, players of today's version of computerized table tennis can enjoy a more sophisticated experience, which incorporates peripherals, such as a fake table tennis bat, which can be located in 3D space and interpreted into a virtual onscreen presence allowing for a much more realistic experience. This rapid change in what a video game is illustrates how our definition of the media needs to change as rapidly as the technology does.

In order to accommodate the rapid changes in media technologies, we have for the purposes of the current book adopted a broad definition of "media." Media will be defined as any method of communication, other than one to one interactions, which is facilitated by some type of technology, such as printed newspapers through to news podcasts. However, the reader should bear in mind that what people mean by media can change over time and that in some situations different academic disciplines may have more specific definitions.

The development of the psychology of media

Psychology is generally considered to be a young science when compared to other more established disciplines, such as biology or chemistry. As a result of the recent birth of psychology, subgenres within psychology, such as media psychology, have only recently become established. In America, media psychology was officially recognized by the American Psychological Association (APA) in the 1980s. The APA defined media psychology, as being interested in the roles psychologists play in assessing the impact that various aspects of the media, such as radio or television have on human behavior (Fischoff 2005). In the UK, the British Psychological Society (BPS) has not been as quick to separate media psychology from general psychology, but there does now appear to be a growing appreciation within the BPS of the need to specifically monitor the important influence the media has on our lives.

Very early work within the field of media psychology includes that of Hugo Münsterberg who working just after the turn of the last century studied audience reaction to films (Fischoff 2005). More research followed, looking at the increasing impact that new media technologies have on our lives, from the social impact of radio broadcasting (Beuick 1927) to experiences of using social networking sites (Pempek *et al.* 2009). In fact, one of the key driving forces within the psychology of the media is to consider the negative influence that certain types of media can have on human behavior.

An early example of the interest taken in how the media can influence human behavior comes from the emergence of horror comics in the 1940s and 1950s, such as *Eerie* or *Tales from the Crypt*. Comics campaign council suggested horror comics were "symptoms of a moral and spiritual sickness which needs urgent treatment" and their campaign eventually led to the Children and Young Persons (Harmful Publications) Act of 1955. Commentary at the time observed the "crusade has left in its wake the smoldering remains of fires on which comics have been burned" (Zorbough 1949: 1).

Although passionate debates took place about the potential impact that exposure to graphic images of aggressive action heroes may have on young readers, little psychological research was undertaken. Today studies, such as Bushman and Huesmann (2006), help present a more scientific and balanced view of the impact of the media and fight against some of the baseless moral panics that have taken place against violent movies or explicit song lyrics. Therefore, media psychology needs to help society avoid moral panics and so stop the media acting as a scapegoat for society's ills. For example, alcohol consumption in young people has been blamed on the positive portrayal of drinking by glamorous movie stars in popular films. Although there is good evidence to suggest that the media influences children's alcohol use, psychological research helps us to keep the media's impact in perspective. Other factors such as alcohol use by a person's peer group are important, but we don't ban children from socializing.

Psychological research on the effects of the media should allow us to have a rational discussion on the topic and so reach a more informed decision. One example of how recent psychological research has helped make a rational decision concerns the studies on the effects of junk food advertising on children's eating patterns. In 2007, the UK banned junk food advertising from any television program aimed at the under 12s. The decision to ban junk food adverting to children was more a rational decision based on solid psychological research (see Dixon *et al.* 2007) and less of a knee-jerk reaction to an unsupported moral campaign.

As well as protecting us from the negative effects of the media, media psychology can also highlight how the media can be used for positive change. Greitemeyer's (2011) research, for instance, suggested that listening to pro-social song lyrics such as Help by the Beatles or Heal the World by Michael Jackson could reduce aggression. So, in conclusion, media psychology is an important tool by which we can monitor both the positive and negative impact that the media can have on individuals, groups within society, and on society as a whole. By keeping abreast of the rapid changes in media technologies and investigating the media's influence on every aspect of our lives, from the impact of advertising to the effects of mobile phone use on children's language development, we can ensure that we protect the vulnerable from the negative effects of the media, while society as a whole benefits from the positive aspects.

The progression of media psychology research

Media psychologists have to keep pace with the rapid developments in media technologies and the more prevalent use of these media in everyday life. New technologies, such as mobile phones and tablet computers, mean that the media can be accessed more immediately. And new methods of communication, such as Twitter or social networking sites, mean that today's media exposure is longer, more intense, and more pervasive than in the past. For example, one hundred years ago, the information about a disaster, such as the sinking of the Titanic, could take days to arrive and media coverage would be limited to newspaper reports up to a week or more after the event. Since then changes in communication technologies, such as the development of the Internet and satellite television, mean that live reporting of disaster events, such as the attack on the World Trade Center on Sept 11th 2001, can unfold in real time on our screens.

Further, advances in mobile phone technologies mean that video footage of major incidents, such as the 7/7 bombings on the London Underground, can be uploaded within minutes of them occurring. The developments in these new technologies coupled with more intensive media coverage on 24-hour news channels mean that people today are exposed to "disaster marathons," which include hours or days of powerful media coverage of major events, which was not possible even thirty years ago.

In addition to the impact that the information presented via the media has on people, media psychologists are also interested in the influence of the method of presentation used. Marshall McLuhan noted to in the 1960s that "[t]he medium is the message," suggesting that the way in which the message is communicated, for example, by radio or by television can have a direct impact on the way in which the message is interpreted by the recipient (McLuhan 1964). So as media technologies change rapidly, the way in which the media is experienced also changes at a rapid pace. Even just the change in the cost of media technologies can change how they are experienced by people. For example, in the 1950s and 1960s the cost of a television set would mean that families would generally have one main set, which would be viewed by the family sitting together. In today's modern world, the cost of a television set has reduced and so families can afford to have several sets in their homes. This increase in television ownership by a family means that where once families enjoyed social time watching a common program, today television programs are likely to be viewed in isolation with families watching a diverse array of programs.

As media technologies develop and our experiences with the media change the way in which we perceive, the information we receive via the media also changes. Consider the case of the 1938 broadcast of the Orson Welles' dramatization of the H. G. Wells' novel *War of the Worlds*. The radio play recounts details of an alien invasion as if it was taking place and reports the story line via a number of very believable news broadcasts. Many listeners to the show took the fictional news reports as genuine and some families actually started to flee from the area. As panicked listeners started to phone local police stations, the radio station bosses were forced to issue a statement to reassure listeners that they had been listening to a fictional play and that the alien invasion was not real. In today's world of instant news and multiple sources of information, it is difficult to imagine a society in which radio was such a trusted form of information that people were taken in by Orson Welles' deception.

Preview

Media Psychology is not a simple historical overview of general research that involves the media. Instead, we have included an in-depth exploration of our current understanding of several important subject areas within this subgenre of psychology. Unlike other areas of psychology that tend to focus on one theoretical or methodological approach (e.g. behaviorism) or on an area of psychological practice (such as clinical psychology), this book encompasses a wide range of theoretical and methodological approaches. In fact, unlike most areas of psychology, media psychology is unique in that it has been shaped by researchers outside the field of psychology. Academics within a wide array of disciplines, such as Journalism, Advertising, Political Science, Public Relations, Media and Communication Science have contributed to our knowledge of how the media impacts on our lives. To reflect the large number of sources that can inform our understanding of media psychology, this book has not been restricted to research conducted by psychologists. Therefore, this book contains a diverse range of material within each chapter, which has been written by a leading academic selected for their knowledge of the specific subject area.

Each chapter should therefore give the readers a good insight into the diverse subject areas covered in media psychology. In addition, each chapter contains a range of references and/or suggested further reading for those wishing to explore the subject in further detail. Of course, once you have obtained a basic knowledge of the topic covered in the book, additional reading of relevant journals such as *American Journal of Media Psychology, Communication Research, International Journal of Advertising, Journal of Broadcasting and Electronic Media* and *Media Psychology* is also recommended.

The book is divided into three sections. The first explores the use of media to persuade the consumer (advertising and health communication) and the potential influence of particular media content (media violence, body image, and eating behavior). The second section considers engagement and interaction with different elements of the media (Internet and interaction, computer games, and celebrity and parasocial relationships). The third section describes media representations (portrayal of crime, gender stereotypes, racial and ethnic stereotyping, and politics). For readers inspired to undertake their own research into the field of media psychology, the final chapter outlines research methodologies, which have been used in media research.

In conclusion, with the media having a more prevalent place in our lives the need to understand and monitor its impact grows. We hope that you find the following chapters give you a good foundation in this new and dynamic area of psychology and inspire you to undertake research of your own!

PART
I

Persuasion and Influence

Media Violence 1

The media often raise the subject of media violence when particularly violent or distinctive crimes are committed. Recent cases attracting attention include the murder of James Bulger, the Columbine High School Killings, and the Hi-Fi murders. In 1993, two children (Robert Thompson and Jon Venables) murdered two-year-old James Bulger in Liverpool, England. As the prosecution and trial of Thompson and Venables progressed, a number of explanations of their crime were publicly debated as people found it difficult to believe that the murder had been committed by perpetrators that were just ten years old at the time of the crime. In the trial, Justice Morland implied that "exposure to violent videos" could partially explain their violent behavior. This comment captured media and public interest, with one film in particular (*Child's Play 3*) often highlighted. In fact the case is often cited as "evidence" that media violence leads to real-life aggression. Despite the widespread acceptance of this explanation, there was no mention of media violence at the trial of Thompson and Venables, no evidence that either Thompson or Venables had ever viewed *Child's Play 3* and police consistently denied the association between the crime and media violence (Barker 1997).

In 1999, two adolescent boys (Eric Harris and Dylan Klebold) entered the Columbine High School (Colorado, US). Harris and Klebold killed twelve students and one teacher before shooting themselves. In the aftermath of the killings, a number of movies, songs, and video games that interested the boys were discussed. Links between the killings and the media were often tenuous; for example, reminiscent of the main character in a film, the boys wore long trench coats during the killing, but the general perception that media violence contributed to the killings continued.

The willingness of the media to relate media violence to real-life aggression may seem contradictory, but largely reflects the distinctions that exist between each media type. For example, it is typically the print or television news and news-based programs (such as documentaries) that criticize television programs and movies for their graphic content. Therefore, while "media" may include song lyrics, newspapers, music videos, etc., the majority of the research (and this chapter) focuses on the violence featured in television and movies. It is also argued that the media violence debate is encouraged by policy makers who view the classification and censorship of violent media as preferable to a wider debate addressing other factors, which may impact on the level of violent crime such as social deprivation, isolation, and intimidation.

For many people, the "copycat" elements of a crime in which the perpetrator recreates acts of media violence, form the most persuasive evidence that media violence causes real-life aggression. For example, during the "Hi-Fi murders" committed in 1974 (Utah, US), the perpetrators (William Andrews and Pierre Dale Selby) forced their hostages to drink Drano (a corrosive drain-cleaning fluid). It is argued that the men chose this method after watching the film *Magnum Force* in which a prostitute is forced to drink the fluid. The imitation of specific scenes understandably draws attention to the relationship between media violence and real-life aggression. However, focusing on the imitation of specific events confuses the likelihood that a person will behave aggressively and the tendency to channel this aggression into a particular type of violent behavior. It could be argued that individuals that are likely to act aggressively (for whatever reasons) repeat particular acts when "inspired" by the media, but the media is not responsible for the aggression per se. As explained by a character in the movie *Scream*, "Movies don't create psychos. Movies make psychos more creative."

This chapter will explore the subject of media violence using a scientific approach. In particular the chapter will describe the extent to which the media contains violence, the evidence both for and against a relationship between media violence and real-life aggression, dominant psychological theories, and two specific forms of media violence that have attracted recent attention.

Media content

Estimates of average exposure to television vary; however, it is widely accepted that people living in Western cultures watch a considerable amount of television. According to Bushman and Anderson (2001), children watch approximately forty hours of television per week, and as a consequence, people have spent nine years watching television by the age of sixty-five (Bushman & Huesmann 2001).

Assessing the level of violence contained within television programs and movies is more problematic than estimating overall media exposure.

Definitions of violence vary between researchers and the content analyses that attempt to report the frequency and level of violence. At the center of most definitions of violence, however, is "the overt expression of physical force" (Signorielli, Gerbner, & Morgan 1995: 280). Using definitions of this type, research indicates that 60% of television programs contain violence (Wilson *et al.* 1997). Therefore most viewers spend a substantial amount of time watching television programs and movies that contain physical violence. Of course, these figures may underestimate the level of violence contained. For example, a character's description of a violent act or the stalking of a victim does not meet the criteria for "physical force" exerted on someone.

Content analyses that record the frequency of violent acts also fail to describe the context in which the violence occurs. For example, children's television programs (and cartoons in particular) contain frequent acts of violence, although many parents would not classify these as violent, perhaps because the violence is unrealistic and includes humor (King 2000; Potter & Warren 1998). In addition, many viewers believe that informative programs such as news and documentaries should be allowed to portray violent acts and should not be compared to other genres that do so for entertainment. Therefore, a relatively superficial list of the number of "violent acts" may ignore a range of issues (e.g. whether the pain of the victim is emphasized) that may influence the way in which the viewer interprets the violence.

The debate surrounding media violence has important implications for all those exposed to potentially harmful media content. The chapter will therefore discuss these issues without reference to a specific culture or country of origin unless these are of particular relevance. The reader should bear in mind, however, that cross-cultural differences may impact on both the type of media that a person is exposed to and the extent to which consumers or policy makers wish to act on research findings. For example, American culture places considerable importance on free speech, which has important implications for the potential censorship of media content.

The scientific evidence

Researchers, policy makers, and the general public have debated the effects of media violence for decades. In response to these concerns and the need to increase understanding, a range of research studies has been conducted investigating the subject in a controlled and scientific way. The current section provides a brief overview of the scientific evidence in this area. Most studies can be categorized as experimental, cross-sectional (including correlational), and longitudinal design (see Chapter 12 for an in-depth description of these approaches and the advantages and disadvantages of each method). Of course, a number of factors may increase the likelihood of aggressive behavior and even researchers that believe media violence is harmful view this influence in the context of multiple causes of aggression. Specifically, the researchers argue that viewing media violence increases the likelihood of a person behaving aggressively but does not automatically lead to aggression.

Experimental evidence

Experimental studies allow the researcher to test cause-and-effect relationships while controlling for a number of other influential variables. The experiments conducted in a laboratory typically present either violent or nonviolent media (usually television programs or movie scenes) to participants. After exposure, participants are given the opportunity to behave in an aggressive way (e.g. competing with another person or believing that they are punishing another person by reducing payment of a reward, etc.). The aggressive behavior of those that have watched the violent scenes can then be compared to the behavior of participants in the nonviolent group. Therefore, most of the experimental research focuses on the short-term effects of media violence. As this subject and methodology has developed, researchers have used increasingly sophisticated approaches that investigate the effects of different media or content types (e.g. cartoons versus news) and the factors that may exacerbate or limit the effects of media violence.

Overall, the experimental evidence suggests that exposure to violent media does increase the incidence of aggressive behavior, although there is less evidence for an increase in criminal violence (Savage 2004). For example, Coyne *et al.* (2008) asked women to view movie scenes featuring either physical violence, nonphysical aggression (see section on *Indirect aggression* for more information), or an equally exciting scene that did not include physical or verbal aggression. Participants were then given an opportunity to administer loud noises to a researcher who had been behaving antagonistically and to provide feedback about the researcher. Women who had watched the scenes featuring either physical or nonphysical aggression behaved more aggressively toward the researcher than those watching the exciting but nonviolent scene. Similar results have been obtained using a range of violent content (e.g. cartoons and dramas) and participant groups (e.g. young children, adolescents, and adults).

Of course, research does not always suggest that exposure to media violence is harmful. Kiewitz and Weaver (2001) exposed men and women to either a violent or nonviolent movie. Each participant was then asked to respond to four written scenarios describing violent conflicts such as an incidence of domestic violence. Participants provided a range of responses including the extent to which they felt that the victim suffered or that the aggressors' actions were justified. In contrast to much of the media violence research, participants that had watched the nonviolent movie were more callous and hostile than those exposed to the movie violence.

One of the most common criticisms of experimental research is that laboratory measures of aggression provide little information about aggression in real life. In particular, popular measures of aggression (such as pressing a button to deliver an electronic shock or punishing a person by giving them poor feedback) have little in common with physically attacking another person. In addition, the experimenter's encouragement or permission to deliver some form of aggression and the fact that participants realize that the victim cannot retaliate do not reflect normal societal responses to aggressive behavior and may in fact encourage the participant to act aggressively.

To address some of these criticisms, researchers have also reported the results of "natural experiments" in which they monitor the effects of real-life changes. For example, Joy, Kimball, and Zabrack (1986) compared Canadian towns that were either already exposed to one (Unitel) or multiple (Multitel) television stations to a town (Notel) as it first received television. Greater increases in aggression occurred in the Notel community after the introduction of television than in towns that were already exposed. Of course, exposure to media violence could not explain why the three towns experienced similar levels of aggression before television made headway into the Notel community.

Centerwall (1989) also investigated the introduction of television by comparing homicide rates in Canada, the United States, and South Africa. The 90% increase in deaths by homicide that occurred in the United States and Canada ten to fifteen years after the advent of television was emphasized by researchers. It was argued that a similar increase in homicide fatalities did not occur in South Africa because the government delayed the introduction of television. The researcher has made a number of particularly bold statements based on this research and the results are widely cited in the academic literature.

In particular, Centerwall (1989) stated that "exposure to television is etiologically related to approximately one half of the homicides committed in the United States, or approximately 10,000 homicides annually ... [E]xposure to television is also etiologically related to a major proportion—perhaps one half—of rapes, assaults, and other forms of interpersonal violence in the United States" (651). Relatively little information is provided by the researchers about the way in which other variables were controlled, however, and there are a number of factors (other than the introduction of television) that may have affected crime levels during this time. Overall it is important to note that the relationship between media exposure and behavior is complex and the advent of television may impact on society in a number of ways (such as increased materialism) which in turn could influence crime rates.

Cross-sectional evidence

Research adopting a cross-sectional (including correlational) design measures the extent to which individuals are exposed to violent media and a form of aggression in the natural environment. Importantly, these studies can provide more realistic (or ecologically valid) results. These studies cannot establish a cause-and-effect relationship (that is more appropriately established with experimental research) but can suggest that media violence is associated with "real-life" aggression. Cross-sectional surveys have consistently shown that exposure to violent television and movies are related to aggression. Krahé and Möller (2011) recruited adolescents from high schools in Germany. All participants were asked to report the frequency with which they were exposed to movies, television programs, and video games. Each genre was rated for violent content by media experts. Measures of adolescents' real-life aggression included the participants' acceptance of aggression in a hypothetical scenario and ratings provided by their teacher. Exposure to media violence predicted the ratings of aggression provided by teachers.

Although this type of research typically produces a weaker association than the experimental evidence, similar results have been obtained with both adults and children, reinforcing the findings of the experimental research. Importantly, cross-sectional research has considered the relationship between media exposure and aggression in a range of audiences in a number of cultures. One of the most rigorous cross-sectional studies (which controlled for a number of potentially important variables) was conducted by Messner (1986). In contrast to much of the research in this area, the study indicated that exposure to violent television was negatively (and significantly) related to rates of violent crime. It could be suggested therefore that watching television (including violent programs) that encourages a person to stay at home actually decreases opportunities to interact with deviant peers or engage in criminal behavior in the wider community.

Longitudinal evidence

The longitudinal method in which participants are assessed at two (or more) time points allows the researcher to both assess real-life aggression and establish a cause-and-effect relationship. Therefore, the longitudinal approach directly addresses public concerns that long-term exposure to media violence leads to real-life aggression. While this method has a number of advantages, a much greater investment by the researchers (compared to experimental and cross-sectional designs) is needed to obtain longitudinal data and so relatively few longitudinal studies have been conducted.

One example of longitudinal research provided by Lefkowitz *et al.* (1977) found that the preference for violent media at age eight predicts aggression at age nineteen. Consistent with these findings, Huesmann (1986) reported that early television preferences predict the number and seriousness of convictions at age thirty and Johnson *et al.* (2002) found a higher number of aggressive acts, assaults, and robberies among adults who watched a greater amount of television during adolescence. Overall, researchers collecting longitudinal research have concluded that "If a child's observation of media violence promotes the learning of aggressive habits, it can have harmful lifelong consequences" (Huesmann 1986: 129). Longitudinal research has also found that while exposure to violent media as a child is related to later aggression, aggression during childhood does not predict if the individual will actively seek violent media later on. Therefore, the relation between exposure to media violence and real-life aggression cannot be explained by aggressive individuals seeking out violent programs. This addresses one major limitation of cross-sectional evidence and highlights the value of using a range of methodological approaches (a technique commonly known as triangulation).

Evaluation, meta-analysis, and reports

No single study or approach can provide a full and accurate description of the relationship between media violence and aggression. However, consistent results based on multiple studies that use a range of methodological approaches provide the "big picture" and increase confidence in the researcher's conclusion. Therefore, researchers attempting to convince policy makers or the wider general public that media violence causes aggression typically cite a number of studies. This inclusive approach addresses the weaknesses of any one research design and provides greater reliability. Results generated in a number of countries also increase the reliability of results and suggest that effects are not limited to one society or culture (Huesmann & Eron 1986).

In addition to individual studies (of all designs), a number of meta-analyses have been conducted. Meta-analyses statistically integrate a number of studies, allowing the researcher to reach a more reliable conclusion and to establish an overall effect size (a measure of the size of the relationship).

Importantly, these analyses can also make comparisons between different methodological approaches or different types of aggression. In this way, researchers can develop a more thorough overview of the research area. Of course, the utility of the meta-analysis depends on the rigor of the studies that are included within it. Overall, meta-analyses have concluded that exposure to violent media increases the level of aggressive and antisocial behavior.

The Paik and Comstock (1994) meta-analysis focused on research published between 1957 and 1990 that explored the impact of violent television and movies. The researchers found that for experiments investigating the effect of exposure on physical violence there was an overall effect size of 0.32. For longitudinal and cross-sectional research, there was a weaker average relationship of 0.19. It has been argued that the media violence effect sizes are "small and lack practical significance" (Ferguson 2002: 447). The effect sizes identified by most meta-analyses are, however, larger than many public health threats. For example, the effect size typically reported is greater than for asbestos and cancer or second-hand smoke and cancer (Bushman & Huesmann 2001) and many researchers argue that the subject of media violence should be afforded the same attention. The extent to which the effect size reported is artificially inflated by poor measures of aggression or publication bias (where research that does not find an effect is not reported) remains unclear, but has been highlighted by researchers in the field (Ferguson & Kilburn 2009).

A number of government agencies have reviewed research in this area. These reviews typically reinforce the conclusion that violent content increases aggression and violent behavior. For example, the US Surgeon General testified to Congress that "the overwhelming consensus and the unanimous Scientific Advisory Committee's report indicates that televised violence, indeed does have an adverse effect on certain members of our society" (Steinfeld 1972: 26). The extent to which politicians believe that media content should be censored to address these concerns varies widely and individual politicians often base their conclusions on public opinion rather than the research evidence. The measures advocated by some politicians often appear excessive or unrealistic, for example, The Children's Defense Act advocated by Representative Henry Hyde (Reid 1999) would have made exposing individuals under the age of seventeen to sexual or violent media a federal felony that could result in a jail sentence.

Nongovernment agencies have also explored this area, reaching similar conclusions. Holding a Congressional Public Health Summit, six medical and public health organizations (including the American Psychological Association and American Medical Association) released a Joint Statement on the Impact of Entertainment Violence on Children, concluding that research refers "overwhelmingly to a causal connection between media violence and aggressive behavior in some children" (Joint Statement 2000: 1). These reviews add considerable weight to the claim that exposure to media violence increases aggression in some consumers.

Important factors

A number of factors associated with the characteristics of the media violence or the individual viewer may strengthen or weaken the impact of media violence. While there is substantial evidence outlining the importance of some factors, others are the product of public opinion rather than established theory or research evidence.

Consequences

The consequences of the violence (both in terms of the suffering by the victim and the punishment or rewards received by the perpetrator) are important. Media that emphasizes the pain and suffering of the victim may be difficult for viewers to ignore or to trivialize. Aggression is less likely to follow exposure to media violence when the victim's pain and suffering are emphasized (Comstock 1985). The importance of this finding should be considered in the context of typical media content. In most cases of media violence, no physical or emotional outcomes for the victim are featured (Lichter & Amundson 1994).

Violent acts that are rewarded (or that do not have any discernable consequences) are more frequently imitated than violence that is punished. Again this finding should be considered in the context of the television content; less than 20% of aggressors featured on television are punished for their behavior (Wilson *et al.* 1997) and most media violence is in fact rewarded (Groebel 1998). The importance of reward and punishment is well established by the scientific evidence, particularly by Bandura and the Social Learning Theory (discussed later in the chapter).

Realism and context

Scenes that contain realistic or graphic violence are more often categorized as violent, with viewers often ignoring other forms of television violence. In particular, media violence that contains some element of humor (e.g. cartoons or slapstick comedy) may signal to the audience that the violence is not serious and that the viewer should not be concerned. Another form of realism—the extent to which the violence featured does or could exist in real life—is also important. According to Bandura (1965), people are more likely to attend to, recall, and imitate media violence that they believe could exist in real life, although there is some evidence that "cartoonish" violence has an impact similar to more realistic or graphic content (Anderson, Gentile, & Buckley 2007).

Television programs often imply that a character's violent behavior is justified, for example, when James Bond punishes the "bad guys" for the greater good. However, "justified" violence is more likely to promote aggressive responses than other violence (Hogben 1998). In part, this may reflect the viewers' willingness to identify with a character that is portrayed in a positive way (e.g. as a hero) and to develop similar traits such as charisma or popularity with the opposite sex. There are a number of theoretical reasons (e.g. Scripts Theory discussed later in the chapter) to believe that this type of identification encourages the viewer to imitate the actor's behavior.

Characteristics of the viewer

Although media violence may increase aggression in any age, gender, or social group, some individuals may be more susceptible than others to these effects. In particular, researchers have suggested that young children are most susceptible to media violence and a number of studies have reported a link between exposure to media violence and children's aggression (Anderson et al. 2003; Gentile 2003). Children may be more likely to display real-life aggression and feel fear or anxiety than other viewers (Valkenburg, Cantor, & Peeters 2000). In part, this reflects the fact that young children find it difficult to distinguish between fantasy and reality, believing all incidences of media violence to be realistic. It is of course difficult for researchers to reliably assess differences between viewers' separate age groups. The violent programs typically viewed by adult participants could not be shown to children and the types of aggression displayed by adults and children would be expected to differ.

In part, individual differences (e.g. personality) may help to explain the way in which different people interpret and react to the same media content (Aluja-Fabregat 2000). For example, people who are generally aggressive are more likely to behave aggressively after watching media violence than people who are generally nonaggressive (Kiewitz & Weaver 2001). Also highlighting the importance of interpretation rather than passive acceptance, adult reactions to media violence or the commentary that they provide may limit the effects of media violence on children (Cantor & Wilson 2003). Specifically, negative comments appear to reduce children's aggression following media violence whereas positive or neutral comments (which may be interpreted by the child as acceptance) result in higher levels of aggression.

Theories of media violence

A range of theories have been proposed that help the researcher to understand, explain, and predict the relationship between media violence and aggression. The current section outlines some of the most frequently discussed theories of media violence, including Social Learning, Scripts, Cultivation, and Desensitization. While some theories (e.g. Social Learning Theory) provide a coherent explanation of both the short- and long-term effects of media violence, other theories are more appropriately suited to either the short-term or long-term effects (e.g. Cultivation Theory).

Social Learning Theory

The dominant theory within this subject area, Social Learning Theory, uses the principles of learning to explain the impact of media violence. Aggression may be learned through both direct and indirect experience. Direct learning depends on the consequences of an aggressive act, for example, a child that uses aggression to steal another child's toy is more likely to repeat the behavior if they are rewarded (e.g. if they obtain the toy) than when punished. Indirect experience, which includes the observation and imitation of aggressive behavior, forms the basis of Social Learning Theory. While much of the research in this area involves young children, it should be noted that observation and imitation remain important throughout childhood, adolescence, and adulthood.

The Social Learning Theory argues that observation of on-screen characters (and not just real-life family members or peers) are influential and provide models to be imitated by the viewer. In fact, even young children have been shown to imitate televised models (Melzoff 1988). Therefore, aggressive behavior can be learned from watching characters behave violently on television. The theory provides an explanation for both short- and long-term media violence effects. Short-term effects occur when the viewer mimics the behavior displayed on screen and the habitual behavior, which results from regular observation and imitation, accounts for long-term effects. According to the Social Learning Theory, the viewer may not intend to learn behavior in this way and may not actually be aware of much of the observational learning that takes place.

The Bobo doll experiments conducted by Bandura, Ross, and Ross (1963) are some of the most famous psychological studies ever conducted and form the basis of all social learning research in this area. In brief, the researchers conducted a series of studies, in which they showed children a televised scene featuring an adult behaving violently toward a Bobo doll (a large inflatable skittle-shaped doll). The children who had viewed the violent scene acted more aggressively. The Bobo doll studies are outlined in detail in the *Subject in focus* section.

Through observation, important information about the effects of the violence and whether it is an appropriate behavior to imitate are relayed to the audience. Therefore, it is not just the level of violence portrayed in the media that is problematic, but also the way in which it is depicted. The rewards associated with the violent behavior such as the increased status or attractiveness of the perpetrator increase the likelihood of imitation (Groebel 2001).

Scripts Theory

Compared to other explanations, Scripts Theory places a greater emphasis on the cognitive processes influenced by the violent media. The theory states that people hold a wide range of cognitive scripts, which guide their behavior. Existing scripts are stored in memory, but can continue to develop as the person observes new behaviors and expands their range of experience. For example, the script that I currently hold for Christmas (which now includes credit card bills and preparation for the new semester) has changed considerably from the script I held as a child (which was dominated by Santa, toys, and vast quantities of chocolate).

Huesmann and Eron (1986) have argued that television can create new scripts and reinforce existing scripts. Therefore, the media impacts on both the development and maintenance of aggressive behavior. In real life, a person selects a script that resembles their situation and assumes an appropriate role within that script to guide their actions. In this way the development of violent scripts can lead to real-life aggression. For example, repeated exposure to on-screen domestic violence may encourage the script that an argument with a partner involves physical violence. When the viewer next argues with their partner, the violent script increases the likelihood that he/she will assume that role and behave aggressively toward their partner.

Of course, the extent to which an individual's future behavior is guided by the script depends on a range of factors, including the similarity of their real-life situation to the media scenario and script. For example, a grocery store owner may be more likely to resist during an armed robbery if they have observed an armed robbery on screen that took place in a grocery store rather than in a bank. Specific triggers and cues may also be important. People are more likely to behave aggressively toward someone that resembles the victim featured in the violent program, even when the resemblance is as superficial as a name (Berkowitz & Geen 1967). Those playing an aggressive video game are also more likely to behave aggressively when using a personalized character (Fischer, Kastenmuller, & Greitemeyer 2010). Therefore, the similarity of both the aggressor and the victim may be important.

Cultivation and fear

Cultivation Theory highlights the fear and anxiety associated with media violence rather than real-life aggression. This is an important subject area that has been ignored by much of the existing research. The immediate impact of media exposure may be small, although most adults can recall being frightened as a child by a television program or movie that affected them for years (Cantor 2000; Hoekstra, Harris, & Helmick 1999). It is argued that the unrealistically frequent violent behavior portrayed by the media can influence the way in which viewers perceive their own environment, and it is the cumulative effect of this exposure that is harmful. Specifically, media violence encourages the audience to believe that the world is a mean, violent, and dangerous place (see Chapter 8 for a more in-depth discussion on this subject). The greater the exposure to the message, the more likely the individual is to accept it.

The skewed perception of the real world that develops is referred to as a "mediated reality" (Wilcox *et al.* 2003: 214). Highlighting the extent to which violent crime is depicted on television and the contrast with actual crime, Medved (1995) states "about 350 characters appear each night on prime-time TV, but studies show an average of seven of these people are murdered every night. If this rate applied in reality, then in just 50 days everyone in the United States would be killed and the last left could turn off the TV" (156–157). With frequent exposure to violent media, it is argued that viewers become fearful of their own environment. In particular, people exposed to violent content are more likely to overestimate the actual level of crime, fear victimization, and mistrust others (Gerbner & Gross 1980). Both children and adults who watch a lot of television are more fearful than light viewers (Dominick 1990).

Cultivation Theory is arguably more inclusive than other theories, as it considers the relative importance of a wide range of material (e.g. news programs and documentaries) rather than only the most graphic fictional violence that many researchers focus on. There is some evidence to support this inclusive approach, as news programs are more salient than other content (Newhagen 1998) and children are more fearful after viewing media violence if it is described as news rather than fiction (Walma van der Molen & Bushman 2008).

The majority of research reported by Cultivation theorists is cross-sectional, and it could be argued that rather than exposure to media violence leading to fear, fearful people watch a greater amount of television, perhaps because they are less likely to leave their home or because they use the media to monitor the outside world. Cultivation Theory has also been criticized for oversimplifying a complex subject area, a criticism that in many respects applies to most theories of media violence.

Desensitization

There is evidence to suggest that violence becomes less upsetting and arousing over time, a process referred to as desensitization. The desensitization and the desire for excitement leads the viewer to select more violent content and increases exposure to graphic material. In a similar way, exposure to media violence also causes the individual to become desensitized to real-life aggression and believe it to be an acceptable form of behavior.

This desensitization removes the barriers (i.e. distress) that typically prevent a person from behaving aggressively and reduces sympathy toward those that are victimized. For example, Drabman and Thomas (1974) found that children who had been exposed to media violence were less likely to tell an adult when a fight occurred, suggesting greater tolerance of aggression. Carnagey, Anderson and Bushman (2007) also found that exposure to media violence reduces arousal after exposure to real-life violence and the amount of help offered to victims. Importantly, people taking part in research are arguably already desensitized to media violence through regular long-term exposure. Investigating the short-term effects of media exposure may therefore underestimate these effects.

Specific content types

Most media violence research has adopted a traditional concept of violence, which involves explicit physical force. As our understanding of aggression has developed, researchers have expanded the scope of media violence research. Two areas of increased interest (indirect aggression and violent pornography) are discussed next. It should be noted that video-game violence has also attracted widespread interest, particularly as the games themselves become increasingly interactive and contain more realistic forms of violence. As Chapter 6 focuses solely on the genre of computer and video games, this issue will be discussed in more detail there.

Indirect aggression

Physical violence (e.g. hitting or kicking) or variables associated with physical violence (e.g. aggressive thoughts and feelings) dominate media violence research. In recent years, however, a number of researchers have sought to expand the definition of aggression. In particular, behaviors that involve verbal abuse and attempts to disrupt social or romantic relationships have attracted attention. In part, researchers' interest in these behaviors reflects a growing understanding of the harm caused by this type of aggression and the extent to which this type of aggression occurs.

Researchers have used a number of terms to describe this type of aggression and overall there are few differences between them. The most frequently used terms are indirect aggression (e.g. Lagerspetz, Bjorkqvist, & Peltonen 1988), social aggression (e.g. Galen & Underwood 1997), and relational aggression (e.g. Crick & Grotpeter 1995). The differences between these concepts largely reflect the emphasis on direct (threatening to terminate a relationship) or indirect (spreading rumors about an individual) methods. Here, the term "indirect aggression" (first investigated by Buss 1961 and extended by Lagerspetz, Bjorkqvist, & Peltonen 1988) will be used.

"Indirect aggression" describes a range of harmful behaviors such as gossiping and spreading rumors (verbal) or intentionally destroying a person's property without the owner's knowledge (physical). Understanding the effects of viewing indirect aggression within the media is particularly important given the fact that television and movie-rating systems do not usually consider this type of behavior when assessing violent content.

Although few studies have been conducted in this area, research suggests that verbal and indirect aggression occurs regularly on programs that are popular with adolescents and in fact occurs more frequently than direct aggression (Feshbach 2005). For example, indirect aggression occurs in 92% of programs popular with British adolescents, with acts of indirect aggression occurring 9.3 times per hour on average (Coyne & Archer 2004). Compared to physical aggression, there is relatively little research describing the potential impact of watching indirect aggression on the viewer.

Recent research finds that viewing indirect aggression is related to increased indirect aggression (Coyne & Archer 2005), providing important parallels with physical aggression and highlighting the need for further research in this area. In addition, it appears that viewing relational media aggression (focusing on the disruption caused to personal relationships) increases both physical and relational aggression (Coyne et al. 2008). These findings have a number of implications for the classification of media content as violent or nonviolent, ratings systems, and the direction and scope of future research (Linder & Gentile 2009).

Violent pornography

A substantial amount of media content could be described as sexually explicit. From the burlesque of Gypsy Rose Lee to hardcore pornography, sexually explicit media have received consistent criticism. In particular, the manner in which material is classified as pornographic and the availability of this material has prompted widespread debate. Pornography is defined here as material developed, selected, and consumed in order to sexually arouse the viewer, rather than material designed to educate or created as artistic expression. The extent to which the term "pornography" should be limited to media whose sole function is to sexually arouse the audience or extended to popular films that contain a degree of sexually arousing material remains controversial. Traditional concerns have centered on the manner in which sexually explicit material portrays women and may "corrupt" society. For example, a number of anti-pornography feminists (Dworkin & MacKinnon 1988) view pornography as a form of exploitation that objectifies and degrades women.

Of particular interest to those working in the area of media violence, it has been suggested that exposure to violent pornography has a number of harmful effects. The term "violent pornography" is perhaps misleading here, as at first glance the term implies a form of hardcore pornography accessed only by those seeking violent material. The inclusion of material featuring physical or verbal sexual coercion of a victim is not, however, uncommon in mainstream television and movies, and exposure to violent pornography is relatively widespread. Demare, Lips, and Briere (1993) reported that 86% of the sampled men had viewed pornography in the previous month; 25% had viewed pornography featuring a rape, and 36% of the men had viewed pornography containing forced sex.

A meta-analysis conducted by Oddone-Paolucci, Genuis, and Violato (2000) reported effects of pornography on sexual deviancy, sexual perpetration, attitudes toward intimate relationships, and belief in rape myths. These myths include a range of beliefs such as "the victim is partly responsible for the rape" and "the rape could be prevented if the victim really wished to resist." Supporting these findings, studies suggest that viewing pornography is related to attitudes to rape victims (Linz 1988) and the sentences given to rapists during mock trials (Zillmann & Bryant 1984).

A number of high-profile crimes have raised awareness of this issue among the general public. For example, Ted Bundy (born Theodore Robert Cowell) provided an interview before his execution in which he claimed that violent pornography influenced his violent behavior, which resulted in over thirty murders. Bundy stated that "The most damaging kind of pornography—and I'm talking from hard, real, personal experience—is that that involves violence and sexual violence. The wedding of those two forces—as I know only too well—brings about behavior that is too terrible to describe." Although Bundy's claims are often dismissed (by those believing that Bundy was simply trying to reduce his own culpability), this association has been widely publicized by those wishing to restrict or eliminate pornography (http://www.pureintimacy.org/piArticles/A000000433.cfm).

Demonstrating the complexity of this issue, Mundorf *et al.* (2007) find that the association between exposure to sexually explicit material and increased acceptance of rape myths and interpersonal violence is not dependent on violent content. This suggests that both violent and nonviolent pornography may influence the consumer. The researchers also report that while viewing pornography increased aggressive behavior, people viewing static images (as presented in pornographic magazines) were less likely to behave aggressively, highlighting the need for further research. Of course, perhaps one of the most fundamental issues with experimental design—the fact that viewing explicit material in an experimental setting may differ in a range of ways from normal consumption—is difficult to control.

Conclusion

To conclude, a wide range of studies have been conducted in this area, the most common using an experimental, cross-sectional, or longitudinal design. Although some studies find no effect of media violence, the general consensus is that media violence increases the likelihood of aggression. These conclusions are supported by a range of meta-analyses and reports. Research suggests that some individuals may be more susceptible to the effects of media violence and that some media content may be more influential than others.

These findings should of course be considered within the context of wider aggression research. In particular, it is important to note that media violence is not the only factor that impacts on aggression, and exposure to media violence alone may not increase aggressive behavior. As the research base increases, theoretical explanations of media violence have also developed. Of the main theories, Social Learning Theory remains the most prominent. Despite a greater understanding of this subject area and the concerns expressed by various public bodies, few practical developments have been made. In part, this reflects an unwillingness to censor material and the difficulties posed by specific content types such as news programs and cartoons.

Subject in focus

The Bobo doll studies

Bandura, Ross, and Ross (1963) conducted one of the most important studies to investigate children's development of aggressive behavior. Taking into account existing levels of aggression, the researchers separated the participants (forty-eight boys and forty-eight girls aged between thirty-five and sixty-nine months) into three experimental groups and one control group.

In the first experimental group, children observed a real-life aggressive model (an adult). As the child engaged in another task (e.g. designing pictures), the model started to play with a separate set of toys. For most of the session, the model behaved aggressively toward a Bobo doll. This aggression included a number of specific acts such as punching the doll and hitting the doll with a mallet, which allowed the researchers to later assess the children's imitation of specific acts in addition to general aggression. While behaving aggressively, the model also used a number of standardized phrases such as "sock him in the nose" and "pow."

In the second experimental group, the child watched a movie of the model (described previously) while also engaging in a design task. Children allocated to the third experimental condition were able to view a cartoon-type program while they carried out their task. The program featured a model dressed as a cartoon cat behaving aggressively toward the Bobo doll. A range of other features such as backdrop and title were included to make the cartoon appear more authentic. The same acts and standardized phrases used in group 1 were also included in groups 2 and 3. Children in the control group did not view any aggression.

In order to frustrate the children, each participant was then taken to another room and allowed to play with some attractive toys. After a short period of time, the child was told that these were the "best" toys and had been reserved for other children. After being taken to a different room, the child was allowed to play with a new range of toys. These included both aggressive (e.g. a gun) and nonaggressive (e.g. crayons) toys. The playroom also contained a Bobo doll. For twenty minutes, the child was observed playing with the toys.

Children in the three experimental groups were more aggressive than the children (in the control group) who had not observed an aggressive model. Importantly, there was no difference in the aggression shown by children watching the real-life model and those watching a movie. These results suggest that children learn from and imitate the violent behavior viewed on screen. While this study has had a substantial impact on both the scientific community and the wider public debate, the methodology employed by the researchers has attracted criticism. In particular, it argued that the children participating in the study responded to a number of cues that identified the "appropriate" behavior, with one child reportedly commenting, "There's the doll we have to hit" (Gauntlett 1995).

Discussion question

To what extent would the children in the Bobo doll study have behaved differently, if they had not been frustrated by the researchers?

Further sources of information

Bandura, A., Ross, D. & Ross, S. (1963). "Imitation of film-mediated models." *Journal of Abnormal Social Psychology*, 66, 3–11.

Bowling for Columbine (2002). A documentary film exploring issues of fear, culture, the media violence debate, and aggression.

Boyle, K. (2005). *Media and violence: Gendering the debates*. Thousand Oaks, CA: Sage.

Grimes, T., Anderson, J. A., & Bergen, L. (2008). *Media violence and aggression: Science and ideology*. Thousand Oaks, CA: Sage.

This Film Is Not Yet Rated (2006). A documentary film exploring issues of film classification and censorship.

2 Health Communication

Health communication is the use and study of communication strategies to inform and influence personal and community decisions that improve health (United States Department of Health and Human Services (USDHHS) 2000a). It bridges the fields of health and communication and is increasingly recognized as a necessary aspect of influencing individual and public health (USDHHS 2000a) (see Figure 2.1).

Health communication encompasses two distinct areas. One revolves around interpersonal and group communication in clinical settings, such as communication between patients and health providers (physicians, nurses, pharmacists, etc.) and among providers themselves. The other area involves the mass media and health messages disseminated through it. This includes people's search for and use of health information from the media, images of health and illness, dissemination of risk communication, and use of mass media for public health campaigns (USDHHS 2000a). This chapter will focus on public health campaigns, their history, elements and influences on health outcomes.

The World Health Organization (WHO) defines health as "a state of complete physical, mental, and social well-being and not merely the absence of disease or infirmity." The focus on well-being shows a holistic view of health. It also connects the medical and public health perspectives through emphasizing the biological, psychological (addressed by medicine), and social (addressed by public health) aspects of well-being. These elements will be revisited as we discuss how health communication campaigns can improve the health of individuals and societies.

Historical background

Reports of the first mass media health communication campaign in the United States date back to the eighteenth century. During the 1721–1722 smallpox epidemic in Boston, Reverend Cotton Mather launched a campaign to promote inoculation through personal appeals and thousands of pamphlets

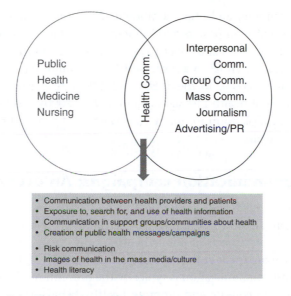

Figure 2.1 The origins and major areas in health communication
Source: USDHHS (2000a).

(Paisley 2001). By the end of the century, the smallpox vaccine was developed and become popular in England, largely due to a word-of-mouth campaign by its creator Edward Jenner and other physicians (Riedel 2005).

Health care emerged as a field in the United States and Western Europe during the twentieth century (for example, Hoving *et al.* 2010; Thomas 2006) and influenced the development of health communication as a distinct discipline. In the 1950s, scientific advances led to new medical models in the United States and much of Europe, and health was discussed unlike ever before (Thomas 2006). This new objective and detached approach to medicine, however, largely ignored the patient and communication. Doctors and medicine were not as concerned with preventative education and instead focused on disease treatment (Hoving *et al.* 2010; Thomas 2006).

In the 1970s, a backlash to this reductionist and reactive approach emerged. It was driven by the consumerist trends and the feminist movement in the United States and Western Europe, the Lalonde report in Canada, the advocacy of patient's rights in the Netherlands, and others (Hoving *et al.* 2010; Thomas 2006). The newfound emphasis on the doctor-patient relationship and understanding the nature of health began to establish what we now call health communication (Thomas 2006). Mass media use for health communication campaigns grew during the 1970s in the United States and Western Europe (Wartella & Stout 2002). Informational pamphlets and posters were common and often combined with other media. Good examples are the anti-alcohol posters and billboards in Poland between 1948 and 1990 (Gorsky *et al*. 2010) and other Eastern European countries. Mass media is now considered essential to a successful health communication campaign (Wartella & Stout, 2002). In the 1980s and 1990s, television greatly influenced the spread of health messages (Kreuter *et al*. 2000). Most recently, the Internet became a platform for many campaigns and changed the dynamics of the field yet again.

Health communication campaigns: An overview

As stated earlier, medicine, public health, and nursing are part of health communication (Figure 2.1). Campaigns often address prevention and human behavior, which are aspects of public health, rather than medical treatment and cure, which are staples of medicine (Hornik 2002a: 13). Because the goal of public health communication is typically the prevention of illnesses, using the mass media to educate and promote healthy behaviors has become the norm (Wartella & Stout 2002).

Health communication campaigns typically do the following:

- Provide direct education to the audience expected to adopt or change to a healthier behavior.
- Affect large audiences and require substantial resources (money, time, labor, and personnel).
- Use multiple communication approaches, and may combine mediated (broadcast, print, Internet) with interpersonal (health professionals, outreach workers, peers) channels.
- Aim to change awareness, attitudes and beliefs, actual and/or perceived social norms, and self-efficacy, all of which influence behavior.
- Are sponsored by the government, advocacy, or professional organizations.
- Are often parts of broader social-marketing programs, which complement communication efforts with other intervention components.
- Try to change public policy, such as taxes or regulation (Institute of Medicine 1989: 82–83).

Social marketing could increase the potential for success (Wallack & Dorfman 2004) and is credited with the integrated strategy of matching intervention messages to audiences via multiple channels (Wartella & Stout 2002: 27). Essentially, social-marketing campaigns sell healthy behavior in the way commercial marketers sell shampoo or insurance. When social marketing is used for the creation of health communication campaigns, it involves the following steps:

Step 1: Assessing the campaign's environment, also called a situation analysis. The big question here is: Where are we? Answering it includes determining the focus of the program, identifying the purpose of the campaign, conducting an analysis of Strengths, Weaknesses, Opportunities, and Threats (SWOT), reviewing similar past efforts.

Step 2: Identifying and analyzing the target audience, segmenting (dividing) the audience into smaller groups with common characteristics. This step is part of the question "Where do we want to go?"

Step 3: Identifying campaign goals and objectives. This step also answers the question "Where do we want to go?" Goals describe the general impact one hopes to achieve (Wason 2004), such as reduce the number of teenagers who smoke in London. The objectives are measurable steps toward the goal (Wason 2004: 196). A related objective could be to implement a peer-led anti-smoking program in 80% of secondary schools in London. Objectives describe the expected outcomes of the campaign and impact of the implemented program (Wason 2004: 199).

Step 4: Determining the strategies under the marketing mix or 4Ps: product, price, place, and promotion. This analysis will answer the question "How will you get there?" and includes the following:

(a) What behavior the campaign aims to influence (product);
(b) Physical, social, and psychological costs of adopting the behavior (price);
(c) Availability of the recommended response (place);
(d) Packaging and presentation of the behavior, which includes messages and media/communication channels (promotion).

Step 5: Planning for implementation, monitoring, and evaluation of the campaign.

(Kotler & Lee 2008: 35; Wartella & Stout 2002: 28).

These steps are the foundation for the chapter. While our overview thus far leans to the applied side of health communication, the field is in fact deeply rooted in theory. Models and theories often provide "a basis for communication planning and evaluation, inspire specific communication approaches, help implement a specific phase of a health communication program, support a true understanding of target audiences and groups," and others (Schiavo 2007: 31). Theories typically come from the social and behavioral sciences. The influence of culture and context will also be addressed. As people live within the boundaries of their own culture, health and health communication are often seen as socially constructed (e.g., Brumberg 1997; Lorber & Moore 2002) and subject to cultural influences (Schiavo 2007).

Important features of health communication campaigns

Target audience

One of the first steps (step 2) of a health communication campaign is to identify, analyze, and possibly segment the target audience. As Schiavo (2007) states, "Only health communication interventions that are based on a true understanding of the audiences have any chance of succeeding and meeting expected program outcomes" (247).

Understanding the target audience means knowing about (1) demographics, such as age, gender, race, ethnic background, language, marital status, number of children, literacy level; (2) needs, values, attitudes, social norms, and behavior (including perceived or existing barriers to adopting the new behavior); (3) geographic factors, such as location, rural/urban setting, climate, and transportation means; (4) socioeconomic factors, such as income level, education, and professional status; (5) lifestyle, such as preferred pastimes, work-family balance, cultural values, ideas about health and illness, religious beliefs, media habits and preferred channels; (6) physical or medical factors, such as health status, medical history and comorbid conditions, health risk factors; (7) other specific characteristics (Schiavo 2007: 239–248).

One example comes from the Health System Reform Project led by the Croatian Ministry of Health and the World Bank. One of the project's goals was to reduce the rate of cardiovascular disease. Heart disease and decreased life expectancy have been increasing in many former Communist countries (Wood 2010). Croatia is no exception, where economic and political turmoil has led to high stress, alcohol and tobacco abuse, and poor nutrition (Ana 2004). A campaign had to address the common risk factors for cardiovascular disease in a very unique context of a country that has experienced a devastating war, and financial and political instability (Ana 2004). The slogan "Say Yes to ... " encouraged positive health practices. The goal was to make the campaign easily recognizable and identifiable as a brand name for behaviors (Ana 2004: 539). The focus was on community-based activities, such as a national "smoke out" day, and attempts to gather large groups of people together for traditional and healthy breakfasts. The campaign became so successful that it was recognized by the World Health Organization and the Council of Europe (Ana 2004: 539).

Primary and secondary target audience

A target audience can be divided into primary and secondary. The primary audience represents the people the campaign seeks to influence, while the secondary audience is the people, groups, communities, and organizations that can influence the decisions and behaviors of the primary audience (Schiavo 2007: 243). Occasionally, media health campaigns must target the behaviors of the secondary audience in order to reach the desired outcomes in the primary audience. One example comes from New York City, when a law required restaurants to stop preparing food with Trans fats. Although the goal was to reduce the rates of cardiovascular disease and obesity, the behavior change targeted the food and restaurant industry (Angell *et al.* 2009). Another example occurred with general medical practitioners in Australia. There the goal was to reduce the number of Chlamydia outbreaks and transmissions in sexually active people aged fifteen to twenty-four. Before creating any messages for the primary audience, the campaign targeted general health practitioners to raise awareness about Chlamydia and routine screenings among patients in the specified age range (Smith *et al.* 2008).

Segmentation

Segmentation is an important part of target audience research because it uses the audience's diversity to tailor the campaign and improve its chances of success. As Slater (1995) noted, it is more efficient to identify people similar in important aspects and tailor message content and delivery to them (187). Audience segments have similar qualities influencing the targeted health behavior and that allows for similar tailored messages that are disseminated through similar media, interpersonal and organizational channels (Slater 1995). But while the benefits of segmentation are clear, the challenges of its execution often prevent health communication planners from fully using it, as no "simple formula or 'cookbook recipe'" exists for identifying segments (Slater 1995: 188). Segmentation could be based on all the audience features discussed earlier (Schiavo 2007).

The role of theory

Theory plays a major role in understanding, analyzing, and segmenting target audiences for health communication campaigns. The Theory of Planned Behavior and Theory of Reasoned Action (Fishbein & Ajzen 2010) are behind attitudinal beliefs and perceptions of social norms being used as segmenting variables, because the theories postulate that human behavior results from one's relevant salient beliefs. Segmenting based on self-efficacy and presence of behavioral models comes from the Social Cognitive Theory, which states that people often model their actions and build self-efficacy through observing others (Bandura 1986, 2001). Attention to perceived preventability and cost of alternatives is based on the Health Belief Model (Maiman & Becker 1974), which states that rational people weigh risk, benefits, and barriers to action when deciding whether to change behaviors. The Stages of Change (Transtheoretical) Model (Prochaska, DiClemente, & Norcross 1992) is considered by many the most useful framework for behavior change (Kotler & Lee 2008) and is applied widely for segmenting audiences.

Objectives and expected outcomes

Before planners consider messages, media channels, and overall strategies, they need to establish expected outcomes. Identifying expected outcomes (objectives) early on contributes to more targeted messages, more appropriate communication channels, and to evaluating the campaign based on actual expectations. Some of the most important elements of an effective campaign are early agreement on expected outcomes, well-defined communication objectives, and strategies meant to meet these objectives (Schiavo 2007: 227).

Typically, health communication campaigns aim to influence behavior. The main causes of death in Europe and the United States result from individual lifestyle choices. Cardiovascular disease (heart disease and stroke) is the number one killer in Europe and accounts for 52% of all deaths (WHO 2006a). Cancer is second, accounting for 19% of all causes of death (WHO 2006a). The same is true for the United States (Xu et al. 2010). The main lifestyle choices related to this are smoking/tobacco use, physical activity patterns, and diet/nutrition (Turnock 2004: 60).

But while influencing behavior may be a campaign's final goal, target audiences often go through several stages before even considering a new behavior. Behaviors are based on many factors: knowledge, attitudes, beliefs, social norms, risk perceptions, and others. Thus, a health campaign must account for and influence one or several of these antecedents before impacting the behavior itself. These stages of influence emphasize again the difference between goals and outcomes. A campaign goal may be a behavior change, but the objectives (expected outcomes) would be changes in knowledge, attitudes, or perceived risk.

For example, social norm campaigns to reduce the number of college students who binge drink are popular in the United States (Lederman et al. 2008). They often include "reality check" messages on how rare this behavior is, which aims to persuade binge-drinking students that their actions are not the "norm" (Lederman et al. 2008).

Types of behavior change

Behavior change can be of several types: begin a healthy behavior or cease an unhealthy one. Campaigns can promote adoption of a new behavior (e.g., for

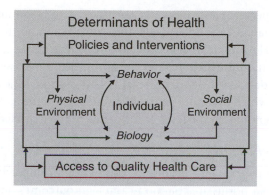

Figure 2.2 Determinants of health
Source: USDHHS (2000b).

a mother to start immunizing her children or for a woman to begin mammograms after a certain age) or the substitution of one behavior with another (e.g., for children to substitute drinking soft drinks with milk). Campaigns can also promote the elimination of a risky behavior (e.g., for young adults to stop texting while driving or to stop smoking).

It is important to emphasize that while much of today's causes for morbidity and mortality are due to individual lifestyle choices, these behaviors occur in a social setting and are often influenced by larger societal factors. Thus, the adoption of healthy behaviors often depends on community-level changes. Often, when community interventions occur, they impact individual behavior through perceived social norms and expectations. This is evidenced in communities that ban smoking in restaurants and later experience fewer new smokers (Siegel *et al.* 2008). Therefore, individual-level changes must be accompanied by changes in the physical and social environment, policies, and access to quality health care (see Figure 2.2).

Outcomes and theory

As stated earlier, campaigns must apply theory to be successful (Lapinski & Witte 1998). These theories differ in their level of influence: individual, interpersonal or organizational/communal/societal (Lapinski & Witte 1998; Thomas 2006). At the individual level are the Theory of Planned Behavior and Theory of Reasoned Action (Fishbein & Ajzen 2010), Health Belief Model (Maiman & Becker, 1974), Stages of Change (Transtheoretical) Model (Prochaska *et al.* 1992), Extended Parallel Process Model (Witte, Meyer, & Martell 2001), Elaboration Likelihood Model (Petty & Cacioppo 1986), and other information processing models. They all focus on individual outcomes, and inner ways to process information and respond to persuasive messages.

At the interpersonal level is Social Cognitive Theory (Bandura 1986, 2001), which sees behavior as an interplay between a person and the environment. The Two-Step Flow model is also situated at this level (Katz 1957) and examines interpersonal influences on the spread of media messages and the role of opinion leaders. At the societal level is Diffusion of Innovations Theory (Rogers 2003), which examines how society adopts new ideas. A theory should be chosen depending on the level of influence of the expected outcomes.

Outcomes and culture

Outcomes also depend on the cultural context of a campaign. For example, changes in social norms are common campaign outcomes. But social norms heavily depend on the local context and sometimes could be influenced by local opinion leaders. Such was the case of an intervention in several small towns in southern United States (Mississippi and Louisiana), which aimed to promote AIDS prevention through opinion leaders in the gay community (Kelly *et al.* 1991). The dynamic interaction between a person and the environment posited by Social Cognitive Theory could also be different depending on whether one lives in an individualistic or collectivistic society. The environment exerts a much stronger overall influence on a person in collectivistic than individualistic cultures (de Mooij 2010).

Types of media

Media type and creation of messages depend on the target audience, goals, and objectives. The selected media channel should be the most efficient way to reach the target audience and offer exposure, so that the message is noticed and remembered. Health communication scholars and practitioners have spent much time and effort researching and creating the right messages, but far less attention goes toward how to get messages to the target audience and provide repeated exposure (Hornik 2002a). Hornik argues that this secondary attention to dissemination "may be a crucial failing," because success of a persuasive message depends not only on the message itself but also on how many people it reaches and how many times the same people see it (13). Reaching maximum saturation during a campaign can ensure that the target audience has seen the message several times and will increase the chances that they comprehend and recognize the message and, in addition, see the issue as a significant problem (due to the agenda-setting role of the media) (Salmon & Atkin 2003).

Health campaign planners typically rely on television, radio, newspapers, and printed materials (press releases, pamphlets). Some authors see this as a narrow approach to dissemination and suggest a diversification of media channels by adding billboards, posters, theater slides, entertainment-education materials, and interactive media (Atkin 2001). Atkin argues that the differences among media channels should be considered. These differences include

- reach (proportion of the community who will be exposed to the message),
- specialization (whether specific subgroups can be reached),
- intrusiveness (whether the media channel creates exposure without initiation by the user),
- safeness (whether the media type can avoid creating a boomerang effect or irritation in the audience),
- participation (whether the recipient can interact with the media channel),
- decidability (the mental effort required to process messages on a channel),
- depth (the channel's capacity for showing detailed and complex content),
- agenda-setting (the channel's ability to influence the priority of issues in society),
- accessibility (ease of placing messages in the channel),
- cost (of producing and disseminating messages on the channel),
- efficiency (simplicity of arranging for production and dissemination) (Atkin 2001).

The Internet and social media

Since the late 1990s, a growing number of health campaign planners have used the Internet to disseminate messages to target audiences. The Internet has certain features that differentiate it from other media types and make it especially appropriate for health communication campaigns. Some of these are multimedia applications, interactivity, customization, and hypertext (Pavlik 2001), which cost less than traditional media, make user tracking possible, and have a more segmented targeting. These features can contribute to more targeted, less expensive, and more effective campaigns.

In terms of targeting, web sites and microsites can reach very small segments of an audience who would otherwise be unreachable or too costly to approach. A campaign web site can provide almost unlimited space for content and give the technical opportunity to tailor parts of the content to the needs of different audience segments, which stems from the medium's customization feature. The same campaign web site can attract people with different communication needs (connectivity, information, entertainment, shopping) (Duffy & Thorson 2009) and meet them under the same roof.

Thus, while responding to the specific communication and health needs of various audiences, a campaign web site would create an integrated image in the minds of these users, since they'll be coming to the same domain for various purposes. This can make the campaign and its overall message more memorable. This kind of one-stop shop available through web sites can be very hard to achieve with traditional media. Further, a campaign web site also integrates different media formats—text, photos, videos, sound—which are parts of the multimedia capabilities of the Internet. The hyperlink function, which allows the hosting of multiple links within a text, can provide additional information to those who need it but will not disrupt the experience of those who do not.

Additionally, the overall use and maintenance of a campaign's web presence is much less costly than use of traditional media channels. For evaluation purposes, users can be tracked for how much time they spend on the web site, how they find out about it, how many and which specific pages on the web site they visit, and where they are from geographically. All this information and more come from web metrics. The detailed information that web metrics provides is impossible to obtain with traditional media channels.

The Internet allows for health communicators to not only display their messages online but also to directly interact with the target audience, receive feedback, and engage them more actively. Bailey and colleagues (2010) analyzed fifteen randomized controlled trials of computer/Internet-based interventions since November 2007 aiming to improve sexual health and involving 3917 people of any age, gender, sexual orientation, ethnicity, or nationality. The authors concluded that these interventions were effective tools for learning about sexual health, and improved self-efficacy, intention, and sexual behavior, but that more research was needed to establish whether they can change outcomes such as sexually transmitted infections and pregnancy and to assess cost-effectiveness (Bailey *et al.* 2010).

More recently, social media has entered the online landscape and occupied much of American users' Internet time ("What Americans do online" 2010). Blogs, social networking sites, microblogging sites (e.g., Twitter), and file-sharing web sites (e.g., YouTube) have developed rapidly over the past five years. Many health communication practitioners have begun to use them for campaigns. One example is The Heart Truth® campaign featured as a *Subject in focus*.

The communication advantages of the Internet and social media do not mean that they should be adopted for all campaigns. The choice should still depend on the target audience and the message. Some populations are unequally active online and traditional media could still provide better exposure for certain audiences. Issues of technological disparities should be considered carefully when involving these particular media types.

The impact of theory and culture on media type

The choice of media type can influence which theories are used by campaign creators. Cultivation Theory (Gerbner 1994) and Social Cognitive Theory (Bandura 2001) can be applied for television, especially for entertainment education. They posit that viewers create impressions about the real world and model their behaviors based on what they see on television. When elite newspapers cover a health issue, they can influence the success of a campaign related to that issue, according to Agenda-setting Theory (McCombs & Shaw 1972). The theory states that extensive or visible media coverage raises the salience of a topic in the public's mind. The *New York Times* and other elite media are seen as agenda-setters for smaller media outlets (Vliegenthart & Walgrave 2008), and for bloggers (Sweetser, Golan & Wanta 2008). When considering the Internet, campaign planners must revisit theories and models related to interactivity and how people process persuasive messages in an online environment (Rodgers & Thorson 2000).

As with the other aspects of a campaign, the use of media types is also culture specific. For example, Middle Eastern mobile customers are most active worldwide in the use of smart phones ("Mideast consumers 'top in smart phone use'" 2010). The Internet has unequal penetration around the world and in many countries certain web sites are censored by the government. Culture influences how people watch television and what programs are most popular (de Mooij 2010: 196). Ownership of radios and time spent in listening correlate with individualism, while reading newspapers relate to several aspects of culture (de Mooij 2010: 198).

Media messages

Probably the most developed aspect of health communication research is the study of persuasive messages and, particularly, how different message features influence effectiveness. The substantial research literature can definitely benefit campaign creation. However, planners can fall into many pitfalls once their messages meet the public. Messages may be regarded as "offensive, disturbing, boring, stale, preachy, confusing, irritating, misleading, irrelevant, uninformative, useless, unbelievable, or unmotivating" (Atkin 2001: 51). Therefore, in addition to consulting research, communicators also should consider the information gathered during the earlier steps of the planning process.

Step 1 can help in the message design through the SWOT (Strengths, Weaknesses, Opportunities, and Threats) analysis and the review of past efforts and possible competitors. For example, a SWOT analysis of an upcoming campaign to raise support for higher tobacco taxes may identify its strength that the campaign organizers are public health experts and researchers, who have high credibility on health issues. Messages can use this strength by talking about health-care costs of smoking and secondhand smoke and the need to raise tobacco taxes to offset these costs. Also, a review of past efforts can show if any messages should be avoided because of poor reception by the target audience.

The information gathered during **step 2** should be a key aspect of message design, as audience characteristics (demographics, psychographics, behaviors) can influence information processing. For example, teenagers' race and gender influence the perceived message bias in health public service announcements (Shen *et al*. 2009). Adolescents' gender and age influence behavioral intention, message perception, and retention for certain message types (Greene *et al*. 2002). Cultural background is related to the effectiveness of persuasive health messages framed as affecting one's self or one's relationships (Ko & Kim 2010).

The psychographics of the target audience also influence how messages are processed. Sensation seeking is one personality trait that has received much attention from researchers. Sensation seekers are more likely to use and abuse alcohol or drugs, and process related messages differently (e.g., Lang *et al*. 2005). Sensation seekers generally reported more positive feelings than their counterparts after watching substance abuse-related public service announcements (Lang *et al*. 2005). Stephenson and Southwell (2006) theorized that while sensation seeking has been studied mostly in substance abuse, it can apply to cancer communication, especially to lung, breast, oral, and cervical cancers, which relate to the risky behaviors of alcohol/tobacco use and unprotected sex.

The objectives of a campaign (**step 3**) also influence message design. One way is through the cue to action inserted in the message. If the objective is simply to raise awareness, no call to action is needed, because the audience would become aware simply by being exposed to the message. If the objective is a behavior, then a call to action would point the audience toward that behavior. A call to action is a request toward the audience to do something. "Talk to your doctor about [drug X]" is a common call to action in direct-to-consumer television advertisements about prescription drugs, which are popular in the United States. In 2009, the American Heart Association and the Ad Council launched a national campaign to publicize the new guidelines for performing CPR (cardiopulmonary resuscitation), which involve hands only and no mouth-to-mouth breathing. The ads featured the following call to action: "Call 911 then push hard and fast on the center of the chest" ("Hands-Only CPR" 2009).

The main purpose of media messages is to "sell" pro-health attitudes, knowledge, and behavior and therefore the overall approach to promoting these "products" (**step 4**) is central. Messages can be discussed in terms of their structural or content features (Lang *et al.* 2005). Structural features of television/video messages include strong sound effects, fast pace, cuts, edits, zooms, pans, and movement from off screen to on screen (Lang 1990; Lang *et al.* 2005). Content features include a message's emotional or informational appeal, positive or negative valence, use of a narrative or factual information, etc. Many messages fall along the positive—negative valence spectrum. Health campaigns tend to use negative approaches and health outcomes over positive ones (Monahan 1995; Salmon & Atkin 2003).

Negativity bias

One reason for the popularity of negative messages is that people tend to give them more weight than to positive messages: a phenomenon called negativity bias. It occurs because negative cues are perceived as more diagnostic than positive cues (Herr, Kardes, & Kim 1991; Skowronski & Carlston 1987, 1989). For example, negativity bias occurs in morality judgments about people, where dishonest behaviors are weighted more heavily than honest behaviors and thus it becomes easier for one to be categorized as dishonest rather than honest (Skowronski & Carlston 1987). Bad news attracts more attention than good news (see Grabe & Kamhawi 2006 for a review) and people spend more time reading bad news (Zillmann *et al.* 2004).

Fear appeals

One very popular negative approach is the use of fear appeals in health messages. Fear appeals are "persuasive messages that arouse fear" (Witte & Allen 2000) and have been used in health promotion since the 1950s. In general, the stronger the fear appeal, the greater the changes in attitude, intention, and behavior, but these relationships have been weak (Boster & Mongeau 1984; Mongeau 1998; Witte & Allen 2000). Scaring people into action can be counterproductive. Audiences also need to hear how to address the threat through the presence of response efficacy and self-efficacy in a message (Witte, Meyer & Martell 2001). Stronger response efficacy and self-efficacy produce stronger attitudes, intentions, and behaviors toward the recommended response (Witte & Allen 2000). Campaign designers can go beyond fear appeals and create additional negative features, such as disgusting images, to increase the message effectiveness. This strategy may backfire, as people show worse cognitive processing when both high fear and high disgust are present in a message (Leshner, Bolls, & Thomas 2009; Leshner *et al.* 2010).

Media messages, theory, and culture

Many of the theories discussed earlier apply for the creation of messages. These include Theory of Planned Behavior and Theory of Reasoned Action

(Fishbein & Ajzen 2010), Social Cognitive Theory (Bandura 1986, 2001), Health Belief Model (Maiman & Becker 1974), Extended Parallel Process Model (Witte, Meyer, & Martell 2001), and Elaboration Likelihood Model (Petty & Cacioppo 1986). In addition, the Limited Capacity Model of Motivated Mediated Message Processing (LC4MP, Lang 2006) theorizes how people attend to, process, and remember messages and the different factors that affect these cognitive processes. The model argues that humans have limited cognitive resources and the distribution of these resources to any media-related task affects how much of the presented information they encode, store, or retrieve. Theories about discrete and dimensional emotions can educate campaign planners how to evoke emotion with their messages and how individuals will process that (Bolls 2010; Nabi 2010).

Culture influences people's ideas about health and illness (Schiavo 2007: 79) and therefore should be considered when designing persuasive health messages. Most studies on health message framing have used partici-pants from individualistic cultures, such as in Western Europe or North America (Ko & Kim 2010). Cultural background (individualistic versus collec-tivistic) is related to the effectiveness of persuasive health messages framed as affecting one's self or one's relationships (Ko & Kim 2010). The use of symbols, numbers, and narrative techniques in messages also varies across cultures.

Effectiveness and evaluation

Evaluation is becoming ever more important as funding agencies pay increasing attention to measurement and accountability (Wason 2004: 36). Campaign evaluations should serve three functions: (1) Determine the degree to which the campaign reached its objectives, (2) Help planners and scholars understand how or why a campaign worked, (3) Provide relevant information for planning future activities (Valente 2001). A major failure of many health campaigns is that evaluation measures and plans are only developed at the end of the planning process. Developing evaluation measures early can help members agree about the ultimate goals and expected outcomes of a project, and what can/should be done to reach them (Schiavo 2007).

Schiavo argues that all evaluation reports should include the following: key theoretical assumptions and models; expected program outcomes; research objectives; methods for data collection and analysis, and the position of the evaluation team; progress report on process indicators, and specific activities and materials; evaluation findings and implications for current or future programs; lessons learned and future directions; existing barriers to expected outcomes and potential approaches to overcome them (350). Hornik (2002b) suggests incorporating measurements at multiple time points, conducting comparisons with unexposed (control) populations, and triangulating evidence by showing effects through several analytic approaches (390). Benchmarking is extremely important for measuring progress in ongoing tasks that occur on a regular basis (Thomas 2006). Indicators measured during evaluation include the context of the communication, number of people reached, characteristics of these people, type and amount of resources expended, and media response (Thomas 2006: 171).

Critical to evaluating any campaign's effectiveness is clearly measuring the appropriate behavioral changes, which means making the connection between attitude and behavior change resulting from the campaign (Devine & Hirt 1989: 247). Campaign effectiveness is a highly subjective topic. Campaigns are often evaluated for success based on definitional effectiveness, ideological effectiveness, political effectiveness, contextual effectiveness, cost-effectiveness, and programmatic effectiveness (Salmon & Murray-Johnson 2001).

The time of measurement is crucial. Typically, for campaigns whose objectives involve behavior change, results will not happen rapidly but will take a more gradual path (Hornik 2002b: 387). This is especially true when the target behavior involves social norms, which also have to change, Hornik explains. Therefore, if an evaluation measuring behavior change occurs too soon after the campaign is completed, results may be disappointing not because the campaign was ineffective but because it takes time for people to change their behaviors.

When discussing campaign effectiveness, attention should be paid to not only whether attitudes, knowledge, or behavior were changed, but also how much they were affected. Often communicators expect radical changes, when in reality they are much more subtle (Kreps & Thornton 1992). In the United States, health communication campaigns that use mass media and avoid coercion have an average effect size of about 5% (Snyder 2007). Thus, if 50% of the target audience were engaged in a certain behavior before a campaign, 55% of them will most likely perform the behavior after a campaign. This number is only an average though and campaigns targeting different behaviors have had varying effects. Most effective have been campaigns about seat-belt use (15% difference), dental care (13% difference), and reduced alcohol use among adults (11% difference), while campaigns discouraging drug and marijuana use among the youth have been least successful (1–2% difference) (Snyder 2007). In the middle and around the average of 5% fall campaigns about family planning, youth-smoking prevention, heart-disease prevention, sexual risk taking, mammography screening, adult-smoking prevention, youth-alcohol prevention, and cessation and tobacco prevention (Snyder 2007).

These modest results are due to "meager resources, poor conceptualization, and narrow strategic approaches," according to Atkin (2001: 67). Other barriers include reaching the audience and attracting attention to the messages, and overcoming audience resistance; misperception of susceptibility to negative outcomes; denial of applicability to self; rejection of unappealing recommendations; and audience inertia or lethargy (Atkin 2001: 51). Thus, audience members can be lost at each stage of response to the message.

Conclusion

Health communication is the use and study of communication strategies to inform and influence personal and community decisions that improve health (USDHHS 2000a). This chapter focuses on health communication campaigns, their history, and features. Health communication campaigns typically provide direct education to a target audience; affect large numbers of people; require substantial resources; use multiple communication approaches; aim to change awareness, attitudes, social norms, self-efficacy, and ultimately behavior; are sponsored by the government, advocacy, or professional organizations; often become part of broader social-marketing programs; and may try to change public policy (Institute of Medicine 1989).

Social marketing could increase the potential for success of campaigns and involves several specific steps. Those are: (1) assessing the campaign's environment; (2) identifying, analyzing, and segmenting the target audience; (3) identifying campaign goals and objectives; (4) determining the strategies under the marketing mix (product, price, place, promotion); (5) planning for implementation, monitoring, and evaluation of the campaign (Kotler & Lee 2008: 35; Wartella & Stout 2002: 28). This chapter discussed health campaigns from the perspective of the social-marketing steps outlined earlier. From its origins in pamphlets and word-of-mouth campaigns in the eighteenth century to the often sophisticated multimedia campaigns of today, health communication has evolved as a field guided by applied and theoretical practices, and strategic planning.

Subject in focus

The Heart Truth® campaign

The Heart Truth® campaign, sponsored by the National Heart, Lung, and Blood Institute (NHLBI), part of the National Institutes of Health at the USDHHS, began as result of a 2001 meeting of women's health experts to discuss the impact heart disease was taking on American women. See Figure 2.3 for data. A year later, the media campaign officially launched and introduced the Red Dress® as the official symbol (NHLBI 2010).

NHLBI targeted women aged forty to sixty, when most women's risk factors for heart disease begin to increase significantly (Long *et al.* 2009). The campaign emphasizes awareness in African-American and Hispanic women, since they are generally disproportionately affected (Long *et al.* 2009). Understanding this demographic group depended on research ranging from psychographic and lifestyle characteristics to attitudes and behaviors (Long *et al.* 2009). Besides the primary audience (women aged forty to sixty), women of all ages were targeted and made aware of heart disease and the appropriate measures to protect their health (NHLBI 2010).

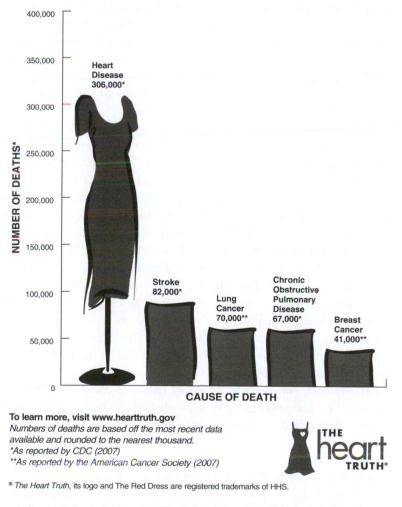

To learn more, visit www.hearttruth.gov
Numbers of deaths are based off the most recent data available and rounded to the nearest thousand.
*As reported by CDC (2007)
**As reported by the American Cancer Society (2007)

® The Heart Truth, its logo and The Red Dress are registered trademarks of HHS.

Figure 2.3   Leading causes of death for American women (2007)
Source: NHLBI (2007).

The goal of the campaign, ongoing since 2002, has been to raise aware-ness about heart disease in women, encourage them to understand the risks, and take action to reduce them (NHLBI 2010). The campaign also addressed barriers to knowledge, which included societal perceptions and media messages that heart disease was a men's problem. The campaign conveyed a sense of urgency in the messages, coupled with information on the disease's deadly effects, and ways to lower the health risks (Long *et al.* 2009).

The Heart Truth® creators felt that the best way to reach their audience was with an edgier approach compared to traditional wellness campaigns (Long *et al.* 2009). They developed the name The Heart Truth® to signify the need for a reality check, and the Red Dress® and accompanying tagline "Heart Disease Doesn't Care What You Wear—It's the #1 Killer of Women" (NHLBI 2010) as a provocative and women-centered message (Long *et al.* 2009). They also included real women's stories about heart disease as an integral part of the campaign (Long *et al.* 2009).

The Heart Truth® campaign, and its partner campaigns, relied heavily on media coverage to help drive home their message. To keep control over the campaign messages, they maintain consistency across all partnerships, including the well-known American Heart Association (2010) "Go Red For Women" campaign. During its initial stages, the campaign partnered with the fashion industry as part of Mercedes Benz Fashion Week in 2003 (Long *et al.* 2009). This high-profile event gained attention among the fashion community and mainstream media. Following this event, the campaign enlisted the help of then First Lady Laura Bush, who made several public appearances wearing the Red Dress® pin and speaking about the need for attention to this issue. Once The Heart Truth® began gaining attention, it launched partnerships with the American Heart Association and other well-known nonprofits to reach a larger audience.

Since its inception, the campaign has expanded its reach to the local level, with many cities, towns, and workplaces now hosting Heart Truth® events and observing National Wear Red Day held on the first Friday of February. The campaign has also expanded its media use, which now ranges from televised events and news to a specialized women's magazine, movie mentions, and informational web sites. As of 2006, awareness of heart disease among women had increased by 29% in Hispanic women, 31% in African-American women, and 68% in Caucasian women (Long *et al.* 2009). Further, a majority of women could now recognize the Red Dress® as the official symbol of the campaign (Long *et al.* 2009).

Discussion question

To what extent would the type of health behavior or condition targeted, impact on the development of a health-care campaign?

Further sources of information

De Mooij, M. (2010). *Global marketing and advertising: Understanding cultural paradoxes* (3rd ed.). Thousand Oaks, CA: Sage.

Kotler, P. & Lee, N. (2008). *Social marketing: Influencing behaviors for good* (3rd ed.). Thousand Oaks, CA: Sage.

National Cancer Institute. (2005). "Theory at a Glance: A Guide for Health Promotion Practice," (2nd ed.).

Thompson, T. L., Dorsey, A., Miller, K. I., & Parrott, R. (2003). *Handbook of health communication.* New York: Lawrence Erlbaum.

Wason, S. D. (2004). *Grant writing handbook.* Hoboken, NJ: Wiley.

Witte, K., Meyer, G., & Martell, D. (2001). *Effective health risk messages: A step-by-step guide.* Thousand Oaks, CA: Sage.

3 Body Image and Eating Behavior

Body image is a psychological construct that comprises of cognitions and feelings about one's physical shape and appearance. Dissatisfaction with own body shape is especially likely when there is a wide gap between the body shape individuals perceive themselves to have and the body shape that they would like to have. Surveys carried out over the last two decades of the twentieth century indicated a gradual and persistent growth in prevalence of body-image dissatisfaction among both women and men (Cash & Henry 1995; Cash, Winstead, & Janda 1986). While nearly one in three American women were not satisfied with their bodies in the 1980s, this figure grew to nearly one in two by the mid-1990s (Cash & Henry 1995).

Subjective "body image" is not only important at a personal level in determining how good individuals feel about themselves, it also has wider social implications for the way individuals behave, particularly with respect to their dietary habits and how concerned they are about their weight (Streigel-Moore *et al.* 1996). Where a poor body image leads to extreme intervention on the part of the individual in the way they consume food, it can give rise to deep-seated psychological problems that in turn result in behavior patters that can be harmful to health and ultimately, if carried to the farthest extremes, be fatal (Crisp 1992). Put simply, a faulty body image can result in either mild or serious clinical disorders that become manifest in the form of distorted eating habits. Such behavioral syndromes are most usually associated with girls and young women, but they also affect boys and young men, and older people, both female and male (Augustus-Horvath & Tylka 2009; Daniel & Bridges 2010; Grogan & Richards 2002; Shomaker & Furman 2010).

There are growing concerns about both the prevalence of body-image dissatisfaction and the age at which it starts to appear. It is well established as a phenomenon among young adult women (Dolan 1989; Stoutjesdyk & Jevne 1993), but it has also been observed to surface among girls as young as eleven years old as they reach puberty (Williams & Currie 2000). The latter development is a source of particular concern, because if it leads to the subsequent appearance of disordered eating at this age, it could disrupt physical growth and create the conditions for long-term, chronic health problems (Griffiths & McCabe 2000).

Epidemiological statistics have shown that the incidence of clinical eating disorders such as anorexia and bulimia are widespread and have been increasing over several decades (Crisp 1992; Crisp, Palmer, & Kalucy 1976; Disordered Eating 2010; Johnson & Connors 1987). Preoccupation with dieting, while not necessarily to a distorted degree, is wider still. Such phenomena are not recent developments. In the late 1980s, research among American girls aged thirteen to seventeen years, found that more than three in four said they wanted to lose weight and two-thirds claimed recently to have been on a diet. More poignantly, around one in six said they had used diet pills and nearly one in ten claimed to have made themselves vomit to expel food to lose weight (Whittaker *et al.* 1989). In the United Kingdom, the picture is much the same where the number of cases of anorexia admitted to UK hospitals increased from 419 in 1996–97 to 620 in 2005–06 (Disordered Eating 2010).

This chapter will examine the role that might be played by the media in relation to body self-concept development and the occurrence of distorted eating patterns. This is a topic that has attracted increased research attention over the past thirty years and provides a useful demonstration of how psychological theory and research can inform our understanding of media effects.

Media and cultural context

Body-shape ideals are frequently culturally embedded. Western societies or cultures have typically adhered to aesthetic norms that define a slender body shape as most pleasing and acceptable, while others are more accepting of fleshier body shapes, especially in the case of women (Rudofsky 1972; Swami *et al.* 2010). The Western norms are in turn reflected in the body-shape preferences exhibited by young women in these societies (Nylander 1971).

The societal norm can be conditioned and internalized by the individual in different ways. Evidence has emerged that role models in the individual's own life, and most especially parents and peer groups, can be influential. Children and teenagers pick up messages about body-shape ideals from these sources and the body shape and eating-related attitudes and behaviors they display (Vincent & McCabe 2000). The transference of cultural norms from one culture to another can also occur and influence body-shape preferences. Thus, women from Eastern cultures where a more rounded female body shape is valued can exhibit Western women's concerns with slimming and fitness after spending time living in Western societies (Bardwell & Choudry 2000).

On a global scale, a survey of women and men in ten different world regions found that Western media exposure was associated with a preference for slimness (Swami *et al.* 2010). Children and teenagers consume messages about and observe images of human body shapes via the mass media. Celebrity role models can be important here, such as with respect to the use of age-inappropriate role models for preadolescents (Fabrianesi, Jones, & Reid 2008). Beyond these iconic figures, research on media forms popular with young people, such as fashion and fitness magazines, and video games, have identified the greater use of thinner and often highly sexualized models, and the prevalence of a discourse that equates an idealized body shape with success (Ballentine & Ogle 2005; Burgess, Stermer, & Burgess 2007; Dill & Thill 2007; Smith Maguire 2002). These editorial decisions taken by media professionals represent a dominant ideology about what represents beauty in the human frame. With the increased globalization of mass media and fashion, such mediated effects can span cultures resulting in cultural norm shifts that drive the onset of eating disorders among women where they may not have been present before (Wassenaar, Le Grange, & Winship, 2000).

Across the 1950s, 1960s, 1970s, and 1980s, the media also displayed a progressive movement away from a voluptuous body shape for women (especially in relation to the upper torso) towards a slender body shape (Byrd-Bredbenner, Murray, & Schlussel 2005; Cash 1990; Spitzer, Henderson, & Zivian 1999). From the start of the 1990s onwards, a growing body of empirical research has explicitly identified the mass media (most especially glossy magazines, movies, and television) as having direct and indirect influences on media consumers' self-perceptions of body shape and propensity to diet and develop eating disorders (see Grogan 2008; Wykes & Gunter 2005).

Theories of media influence on body image

The impact of media representations of body image upon media consumers has been explained by a number of theories. Theoretical models vary between those that attempt to explain how media depictions of human body shapes can influence individuals' self-perceptions, and those that examine how broader social beliefs about gender and body shape can be cultivated by the media.

Social Comparison Theory

In its original form, the Social Comparison Theory was used to explain how any social comparison could underpin self-perceptions (Festinger 1954). More recently, however, Social Comparison Theory has been used to help us understand media effects on body self-concepts. In essence, if an individual compares their own body with those of actors and models seen in the media, the outcome could be favorable or unfavorable. If the outcome is unfavorable, that is, if the individual regards their own body shape as less attractive than ones seen in the mass media, this could result in lowered body self-esteem (Thompson, Heinberg, & Tantleff 1991). The bodies of celebrities or anonymous models that populate glossy magazines, movies and television programs and the body shapes of actors and models in advertisements can be particularly important in this context (Heinberg & Thompson 1992b; Smolak, Levine, & Gralen 1993).

Some individuals exhibit a greater propensity than others to make these social comparisons. Research among women has found that those with stronger social comparison tendencies also displayed greater dissatisfaction with their own bodies (Heinberg & Thompson 1992a, 1992b; Streigel-Moore, Silverstein, & Rodin 1986; Thompson, Heinberg, & Tantleff 1991). There are gender differences in social comparison-making tendencies. Boys and men are less likely to exhibit this propensity than are girls and women. This can sometimes explain why female consumers react more profoundly than male consumers, in terms of their body self-perceptions, after exposure to advertisements that depict idealized physical specimens of their own gender (Fischer & Halpenny 1993).

A different version of Social Comparison Theory called "Self-Ideal Discrepancy" has been invoked to analyze the way that some individuals do not simply make comparisons between themselves and specific others, but between their body shape as they currently perceive it to be and an "ideal" body shape that they hold in their heads (Fallon & Rozin 1985; Thompson 1992). To the extent that the perceived "real self" and "ideal self" are different, dissonance is created and the individual is motivated to close the gap (Cash & Szymanski 1995). A large gap between these two self-concepts has been seen among women who are more dissatisfied with their current body shape (Thompson 1990, 1992). Even more seriously, large self-discrepancies have also been linked to a greater likelihood of exhibiting eating disorders (Strauman *et al.* 1991).

Cultivation Theory

Media representations of social phenomena can influence media consumers by providing examples for them to follow and also by presenting a broader view of the world that presents a distorted or exaggerated perspective of everyday reality. Regular exposure to this distorted media world can cultivate stereotyped or biased impressions of the depicted aspects of reality (Gerbner *et al.* 1980; Signorielli & Morgan 1990). In the context of body-image perceptions, the constant use of thin female actors and models in televised entertainment and popular magazines could create an impression that "thin is normal" or that "thin is best." If this norm is transferred from the media world to the real world, it could affect the self-perceptions of women and their satisfaction with their own body shape, especially if they perceive it to be different from the "norm" (Harrison & Cantor 1997). Experimental research assessing whether such stereotyped media portrayals can produce immediate post-exposure shifts in relevant social attitudes and beliefs is discussed in the next section.

Social comparison processes can mediate the degree to which such cultivation effects occur. Girls and women who display high social comparison-making tendencies could be more sensitive to media representations of female body image and pay more attention to them. It is known that women who are dissatisfied with their body weight and physical appearance seem to pay greater attention to messages about body shape and appearance (Cooper 1997; Jackman *et al.* 1995). Personal sensitivity to own weight and appearance can affect the way women rate the attractiveness of on-screen female actors in terms of their weight and appearance (Tantleff-Dunn & Thompson 1998). Social comparison processes and cultivation effects have been shown to be mediated for individuals within the same societal context by a host of factors, including race/ethnicity, age, and sexuality (Augustus-Horvath & Tylka 2009; Baker & Gringart 2009; Debraganza & Hausenblas 2010; Fujioka *et al.* 2009; McArdle & Hill 2009; Zhang, Dixon, & Conrad 2009).

Research evidence

Print media, television, and advertising have been highlighted as media that are potentially influential with respect to providing points of comparison for readers and viewers when making judgments about their body shape; however, similar research findings extend to such media forms as video games and toys (Barlett *et al.* 2005; Behm-Morawitz & Mastro 2009; Dittmar, Halliwell, & Ive 2006). Studies differ with respect to whether they examine media forms in isolation or combination. Most empirical investigations comprise self-completion questionnaire surveys, but a few have used interventionist designs to examine the immediate effects of mediated body-shape depictions. The main focus has been placed on the potential effects of visible media displays or depictions or body shapes. These can occur in entertainment or information content and also in advertisements. Some researchers have also examined the effects of narrative content that discusses body-shape themes. The key dependent measures in this context comprise attitudes towards and perceptions of own body shape, self, and the ideal body shape an individual would like to attain.

Self-reported exposure to magazine articles and advertisements that depict or make reference to human body shape have been found to predict teenage girl readers' perceptions of the body shape they would like to have (Levine, Smolak, & Hayden, 1994). Similarly, greater claimed readership of fashion magazines among teenage girls was associated with lower body self-esteem (Botta 2003).

There is evidence that greater frequency of watching television is associated with high body dissatisfaction scores among preteen and teenage girls (Borzekowski, Robinson, & Killen 2000; Gonzalez-Levin & Smolak 1995; Tiggemann & Pickering 1996). Reported exposure to televised movies and soap operas were especially closely related to body dissatisfaction (Tiggemann & Pickering 1996). What this type of evidence does not show, however, is whether there are particular types of body-image portrayal that are especially potent in this context. These general "reported frequency of viewing" measures therefore represent blunt instruments in understanding anything about the nature of media impact on body-image perceptions.

The importance of differentiating between different types of media content has been underlined by research showing that while study of American teenage girls showed no relationship between overall television viewing and body-shape perceptions, those who were especially strongly attracted to thin characters in television programs were more likely to perceive themselves as fatter than they really were (Harrison 2000a) and viewing of a specific program with conspicuously thin and attractive characters was related to greater dissatisfaction among college-aged women in Canada (Want, Vickers, & Amos 2009).

The apparent potency of attraction to specific celebrity characters in the media in relation to the adoption or conditioning of specific body-image preferences can perhaps be explained by Social Comparison Theory. This point is confirmed by evidence that the more young people make comparisons between themselves and physically attractive celebrity figures, the more dissatisfied with their own bodies they seem to become (Heinberg & Thompson 1992a). Although reported viewing of programs on television that featured lead characters with thin body shapes was statistically related to body dissatisfaction, it accounted for only a tiny portion (2%) of the variance in this perception. Of far greater significance was the degree to which viewers make active comparisons between themselves and television actors (Botta 1999).

Body-shape ideals are known historically to vary between cultures and ethnic groups (Grogan 2008). Research in the United States has shown that African-American girls in their mid-teens were on the whole more satisfied with their bodies than were European American girls. However, both groups were equally likely to enjoy watching television shows with attractive lead female characters with thin body shapes. Both were also more likely to exhibit body dissatisfaction if they idealized these thin celebrity television role models and their body shapes (Botta 2000).

Survey studies of media and body-image perceptions are limited to measuring association between these variables. A standard experimental research design is to measure body esteem or satisfaction, present images of female or male models, and then retest body esteem or satisfaction. Participants are randomly allocated to conditions in which they see a series of images that represent one particular type of body shape: thin, average, fat, muscular. In a controlled condition, participants may be shown pictures of landscapes or other scenes that can be evaluated but have no relevance to body shape.

When shown pictures of attractive female models, it is not unusual for women to exhibit a drop in how positively they feel about their own physical appearance (Cash, Cash, & Butters 1983). Studies of the impact of exposure to images of thin female models taken from magazines have produced mixed evidence, including no apparent impact (Richins 1991) versus higher post-exposure levels of body-shape insecurity and dissatisfaction (Stice & Shaw 1994). Similar studies of men found that viewing images of muscular or idealized male models resulted in decreased body satisfaction (Agliata & Tantleff-Dunn 2004; Lorenzen, Grieve, & Thomas 2004) and detrimental effects were also detected in an experimental study that compared men's and women's psychological affect following exposure to fitness magazines (Garvin & Damson 2008).

Both men and women are susceptible to the influence of an intensive dose of body images upon their own body self-perceptions. Whether body dissatisfaction grows stronger or weaker depends, however, on the types of images shown. Exposure to a series of images of thin role models increased levels of body dissatisfaction while seeing images of over-sized role models led to improved body satisfaction among medical students (Ogden & Mundray 1996). A replication of the previous study among adolescent girls aged twelve to seventeen years failed to reproduce the main effect of body-image exposure. However, body exposure interacted with preexisting body dissatisfaction to enhance the extent to which the girls thought about their weight. Exposure to images of over-sized models led already dissatisfied girls to think less about their own weight (Champion & Furnham 1999).

Enhanced concern about own weight emerged as an effect of exposure to pictures of glamorous-looking women among female participants who in pretesting had disclosed dissatisfaction with their own body shape. This effect emerged whether the depicted women were fashion models or other students. It did not emerge among women who exhibited pre-exposure self-confidence in their own bodies (Posavec, Posavec, & Posavec 1993). A further study of teenage girls reinforced the previous findings by showing that girls who exhibited low body self-esteem found female models in magazine advertisements more attractive than did girls with high body self-esteem (Martin, Gentry, & Hill, 1999).

Television and video images have also been tested for their impact upon body self-perceptions. Exposure of college-going women to video vignettes containing text and images that extolled the virtues of thinness as attractive produce post-exposure increases in body weight and appearance dissatisfaction among women who already lacked confidence about these attributes (Heinberg & Thompson 1995). Thus, individuals can vary with respect to their general self-confidence about their bodies and the degree to which they adhere to a specific ideal of physical attractiveness. While self-confidence can mitigate the impact of media images, even relatively self-confident individuals can display lowered body self-esteem after being shown a series of photographic images of attractive models (Thornton & Maurice 1997).

Another experimental study with television images utilized a nonverbal measure of body image—the Body Image Detection Device (BIDD) (Myers & Biocca 1992). Participants could manipulate three bands of light that represented their chest, waist, and hip measurements. The stimulus materials comprised programs that featured thin lead female characters or no such characters and advertisements that featured actors/models with thin body shapes or no such actors/models.

In general the young women who took part overestimated their actual body size. Rather than enhancing body dissatisfaction and other negative feelings about own body shape, however, exposure to media materials that depicted thin actors/models had the opposite effect. This was especially true in relation to exposure to the body-image advertisements on their own and when paired with body-image programming. The authors concluded that mediated ideal body shapes might have some therapeutic value by helping young women, many of whom already exaggerate their actual size, to adopt a more realistic view of themselves.

Elsewhere, television advertisements that depicted highly attractive women as sex objects caused young women aged eighteen to thirty-five to adjust their self-perceptions and rate their body size as larger and to depart more significantly from their ideal body shape. Young women shown advertisements devoid of this kind of imagery did not change their body self-perceptions (Lavine, Sweeney, & Wagner 1999).

It has been observed previously that some individuals have a greater proclivity than others to draw comparisons between their own appearance and that of others. This notion of social comparison has generally been tested in self-report research settings with social comparison measures used as control measures in correlation analyses. The social comparison process was, however, manipulated in one study by varying the instructions given to participants in regard to the way they should process images of attractive female models. Mere exposure to advertisements or video materials that depicted physically attractive models or actors on its own did not influence body-image perceptions. In contrast, when participants were encouraged to make comparisons between the models/actors shown in these media images and themselves, they tended to produce less favorable comparative judgments about themselves (Cattarin *et al.* 2000).

A meta-analysis of published research on relationships between exposure to media representations of female body shape and body self-esteem found that the propensity to make social comparisons between the self and others and the presence or absence of instructions concerning how to evaluate media body images were critical variables. Young women who routinely compared themselves to media role models were more likely than their peers who did not do this to disclose diminished body self-esteem after exposure. This effect could be minimized, however, when female participants in studies were instructed to focus on the appearance of mediated role models. Want (2009) concluded that social comparison processes occur automatically, but cognitive processing strategies can be invoked in relation to body-shape image in the media that can counteract comparison process effects.

Male body image

Concerns about media choices of female body shapes to put on display have attracted high-profile public debate (e.g., Woolf 2010) and widespread empirical investigation (Wykes & Gunter 2005). There are, however, also media biases in choices that are made for ideal male body shapes (Henwood, Gill, & McLean 1999, 2002). While a thin body shape is emphasized for women, a muscular frame is the ideal depicted most prominently for men. Consequently, for women, mediated female body shapes could make women feel bigger (or fatter) than they really are. For men, mediated male body shapes could make them feel too small or inadequately muscular (Harmatz, Gronendyke, & Thomas 1985; Mintz & Betz 1988).

There is mounting evidence—both qualitative and quantitative—that effects of media representation can also occur among men. Grogan and Richards (2002) reported that in focus group interviews with boys aged eight, thirteen, and sixteen, and with young adult males, the participants—especially from their teen years—identified being lean and muscular with being healthy and fit. They also noted that there were growing social pressures on them to adopt this "look." Some of these social pressures would seem to be driven by the mass media. One review of fifteen studies concluded that there was consistent evidence that exposure to idealized media images of muscular male bodies had a statistically significant effect on men's body dissatisfaction. Boys and men who lacked confidence in their physical appearance emerged as the most vulnerable to this effect (Blond 2008).

Research on media effects on men's body satisfaction may have mixed findings. In a study that depicted images taken from advertisements of male models with average-sized slender body shape, average-sized large body shape, or a muscular physique, men disclosed a more positive body image of themselves after seeing an average-sized model as compared to no model at all. Exposure to an advertising image showing a muscular male made no significant difference to male participants' body self-esteem (Diedriche & Lee 2010). In contrast, other studies of men have demonstrated decreased body satisfaction after viewing images of idealized, muscular models (Agliata & Tantleff-Dunn 2004; Lorenzen, Grieve, & Thomas 2004). These effects may be mediated by sexuality: a study of gay and heterosexual men found that while both groups had approximately the same strength of relationship between their self-esteem and body dissatisfaction, gay men reported more body dissatisfaction, and this was more strongly related to media influence than for straight men (McArdle & Hill 2009).

Eating behavior and disorders

Research into the effects of the media on eating disorders includes studies with clinical and nonclinical populations. The former studies, which are few in number, have explored the media habits and their potential influences among samples of women diagnosed as suffering from anorexia or bulimia. In one such study, women clinically diagnosed with eating disorders were found to display lower body self-esteem after being exposed to images of thin models compared to similar women shown pictures of average- or over-sized models. In the absence of a pretest, however, there was no opportunity to discover what pre-exposure differences existed in terms of body self-perceptions in each group (Irving 1990).

The latter studies have drawn mostly female samples from nonclinical populations and explored relationships between exposure to media representations of body shapes and self-reported, but not clinically diagnosed, indications of disordered eating. Exposure to magazines with visible body images and narrative themes concerning body shape has been statistically related to propensity to seek weight loss and to engage in extreme dieting among teenage girls (Levine, Smolak, & Hayden 1994). Greater reported reading of fashion magazines among teenage girls was associated with increased bulimic tendencies and greater reading of fitness magazines was linked to increased bulimia and anorexia (Botta 2003). Elsewhere, the frequency with which adolescent girls reported reading women's health and fitness magazines was positively linked to unhealthy weight control practices, such as the use of laxatives and over-restricting calories (Thomsen, Weber, & Brown 2001).

Survey research with nonclinical populations has provided little consistent evidence that television viewing per se is related to behavioral changes associated with eating. Frequency of television viewing was not found to have any link to dieting or propensities to engage in disordered eating among American preteen and teenage girls (Gonzalez-Levin & Smolak 1995) or to aspirations for thinness among another American teenage girl sample (Tiggemann & Pickering 1996). Despite showing some links to body self-esteem among Flemish teenagers in Belgium, self-reported television viewing was not related to levels of behavioral activity linked to weight loss or obesity (van den Bulck 2000).

When print and television exposure have been examined together, self-reported media exposure measures have been found to predict the internalized desire for a thinner body shape and body dissatisfaction, and via these constructs, a propensity for disordered eating has emerged among female college students (Polivy & Herman 1985; Stice *et al*. 1994). What this research shows is that any failure to find direct statistical links between media exposure and eating disorders does not necessarily mean that such links do not exist. Instead, disordered eating may be indirectly linked to media representations that first condition internalized body stereotypes that are often gender related, and then these constructs in turn establish the psychological conditions under which disordered eating patterns emerge.

Harrison (1997) examined relationships between both magazine reading and television viewing and disordered eating among American college-going women. On this occasion, respondents were also shown photographs of well-known female television characters and models from magazines and asked to evaluate these images in terms of their likeability, similarity to self, and wish to be like them. Harrison found that self-reported watching of named television shows with thin female leads was related to the drive to be thinner and to anorexic tendencies. Reported reading of fitness and fashion magazines was also related to anorexic and bulimic tendencies. In more complex statistical tests, however, which were designed to identify whether specific media variables were particularly significant as predictors, she found that the propensity to show anorexic symptoms was predicted most of all by reading fitness magazines and that both anorexia and bulimia were predicted also by attraction to thin media role models. This research was then extended to a young cohort of adolescents aged eleven to seventeen years. In this case, greater exposure to television programs that contained obviously fat characters was related to stronger bulimic tendencies and exposure to magazines that contained lots of thin models was related to stronger anorexia tendencies among teenage girls (Harrison 2000b).

General measures of television viewing, even at the program level, proved to be far less effective at predicting bulimia than the degree to which viewers made comparisons between themselves and on-screen characters (Botta 1999). Among adolescent girls then, it is not simply important to know whether they watch television programs with thin role models, but also whether these role models represent significant points of comparison for them. This argument is reinforced by qualitative research evidence showing that for the under-twenties, celebrity figures are especially important reference points when judging their own physical appearance (Grogan 1999); and—more broadly—when quantitative research demonstrates that media exposure, though a statistically significant factor, explains relatively little variance in feelings of dissatisfaction or body weight preferences (Botta 1999; Swami *et al.* 2010).

Turning to experimental research in which cause-effect hypotheses could be more directly assessed, mixed evidence has emerged that exposure to body-image ideals triggers changed eating habits. Much of the research has been conducted among populations classified as clinically "normal." This means that participants had not been medically diagnosed as suffering from a clinical eating disorder, such as anorexia or bulimia, in which they could cause harm to themselves or had already done so. In these studies, some evidence emerged that under controlled exposure conditions, young women exhibited shifts in their self-perceptions and even in their immediate eating choices after watching television programs or advertisements that featured female actors and models with slender body shapes (Lavine, Sweeney, & Wagner 1999; Myers & Biocca 1992; Seddon & Berry 1996).

A limited amount of evidence has emerged that when shown photographs of attractive, thin fashion models, women with eating disorders display lowered body self-esteem, greater body dissatisfaction, and also further exaggerate their estimates of their own body size (Hamilton & Waller 1993; Waller, Hamilton, & Shaw 1992). Qualitative research with women aged between eighteen and forty-three years, who were receiving outpatient treatment for eating disorders, indicated that they often made comparisons between themselves and models in beauty and fashion magazines. Some of these women said that they cut out photographs from magazines and kept them to refer to. In order to emulate the slender body shapes of these role models that they aspired to attain and maintain for themselves, these women reportedly controlled their own eating habits to keep their weight down (Thomsen, McCoy, & Williams, 2001).

Conclusion

Growing concern about the impact of media representations of body shape has led to calls for advertisers, magazine editors, movie and television producers to think carefully about the body shapes and appearance-related attributes they emphasize when selecting actors and models to appear in popular media outputs. The bombardment of young people with unrealistic images of idealized bodies at a time of personal development when their self-identity is malleable and susceptible to influence can, according to some critics, result in potentially harmful distortions of their body self-image (Woolf 2010). Such images are the outcome of not only the choice of slender actors and models for media portrayal, but also the subsequent manipulation of images through digital editing techniques, which "airbrush" the physical appearance of actors and models to render them slimmer than they actually are.

In the context of media and psychology, the study of body image and disordered eating provides potentially fertile ground for testing specific psychological theories about self-identity development and where and why it can go wrong. Psychologists have produced effective standard tests to measure constructs such as body image, body dissatisfaction, drive for thinness, and disordered eating. There is a growing understanding within psychology of the parts played by different personal and social factors that underpin these constructs (Grogan 2008). What is missing in relation to the study of the role played by the mass media is the development of methodologies that effectively represent the complete experiences of media consumers when they engage with media images of the human body. Complex cognitive and social processes are at play when individuals react to media images and media texts—a level of complexity largely absent in the evidence accumulated so far on this subject.

Subject in focus

The pro-ana phenomenon

The pro-ana phenomenon has become constructed around a community of web sites produced by and for young people with eating disorders. It focuses specifically on anorexia although it also embraces discussions about other eating disorders, such as bulimia (Davies & Lipsey 2003).

The membership of these sites tends to be primarily female, and the web sites are used for a variety of purposes, including information and advice exchange, mutual support, and sharing of experiences. Many of the sites incorporate social networking functions that enable users to forge new companionships (Borzekowski *et al.* 2010; Overbeke 2008).

Pro-ana sites have attracted negative publicity surrounding the tendency of some of these sites to seemingly promote anorexia as a lifestyle choice (Dolan 2003; Watkins 2010). Their major harms are that they are used to justify harmful behavior among misguided young women maintaining it among those who already suffer while encouraging others to join in (Paquette 2002; Pollack 2003). Many pro-ana web sites present images of thin and emaciated women under the theme of "thinspiration" that are designed to promote the desirability of being under-weight. Often these images depict celebrities or fashion models who are presented as role models in this context (Borzekowski *et al.* 2010; Dias 2003). These images are frequently accompanied by pro-anorexia narratives, with claims that they are not really harming themselves and that others simply do not understand them (Dias 2003).

Pro-ana sites attract negative comment as well as supporting posts and these so-called "flaming" messages can get very abusive. Online abuse can also sometimes be leveled by anorexics against other users, such as bulimics (also referred as the "mia" community), whose issues are not regarded as relevant or important. Further criticism is targeted at aspirant members (or "wannabes") who are blamed for attracting negative media coverage to the sites (Giles 2006).

A key concern about the pro-ana movement is that it openly seeks to promote anorexia and to encourage girls and young women to control their diets to achieve a slender body shape that is promoted as an "ideal" through posted discourses and images (Riley, Rodham, & Gavin 2009). Analyses of discourses, however, do not yield evidence of effects of pro-ana sites in their users; they merely identify the potential for effects to occur. Survey evidence has indicated that pro-ana sites attract a lot of traffic from young people with eating disorders and that they claim to have been further encouraged in their behavior by these sites (Wilson *et al.* 2006)

Research into the direct effects of these sites has been limited. Nonetheless, some empirical evidence has emerged that controlled exposure to pro-ana web sites can influence young women's perceptions of their appearance and weight, and their overall self-regard, even though they do not currently demonstrate disordered eating patterns. Following controlled exposure to pro-ana web sites, American college undergraduates have been observed to display more concerns about their weight, how much they eat, and exercising (Bardone-Cone & Cass 2007). Furthermore, young women whose test scores revealed a potential to bulimic tendencies had those tendencies strengthened by exposure to pro-ana web sites. Similarly, young women who already exhibited a propensity to go on diets had this propensity strengthened following exposure to a pro-ana web site (Bardone-Cone & Cass 2007).

The emergent evidence on the effects of pro-ana sites coupled with the clearly controversial nature of their discourses and imagery has rightly encouraged scholars working in this area to call for more work to be done into their impact upon vulnerable young people.

Discussion question

Some anorexics claim that pro-ana sites provide a source of support. To what extent should this be taken into consideration when evaluating the potential harm caused by these sites?

Further sources of information

Augustus-Horvath, C. L. & Tylka, T. L. (2009). "A test and extension of objectification theory as it predicts disordered eating: Does women's age matter?" *Journal of Counselling Psychology, 56,* 253–265.

Blond, A. (2008). "Impacts of exposure to images of ideal bodies on male body dissatisfaction: A review." *Body Image, 5,* 244–250.

Grogan, S. (2008). *Body image: Understanding body dissatisfaction in men, women and children* (2nd ed). London, UK: Routledge.

Stice, E., Schupak-Neuberg, E., Shaw, H. E., & Stein, R. (1994). "Relation of media exposure to eating disorder symptomatology: An examination of mediating mechanisms." *Journal of Abnormal Psychology, 103,* 836–840.

Swami, V., *et al.* (2010). "The attractive female body weight and female body dissatisfaction in 26 countries across 10 world regions: Results of the International Body Project I." *Personality and Social Psychology Bulletin, 36,* 309–325.

Want, S. C. (2009). "Meta-analytic moderators of experimental exposure to media portrayals of women on female appearance satisfaction: Social comparisons as automatic processes." *Body Image, 6,* 257–269.

Wykes, M. & Gunter, B. (2005). *The media and body image: If looks could kill.* London, UK: Sage.

Advertising 4

Advertising represents a substantial departure from two of the previous subject areas (Media Violence and Body Image) in which media executives often argue that media exposure has little impact on the attitudes and behavior of the audience. Advertising, conceptualized as "communication intended to persuade the consumer to purchase a product or service" (and the media that rely on advertising driven revenue), is dependent on the influence that the media has on the consumer. The wide range of newspapers and television channels that are free to consumers, but generate their income from advertising alone, clearly demonstrate the extent to which advertising can be desirable and in fact essential to some media.

Compared to other areas of the media, psychologists have made a relatively small contribution to advertising research, with much of the work in this area conducted by advertising agencies or media analysts. While psychologists have become more engaged with the subject in recent years, this tradition has impacted on the scope of work conducted, the development of theory, and the dissemination of findings to the wider public. The current text therefore includes research conducted in a range of fields.

The chapter describes the techniques used by advertisers to attract consumer attention, enhance brand awareness, and increase product sales. The specific importance of product placement and the rise in Internet advertising will also be considered. The dominant theories within the field of advertising, which influence numerous aspects of advertising campaign development, will also be outlined. As public bodies and consumer groups have expressed specific concern at the impact of advertising on children, this issue (with particular emphasis on food advertising) will be covered.

Exposure and avoidance

Advertising involves a wide range of media, including television, radio, Internet, newspapers and magazines, and exposure to advertising is considerable.

The average British consumer views forty television commercials per day (BARB 2007). The amount of advertising in existence and disruption to regular media content (e.g., interruptions to programs on television) has led many consumers to become disinterested or skeptical. In fact, many consumers regularly avoid advertisements (Peitz & Valetti 2008; Tse & Lee 2001), either by physically (e.g., zapping between channels) or mentally (e.g., talking to someone) separating themselves from the advertisement. Overall it is generally accepted that television viewers pay less attention to advertisements than television programs (Abernethy 1991). It is perhaps surprising then that a number of television channels (QVC—Quality, Value, Convenience and HSN—Home Shopping Network) consist entirely of product advertising and sales.

Reasons for avoidance may include general boredom or interest in other activities such as checking e-mail, although consumers' attitudes toward advertisements have a substantial impact on the extent to which they engage in these types of avoidance behaviors. Individuals who have positive attitudes toward advertisements (e.g., believing that advertisements are informative) are less likely to avoid advertisements than those with negative attitudes (Rojas-Mendez & Davies 2005; Speck & Elliot 1997). Culture and prior exposure to advertising may be particularly important when developing attitudes toward advertising. For example, consumers living in former Soviet Bloc countries (with a relatively recent exposure to branded goods and advertising) are more positive toward advertising than those consumers exposed to a greater level of advertising such as those in the US or UK (Andrews, Durvasala & Netermeyer 1994). Similarly, consumers in countries with relatively little experience of advertising are also less skeptical than those with greater previous exposure (Feick & Gierl 1996).

Techniques

Advertisers have developed a number of techniques in order to attract the consumers' attention, increase brand awareness, convey important product information, and shape consumer attitudes and behavior. Of course, a number of factors, including the product category (Geuens, De Pelsmacker, & Faseur 2011) and market, may influence the success of each technique (Jeon & Beatty 2002) and the way in which consumers react to advertisements vary widely (Moore, Harris, & Chen 1995; Ruiz & Sicilia 2004). A number of frequently used techniques are outlined next.

News and information

Some advertisements focus on the transmission of news such as a "new and improved formula" or extension of the brand range. Although the consumer may not necessarily find these advertisements enjoyable or entertaining, if the information is relevant (e.g., the new product is sought after), they may be well received (Kaiser & Song 2009). The current medicalization of food advertising whereby a number of health claims are included (Zwier 2009) represent one recent trend. Of course, the number of advertisements regularly attempting to publicize brand improvements may also make consumers skeptical and distrustful of these claims.

One form of information advertising includes comparisons with other brands (Jeon & Beatty 2002). This may include explicit comparisons in which the brand is named (common in the US) or referenced as "Brand X" or "the leading brand" that is more frequent in the British market. Consumers may find comparative information useful or reliable; alternatively, if each brand makes similar claims about its own product, consumers may believe that there is little actual difference between each brand. This belief may benefit less popular brands if the consumer decides to alternate between brands rather than repeatedly purchase the market leader.

Entertainment, liking, and humor

An entertaining advertisement may encourage the consumer to develop positive associations with the brand, attend to the advertisement (leading to greater recall and recognition of the brand), and build tolerance for long or repeated advertising campaigns. The creation of entertaining advertisements may be particularly appealing to established brands where opportunities to inform the audience about new developments are limited. Two common forms of entertainment involve mini-dramas and humor. While these represent different types of entertainment, both work on similar principles (e.g., capturing attention and reducing distrust) and experience similar challenges. For example, it is important for advertisers using this technique to fully integrate the featured brand and ensure that the brand itself is memorable. Otherwise, there is a risk that the advertisement will be likeable but have little impact on brand awareness, among other things.

One recent advertising campaign for comparethemarket.com (a price comparison Internet site) involved an animated meerkat complaining of confusion with comparethemeerkat.com. This capitalized on consumer fondness of animals (Lancendorfer, Atkin, & Reece 2008) and importantly made the name of the brand a key part of the advertisement. Additional (comparethemeerkat.com and comparethemuskrat.com) Internet sites have been created to support the advertisements. Further highlighting the degree to which consumers may engage with entertaining content, material associated with the campaign features on social networking sites, and YouTube hosts "bloopers" of the advertisements and interviews. Perhaps the most notable achievement is the success of an "autobiography" from one meerkat *A simples Life: My Life and Times by Aleksandr Orlov* and various other merchandise.

Technological advances that allow consumers to avoid advertisements (e.g., Digital Video Recorders (DVRs) such as TiVo and Sky+) or access interesting material (e.g., video sharing sites such as YouTube) have arguably encouraged the development of entertaining and innovative advertisements. Therefore, while traditionally advertisers have spent a large proportion of their budget on distribution rather than production of advertising material, some successful campaigns may increase production costs and benefit from consumer-driven distribution. For example, the Adidas Star Wars Cantina advertisement (2010) incorporated a number of celebrities into the original movie scene and was widely viewed and shared through social networking sites.

Controversy

One advertising technique is to deliberately shock or provoke the consumer. A controversial campaign may attract the consumer's attention and thus raise awareness of the brand (Waller 1999) although there is a risk that a negative association with the brand may develop. In extreme instances, provocative advertising campaigns have resulted in a boycott by consumers or consumer groups. The effects of provocation may vary according to the nature of the controversy, the product category advertised, and the demographics of the target consumers (Waller 2004); therefore, advertisers using this technique require a substantial knowledge of the target consumer in order to minimize risk and obtain the desired reaction. While there is a possibility that those adverts may cause offence (and thus alienate potential consumers), controversial advertising campaigns are more likely to be discussed by individuals (and thus promote the brand to consumers that were not originally exposed to the original advertisement) and be debated within the media, which further attracts attention to the brand.

Provocative or controversial advertising is often associated with the clothing company Benetton. In the late 1980s, the company's advertising typically featured provocative images (often with reference to racism or religion) rather than the products available, accompanied by the company slogan "United Colors of Benetton." The widespread interest in the campaign encouraged a number of other high-profile companies to include provocation within their advertising campaigns. As the use of provocation within advertising becomes more widespread, it is possible that each campaign will become less distinct. This may have important implications for the consumer's reaction to the campaign and recall of the advertised brand.

Popularity

Consumers are often influenced by what they believe is the most popular product and a number of advertising campaigns emphasize the popularity of the brand. In particular, advertisers may refer to the "leading brand" as selecting the popular brand minimizes the risk that the consumer will be marginalized for their purchase. This type of conformity may be particularly important for those concerned with their image or heavily influenced by their peers such as children and adolescents. The popularity of a product may also indicate to the consumer that the brand can be trusted, that others have found it satisfactory and reliable.

Consumers are often attracted to products that appear to be rapidly gaining popularity. In this context, the consumer who also purchases the product demonstrates that they are familiar with popular trends. Of course, there is a potential for brands that become very popular (particularly in a short space of time) to become devalued or rejected by consumers who wish to display their discriminating taste. In this way, many brands have achieved enviable short-term success but become permanently associated with a particular era such as the Cabbage Patch dolls in the 1980s or season such as the Thunderbirds Tracy Island during Christmas 1992.

Brand image: The use of celebrities and characters

If the people featured in the advertisement are the types of individuals that we aspire to be (attractive, popular, etc.) then we may be encouraged to purchase the product in order to "become a member of the group" and develop these qualities. In this way, using or purchasing a particular brand may allow consumers to express or develop a particular self-identity. For some brands, the cultural status associated with the product, rather than a qualitative difference with another brand, is central to its success. Celebrity endorsement may encourage consumers to associate the product with the qualities of the celebrity (e.g., sporting performance or glamour) and their current liking of the celebrity may be transferred to the product endorsed. The selection of a suitable celebrity is particularly important as the consumer's perception of the product may differ depending on the celebrity endorsing the product (Walker, Langmeyer, & Langmeyer 1992).

Directly relating the image of a product with a particular celebrity may, however, be problematic if the celebrity becomes involved in a scandal or behaves in a way that is inconsistent with the brand image. There are numerous examples of a celebrity behaving in a way inconsistent with a brand image, including David Beckham shaving his head when endorsing the

Brylcreem hair product range and the revelations about Tiger Woods' extramarital affairs. Although advertisers may remove the celebrity from all advertising in order to protect brand image (e.g., Hertz terminated the relationship with O. J. Simpson after allegations of domestic violence and murder) an association between the behavior of the celebrity and brand may have developed.

A popular alternative to celebrity endorsement involves the creation of a particular character with which the brand is associated: for example, the creation of "Sue Chard" to promote Suchard chocolates or "Ronald McDonald" to promote the McDonald's chain. The development of a fictional character provides the company and advertisers with total control over the use of the character. In this manner, the addition of a character to relatively innocuous material such as posters and stickers can remind the consumer of the brand.

Presenters

Many advertisements feature presenters who describe the positive features of the brand to the consumer or less directly to another character. The president or owner of the company may act as a presenter, which may make the company and brand seem less impersonal and corporate. When the consumer feels that the presenter is trying to persuade them, they may become defensive and reluctant to believe the claims within the advert. Therefore, in a number of advertisements, the presenter explains the features of the brand to another character. This approach appears less confrontational and typically results in less distrust from the consumer.

Advertisements that feature a presenter are typically more effective than those featuring a voice-over only. Voice-overs continue to be used, however, as they are less expensive than adverts featuring a presenter and they allow the advertiser to modify the message as new promotions or information are available or to provide variation for different national markets. One solution often used is to employ a voice-over recorded by a celebrity with a distinctive voice, allowing a positive association between the brand and celebrity to develop but remaining less expensive and more readily modifiable.

Product placement

Product placement describes the inclusion of branded goods or services into media that is not recognized as an advertisement. Although product placement is most frequently discussed with reference to television programs and movies, the technique is also used (albeit less frequently) in other media forms such as books and song lyrics (e.g., Bacardi in *In Da Club* by 50 Cent). The technique has become increasingly popular (Karrh, Brittain McKee, & Pardun 2003) with advertising companies often diverting funds from their television-advertising budget to invest in product placement (Consoli 2005). In part, this trend reflects the availability of technology such as TiVO and Sky+ that allow the consumer to avoid traditional television advertisements and fragmentation of the media. In this context, product placement may be viewed as a more attractive and reliable way of reaching potential consumers.

Explicit product placement is usually incorporated into a program or movie in exchange for products that reduce production costs (e.g., the supply of cars for an action movie) or a fee (Karrh 1998). Similar arrangements may also occur with quiz shows that offer branded goods as prizes. In return for the placement or integration of their product, companies may also promote the movie when advertising their own product. For example, fast-food outlets such as Burger King (*Star Wars: Revenge of the Sith*) or McDonalds (*Star Wars: The Clone Wars*) routinely offer movie merchandise to children while running advertising campaigns that feature both the movie and product. These types of exclusive arrangements have become increasingly popular over the last decade and can be beneficial for both parties. Product placement should be distinguished from sponsored programming (e.g., Hallmark movies) in which a company funds the production of a program in return for a high-profile advertisement or association with the program.

Investing in product placement may be more financially rewarding than for expensive prime-time television advertisements, particularly when the popularity of repeat programming and the purchase of DVDs (which repeatedly expose consumers to the featured product at no extra cost) are taken into consideration. Lehu and Bressoud (2008) outline the importance of these "second viewings" and report that viewers watching a movie on DVD show better product recall than when they have previously seen the movie at a cinema. Consequently, the "box office" success of a movie does not fully reflect the impact of product placement.

The extent to which the product is integrated within a program or movie varies widely. Characters may use the product but not refer to it; a practice which many media companies claim simply increases realism. The character may explicitly refer to or praise the brand (Converse in *I, Robot* or Omega and Gordon's in *Casino Royale*). And in some (less frequent) instances the brand may be an integral part of the story itself (*Breakfast at Tiffany's*). When products become an integral part of the program, the practice is often described as product integration. Other movies have referred to artificial brands (e.g., Big Kahuna Burger in *Pulp Fiction*. Of course, this has also provided opportunities for manufacturers with, for example, 7-Eleven rebranding some of its stores as Kwik-E-Marts (featured in *The Simpsons*).

Product placement does appear to impact on the viewer's attitudes (Redondo 2006) and recall (Brennan, Dubas, & Babin 1999) of the featured product. After watching a movie clip, over 95% of participants can recall products featured (Vollmers & Mizerski 1994). However, how attractive, identifiable, and memorable the brand is may impact on placement success. Matching the brand with an appropriate movie and audience is important. For example, a placement of a baby food brand may be less successful in an action movie than a family comedy or cartoon targeted at parents and young children. The type of product featured also impacts on viewer responses. For example, while smoking is featured heavily in some movies (e.g., *Coco before Chanel*), the inclusion of cigarettes or other controversial products can impact on the viewers' reaction (Gupta & Gould 1997).

Recent technological developments have allowed large corporations to target regional markets. In particular, a brand name more suitable for a US audience can be replaced with a brand more suitable for an overseas audience depending on the movie distribution. For example *Demolition Man* (1993) featured the Taco Bell chain when distributed in the US and Pizza Hut when delivered overseas. Similarly US versions of *Spider-Man 2* (2004) contained the Dr Pepper brand, which was replaced with Mirinda overseas. New technologies provide additional opportunities for advertising and product placement in particular. Virtual placement refers to the addition of brands to movies or programs post production, which may also allow advertisers to take advantage of movies that are more popular at the box office than anticipated during production.

The controversy surrounding product placement stems largely from the fact that consumers are not prepared for the advertisement and may be less ready to critique the product than in traditional settings. The explicitness of the product placement and whether the consumer believes that the product has been included to reflect typical consumption or purely to promote a product may have a considerable impact on viewers' perceptions of product placement. Critics of product placement include writers who believe that the integrity of their work is compromised when they are asked to include explicit references to brands and products and consumer groups.

The replacement of one brand with another can be particularly problematic. New brands may be rejected by the audience if the replacement is seen as a betrayal of the character or a "sellout" by the producers that place financial rewards above the integrity of the story. For example, Carrie Bradshaw, the central character in the *Sex and the City* series frequently used a Mac in the television series and first movie. In fact, Apple created a web site allowing viewers to access the character's desktop to capitalize on the association. The use of a PC in the second movie was criticized by many viewers. Similarly, fans of the James Bond franchise widely rejected the decision to replace the

Aston Martin with BMWs. If a character changes from one product or brand for no other reason than the product placement agreement, viewers may not believe that the new product is a credible alternative.

Internet advertising

In recent years, Internet advertising has become both more widespread and sophisticated (Low 2000). The initial approach of adapting advertising material to the Internet has progressed to a more in-depth understanding of the way in which consumers engage with the Internet (see Chapter 5 for a wider discussion of consumer engagement with the Internet). In particular, advertisers and companies have increasingly focused on the development of material for consumers searching for information on a brand or product type (e.g., laptop computers and digital cameras) rather than the widespread use of pop-ups, which are unpopular with consumers and largely ineffective. Search advertising has proved particularly popular in recent years and the revenue from this stream has contributed to the development of influential search engines such as Google. This partly reflects the fact that searching for information is one of the most common reasons for Internet use (Rubin 2002). Attitudes, beliefs, and responses to online advertising may of course differ between countries (Wang & Sun 2010).

The Internet has provided valuable opportunities for advertisers to obtain information about an individual, including basic demographic details and purchase history. Sites may offer free services such as e-mail or discounts and rewards to users that register their personal details, although users often provide false information if there are concerns about privacy (Montaner, Lopez, & de la Rosa 2003). This information is especially valuable to advertisers wishing to target particular groups. The use of targeted advertisements (e.g., recommendation of a book or DVD based on previous searches or purchase history) may be of interest to the consumer, which reduces the likelihood that the user will unsubscribe from the service. The use of targeted advertising, particularly if client information has been sold to a secondary source in order to generate revenue, however, has been criticized for increasing the level of unsolicited "junk" mail.

Some of the most controversial online advertising campaigns have involved the use of bait and switch campaigns in which users register to receive free content such as an image or ringtone for a mobile phone, but do not realize that (within the often ignored small print) they have also registered to receive additional content for which they will be charged. Companies may generate substantial revenue in this manner, particularly if the individual charges are relatively small and consumers do not unsubscribe immediately. In the long term, however, this strategy can alienate consumers who develop a negative image of the brand and convey their distrust to other potential consumers.

Advertising theory

A number of theories have guided advertising research. These theories have often been adapted from a wider subject area such as attitude formation and do not necessarily focus on advertising alone. Advertising theories have increased the understanding of both advertising executives and researchers. In particular, a greater theoretical understanding of advertising can inform the content and style of future advertising campaigns. Compared to other subject areas, however, there has been relatively little theoretical development. Advertisers often focus on more specific and practical issues such as the role of repetition and the consumer groups most responsive to specific advertising techniques. In addition, the research conducted (or funded) by the advertising companies themselves is not necessarily disseminated to the wider research community (which of course gives their direct competitors access to the information). The most prominent theories include the Hierarchy of Effects Model and the Elaboration Likelihood Model, each outlined next.

Hierarchy of Effects Model

The Hierarchy of Effects Model has been widely used to describe and explain the influence of mass-media advertising. According to the model, consumers respond to advertising in a predictable and ordered way. First there is a cognitive (thinking), then affective (feeling and emotion), and lastly conative response (action and behavior). Lavidge and Steiner (1961) proposed one of the most commonly discussed versions of the model, which describes the way in which advertising moves the consumer through a series of stages. These stages ultimately lead to the desired behavior, typically the purchase of the advertised brand.

Lavidge and Steiner acknowledged that a number of factors such as the consumer's involvement with the advertisement or attachment to a rival brand would impact on the time taken to be persuaded to purchase the advertised brand. While the length of time a consumer takes to progress through these stages may differ, the researchers argued that the stages were passed through in the same order by consumers regardless of previous preference and experience. Some support for the Hierarchy of Effects Model has been generated by researchers assessing the effects of a health-care campaign (Bauman *et al.* 2008; Craig, Bauman, & Reger-Nash 2009); see Chapter 2 for an in-depth description of health communication.

As with most theoretical frameworks, more recent revisions and alternatives have been proposed. Most criticisms and revisions have focused on the order in which these stages are experienced rather than the actual existence or importance of each stage. Research evidence exists for a range of sequences: for example, understanding of the advertising message may lead to behavioral change (leading to attitude change) rather than the attitude and then the behavior change. Similarly, the purchase and use of a brand (behavior) may influence a consumer's thoughts and feelings (cognitive and affective) about the brand—a situation that may be quite common when our favored brand is not available and we find that the alternate is just as good. Other criticisms focus on the extent to which researchers can distinguish between the cognitive (thinking) and affective (feeling and emotion) stages.

Elaboration Likelihood Model

The Elaboration Likelihood Model (Petty & Cacioppo 1981, 1986) focuses on persuasion and the formation and development of attitudes. The model has been successfully applied to advertising (Petty & Cacioppo 1983; Petty, Cacioppo, & Shumann 1983) and has achieved widespread acceptance within the field.

According to the model, there are two routes to persuasion (and a change in attitude toward the advertised brand): the central route and the peripheral route. The central route involves high elaboration and occurs when the consumer considers the advertisement in detail. For example, an individual may assess the arguments and evidence put forward by the advertiser. The thoughts that arise during this process determine whether the consumer accepts the message and the extent to which they are persuaded. Persuasion through the central route requires both the ability to process the message and the motivation. The peripheral route does not involve extensive elaboration. The consumer's interpretation of the advertisement focuses on surface characteristics such as the physical attractiveness of the advertisement rather than the argument presented.

The consumer's desire to process the information (motivation) and proficiency evaluating the message (ability) determine the level to which the advertisement is elaborated and it is this elaboration that establishes the route to persuasion taken. The likelihood of following each route varies as the level of motivation and ability develops. A number of factors may influence a person's ability or motivation such as the presence of distractions and the relevance of the information conveyed. For example, an advertisement for dog food is not relevant to a person with no pets and diapers hold no interest for people with no children.

It is also possible that the consumer will use peripheral cues to guide whether or not to attend to the central arguments. According to the model, attitudes that develop through the central route (involving high elaboration) are stronger than those formed via the peripheral (low elaboration) route. As a result, attitudes that follow the central route are less likely to change and more resistant to contradictory information.

The model has achieved widespread recognition and acceptance within the field of advertising. There are, however, a number of important limitations. First, while the theory acknowledges that under certain circumstances, peripheral cues may guide an individual to attend or not attend to central arguments, there is little distinction between moderate levels of consumer motivation and ambiguity (where interest in the product has not yet been established). Understanding this ambiguity may be particularly important when assessing consumer reactions to new products.

Second, the model suggests that on the peripheral route, cue attractiveness impacts on attitude change. However, initial attitudes toward the product (and not just the quality of the argument provided) may predict attitude change via the central route. Third, the model assumes that a consumer that has started to progress along the peripheral or central route will continue on the same route. This ignores the frequency with which people may stop attending to the advertisement or their attention may be disrupted. For example, although I may accept the general message conveyed by an advertisement "if you do not buy this detergent, your home will be filled with germs and your family will become ill" or "if you do not buy this drink, your peers will find you unattractive and you will become a social outcast," I may find the implicit threat distressing, causing me to select more positive or humorous material.

Measurement and evaluation

Advertising as an industry is clearly established and, as detailed, a number of specific advertising techniques have been identified. It is perhaps surprising then that there is relatively little agreement about the overall effectiveness of advertising or in fact how to actually measure advertising success. It is important to note that the type of product featured and the country in which the advertisement occurs may influence the measurement of advertising success (Jeon & Beatty 2002). For example, an increase in product sales may be more quickly determined for low investment products such as soft drinks that are bought daily or weekly than for infrequently bought high investment items such as a car or vacation.

A clear indication that an advertising campaign is successful is an increase in product sales and this would at first glance be the most straightforward and objective way to determine success. However, a high-profile advertising campaign may encourage stores to display the brand in a more prominent position; sales personnel may have increased confidence in the brand or find it easier to generate orders. In addition, advertising that features a celebrity may benefit from increased coverage of the celebrity (e.g., sporting success, high-profile relationships). In this context, it is difficult to establish the exclusive impact of an advertising campaign on product sales.

In recent years, a more sophisticated understanding of advertising has developed. In particular, the original assumption that repeated viewing of an advertisement automatically increases the likelihood that a brand will be purchased has been challenged. For example, consumers may be unwilling to purchase brands following offensive or irritating advertisements. Consequently, advertisers measuring the success of a campaign have placed a greater emphasis on consumers' attitudes and feelings toward the advertised brand (Mehta 2000), which also relates to purchase of the product (Korgaonkar & Wolin 2002).

Focus groups may be used to establish consumers' liking of the advertisement. The extent to which liking an advertisement encourages sales remains unclear, however. In addition, while focus groups may provide advertisers with important information (e.g., whether the primary message is clear), reaction to one advertisement may not provide feedback about repeated exposure or a response to an integrated campaign (e.g., incorporating radio, print, Internet, and television advertising).

It is also difficult to make generalizations about specific techniques. For example, numerous forms of humorous advertising exist and so simply evaluating the effectiveness of humor may be inappropriate. Important differences also exist between individuals and cultures with respect to what we find humorous. An advertisement that is humorous to one person may be offensive to another. Therefore, both positive and negative effects of the campaign should be considered in the evaluation.

Similarly, the distribution of the advertisement rather than its execution may impact on campaign success. For example, it may be more difficult for consumers to avoid advertisements presented on a cinema screen than to a television at home. In this context, it is important to consider each aspect of an integrated media campaign, in addition to other factors such as the consumers' preexisting perception of the brand. For example, companies reintroducing into market a product that has a poor brand image (e.g., previous poor performance) may regard a campaign as successful if it simply removes the negative perception rather than developing a liking for the product.

Internet advertising has progressed considerably in recent years. This area clearly illustrates some of the difficulties associated with the measurement of advertising success. For example, the frequency with which consumers are exposed to "pop-ups" may reflect the percentage of the target market reached, but not the consumers' reaction (e.g., irritation and frustration). In response, many advertisers developed "pay per click" agreements in which fees were based on the number of users actively clicking through to a site. The number of times that an advertisement is clicked can be a useful measure of advertising effectiveness (Dreze & Zufryden 1997) and does predict recall of the advertisement (Gong & Maddox 2003). Click fraud (Oser 2005) in which a person or program clicks through to a site to make it appear more popular has, however, reduced the reliability of the system.

Children and advertising

Two issues have dominated research in this area: (a) the extent to which young consumers can evaluate an advertisement and differentiate between advertising and other media and (b) the potential impact of the advertising on the child's attitude and behavior. Findings from both areas have been used to suggest that direct advertising to children should be restricted.

It has been argued that children lack the cognitive skills to analyze advertisements with the same level of discrimination and skepticism as adult consumers, making children more susceptible to the influence of advertisers, with young children more vulnerable than older children (Gunter & Furnham 1998). This may be exacerbated by the fact that younger children find it difficult to delay gratification (Metcalfe & Mischel 1999). Understanding the persuasive nature of advertising may be particularly difficult for children when sophisticated techniques such as celebrity endorsement or product placement are used. Even when children understand the persuasive intent of advertising, however, they continue to desire and request products (Mehta *et al.* 2010). Overall, the research suggests that exposure to advertising increases comprehension of the brand, positive associations with the brand, and more frequent selection of the brand advertised (Desmond & Carveth 2007) although the effects are relatively small.

Exposure to advertising is linked to increased materialism in children (Greenberg & Brand 1993). In this context, advertising focuses the child's attention on desirable goods and suggests that happiness will result from the possession of particular products. This may lead to unhappiness (if less affluent children compare themselves and their own situation to the children featured in the advertisements) and increased parent-child conflict (Buijxen & Valkenburg 2003). The term "pester power" is used to describe the way in which a child (often unrelentingly) attempts to persuade a parent to purchase a product. While this continual pestering and subsequent conflict may leave many adults frustrated, parents can influence the child's perception of an advertisement and subsequent "pester" behavior. For example, the relationship between exposure to television programs and the number of gifts placed on a list to Father Christmas is strongest for children who are exposed to television without parental supervision (Pine & Nash 2001).

In many cases, products are developed to accompany a successful program. Children may use pester power to obtain products that feature (and are apparently endorsed) by popular characters without the involvement of traditional advertising campaigns. In fact, products are often introduced to coincide with the release of a movie or television program in which the movie or series itself acts as the advertising campaign. The value of the merchandise associated with a movie can be clearly observed from the vast range of products available to support the *Star Wars* and *Spider-Man* movies. Clearly the complexity of this relationship requires further research. The close association between media content and branded goods is not a recent development. In fact, the toy manufacturer Mattel developed the cartoon series *He-Man: Masters of the Universe* to promote and sell their He-Man products. Corporate awareness of the association between television or movies and merchandise is further evidenced by the way in which the media often parodies the role of branded goods. For example, in the Disney film *Hercules*, one of the main characters own *Hercules* shoes and soft drink.

It is also important to consider the manner in which children's engagement with advertising is changing in response to technological developments. Demonstrating the sophistication of young consumers, a friend's son used digitally recorded commercials as "evidence" to support his Christmas list. As children in modern society are exposed to more advertising than previous generations, some groups have campaigned for a removal of all advertising targeted at children. Others have highlighted the effectiveness of media literacy interventions in which children are educated to become critical consumers (Kubey 1998). It is argued that this type of education will prepare children and adolescents for the increasingly sophisticated advertising techniques that they will be exposed to as adults.

Researchers addressing this area often (as with research focused on adult consumers) neglect the importance of individual differences and the consumer's interpretation of the advertisement. For example, young viewers may categorize products as "boys' toys" or "girls' toys" and only attend closely to the adverts that feature age and gender appropriate products.

Advertising and children's health

Much of the controversy that surrounds direct advertising to children centers on the extent to which advertising exposure may impact on children's health and well-being. This research typically investigates the relationship between the advertising of one product category and subsequent consumption. For example, the likelihood of trying smoking has been related to the exposure to tobacco advertising (Feighery *et al.* 2006) and exposure to alcohol advertising is related to drinking and drinking intentions (Fleming, Thorson, & Atkin 2004; Grube & Waiters 2005). Highlighting the importance of brand identification, ownership of merchandise promoting alcohol also predicts drinking intentions (McClure *et al.* 2006).

A number of particularly bold statements have been made about the effects of advertising on children and adolescents. For example, "Tobacco marketing campaigns between 1988 and 1997 are responsible for 6 million adolescents experimenting with cigarettes. Of those, 2.6 million kids took their first puffs as a result of the Joe Camel campaign; another 1.4 million tried smoking because of the Marlboro campaign" (Thorp 1998, cited in Desmond & Carveth 2007). The strongest claims about the relationship between advertising and behavior are typically made by the general public, consumer groups, and policy makers, however, rather than academics or health professionals researching this subject area.

Food products dominate the advertising directed at children (Harris 1999), with soft drinks, confectionary, breakfast cereals, fast food, and savory snacks most prominent (FSA 2003). These advertisements often associate food and drinks with athletic ability, popularity, and enjoyment (Folta *et al.* 2006). The content of these advertisements combined with the fact that television exposure has been related to childhood obesity (Anderson *et al.* 1998) and weight gain (Proctor *et al.* 2003) has prompted concern. In response to these findings and widespread criticism, advertisers commonly argue that, rather than the eating habits, this relationship reflects a lack of physical activity among children who watch a lot of television.

However, while children's level of physical activity may contribute to the relationship between television exposure and obesity, research demonstrates that this media exposure is associated with greater consumption of food and unhealthy food in particular (Francis, Lee, & Birch 2003). It appears that food advertising influences both the preference for a particular product category (such as soft drinks) and the preference for a particular brand. These findings together with evidence that children eat more after exposure to food advertising on television (Halford *et al.* 2004) clearly highlights the influence of food advertising on eating behavior and the potential impact on health and well-being. In 2006b, the World Health Organization recommended "national actions to substantially reduce the volume and impact of commercial promotion of energy-dense, micronutrient-poor food and beverages to children" (32). In response to the accumulation of research evidence and consumer concerns, many countries have introduced self-regulation to address this issue rather than government intervention.

Conclusion

To summarize, advertisers use a range of media such as television and radio to attract consumers' attention, increase brand awareness, and encourage product sales. Popular techniques include celebrity endorsement and the development of controversial advertisements. The creation of humorous or entertaining advertisements and product placement may become increasingly important techniques, as Sky+ and TiVo allow consumers to avoid television commercials. Although a number of popular techniques exist, relatively little systematic research has been conducted in this area.

In fact, much of the research and theoretical development in this area has been directed by advertising agencies or media analysts, restricting the dissemination of research findings. In recent years, psychologists have increased their presence in the field, a trend that is expected to continue. Psychologists have often investigated the impact of advertising on consumer attitudes and behavior, particularly for more vulnerable groups such as children. Overall, advertising provides an interesting comparison with other areas of media psychology in which industry experts often try to deny or minimize the association between media exposure and consumer behavior.

Subject in focus

Subliminal and covert advertising

The potential for advertisers to manipulate or persuade consumers has caused concern for as long as advertising has existed. In 1957, the techniques used by advertisers and their ability to influence behavior came under particular scrutiny, as it was claimed that subliminal messages had been shown to over 45,000 people watching a movie at a theater in New Jersey (US) over a six-week period. According to Vicary, showing the messages "Eat popcorn" and "Drink Coke" increased popcorn and coke sales by 18% and 58% respectively.

Understandably, the technique captured the attention of advertising agencies, consumers, and others who wished to influence human behavior. For example, in the late 1970s, a Wichita (Kansas, US) television station inserted the message "Contact the Chief" into a news report at the request of the police investigating the BTK Strangler case (Guillen 2002). Despite the interest that his claims received, Vicary later admitted that he had not conducted the research. In fact, although self-help tapes featuring subliminal messages remain popular and the use of subliminal messages continues in other areas of psychological research (Massar & Buunk 2009; Massar, Buunk, & Dechesne 2009), a review of the literature (Pratkanis & Aronson 1992) finds no clear evidence that these subliminal messages influence attitudes or behavior.

Despite the general consensus that subliminal advertising is not effective, a number of researchers have explored the potential use of subliminal messages and argue that subliminal messages can influence behavior but only under specific conditions. For example, Karremans, Stroebe, and Claus (2006) found that presenting subliminal messages could increase the participant's intention to drink and their choice for a specific brand, but only when they were already thirsty.

It has also been argued that advertisers use covert communication (see Crook 2004 for a discussion) in order to manipulate the consumer's emotions and influence their perception of the advertised brand. In particular, Key (1994) suggests that advertisers regularly insert sexually explicit words or images into advertisements. This argument is popular with the general public and speculation has surrounded a number of brands such as Camel cigarettes. There is little research evidence to support this suggestion, although the speculation itself may attract attention to the brand. In a number of cases, the supposed images are unclear and sexually explicit images or words that are inserted into advertising often reflect the sense of humor of the artist that has included the images without the knowledge of the advertising company or brand.

Discussion question

Do advertisers have a responsibility to inform consumers about covert advertising?

Further sources of information

Du Plessis, E. (2008). *The advertised mind: Groundbreaking insights into how our brains respond to advertising.* London: Millward Brown.

Spurgeon, C. (2008). *Advertising and new media.* New York: Routledge.

Sutherland, M. & Sylvester, A. K. (2000). *Advertising and the mind of the consumer: What works, what doesn't, and why* (2nd ed). Sydney: Allen & Unwin.

PART
II

Interaction with the Media

Jon Cabiria

Internet and Interaction

The earliest written information about how the Internet would work was described in memos written in 1962 by an MIT computer scientist, J. C. R. Licklider (Leiner *et al.* 2010). In it, he described a "Galactic network" of computers connected to one other, allowing access to data (and to each other) from any location. By 1973, the US Defense Advanced Research Projects Agency (DARPA) explored technological methods for interlinking various networks, with a goal to develop communication protocols across a variety of networked sites (Cerf 2010).

Over the next decades, Licklider's vision of a world connected through machines came to fruition as computers became ubiquitous in many homes and businesses across the globe. People no longer had to be in one another's presence to communicate, nor did the communication have to be in real time. While telephones and letters were the standard means of distance communication for generations, computer communications advanced the concept of "non-present" interactions to unimagined levels, even by the earliest developers. Forrester Research noted that there would be approximately two billion personal computers in use by 2015 (Yates 2007). This represents the potential for human interaction on an unprecedented scale, whereby creating relationships is as easy as a web link and a click of the mouse.

Today, most of the current one billion plus users of personal computers have access to a dizzying array of methods for interaction. E-mail and texting remain the most popular means of staying connected with each other (Pew 2009). However, other online social options have grown exponentially over the years to include chat forums for people with mutual interests, virtual worlds, video sharing, blogging, podcasting, and a host of other means to connect and to relate. For many, personal relationships exist in multiple venues that blend offline and online activities. From a psychological and sociological perspective, it would seem that there is a need for these ways of connecting as the world becomes more global and people more transient. However, mediated approaches to communicating come at a cost.

Concerns about the lack of sensory cues, so important in our face-to-face interactions and so carefully evolved over the course of human history, have been expressed by a number of researchers. It has been argued that we cannot effectively communicate with each other if we are not aware of the full meaning being conveyed by the other person, with particular concern over the depth, quality, and authenticity of these interactions (Chayko 2002). These debates reveal widespread fears about the perceived proliferation of shallow connections (Douglas 1994), the inability to critically assess information, and of not knowing for certain to whom we are connected (Joinson 1999; Weisband & Atwater 1999). Social scientists wonder at the shifting of social protocols in an online world where there are seemingly little to no boundaries to keep people from doing and saying whatever they want, and possibly having little to no regard for the other partner in the interaction (Coleman, Paternite, & Sherman 1999).

This new paradigm in how we connect not only addresses how we relate to each other, but how we relate to ourselves. In a constant search to discover "Who am I?" and "Who are you?" people have discovered in various online social sites a means of self-exploration, emotional support, identity affirmation, belonging, and strong communities that may have eluded them in real life. In addition, researchers have found these same online social communities to be a vast research laboratory of human behavior from which negative and positive findings continue to emerge.

In this chapter, we will look at the emergence and proliferation of a variety of online social groups, from text-based chat rooms and forums to graphics-based digital gaming and virtual worlds. The exploration of these venues will lead to discussions about the importance of sensory cues in communication and how their absence or mediated facsimiles affect the authenticity of online relationships. Because social constructivism addresses the effect we have on each other as we interact, we will also look at some of the ways in which we approach and respond to each other when online, including disinhibition effects, behavior legitimization, anonymity, and the espousal of extreme views, and positive benefits of online social engagement.

The range of Internet groups and online forums

Online social communities are often regarded as the sole domain of teenagers and young adults. While this may have been true a decade or more ago, those younger users have aged and are still actively engaged in online socializing. But they are not alone. They have been joined by their teenage and young-adult children as well as by their own parents. While teenagers and young adults still make up a very large percentage of online social community members, there is now significant representation among all age-groups (Stroud 2008). Additionally, the selection and sophistication of social communities from which they can pick has increased exponentially from the early days of simple, text-based chat rooms. Today, users have a wide array of options, catering to any number of specific interests.

Several basic functions of online social communities can be identified, such as informational and research, professional or career, educational and skills development, news (archival and current), special interests, advocacy, gaming, and socializing. This is not a comprehensive list, however, as many multipurpose functions exist. These social communities should therefore be conceptualized as an interconnected matrix rather than as separate and distinct entities. Still, for ease of description, there are some basic qualities found in each.

Informational and research

These social sites consist of people who wish to disseminate information and those who seek information. The information contained in these sites might come from professional sources or from the postings of everyday people with experience, insights, and advice to convey. The sense of community one develops from these sites ranges from close-knit and long-term to loose and transient, depending upon the nature of the specific site. Here relationships can become meaningful, and offline and online identities are often merged.

Professional or career

Professional and career sites offer skills development tools and resources for those who are employed and for those seeking employment. In these, relationships tend to be weak, in general, and professional online identities often reflect professional offline identities.

Educational and skills development

These sites provide access to a wide range of educational information and opportunities for students of all ages. From lectures, videos, seminars, online classes, and other resources, students, potential students, alumni, faculty, and education administrators are able to join communities that align with their specific interests. Here relationships tend to be weak, in general, depending on the site. Closed-system sites tend to engender stronger relationships whereas general-access sites create weaker relationships. Also, online identities tend to reflect offline identities.

News (archival and current)

Related to informational communities, news communities have flourished in recent years. Online communities have grown around specific newsworthy topics, some of which are persistent (lasting years), while others are short-term (lasting a day or two). In these, relationships tend to be weak, in general, and online identities are typically related with offline identities.

Special interests

Unwavering in popularity, special interest groups (SIGs) bring together people with similar interests, often creating strong, long-lasting communities. From orchid enthusiasts to amateur astrologers, lovers of Texas chilli to dieters, and everything in between, SIGs provide a means by which people can share information and perhaps make friends in the process. Relationships can become strong in smaller groups and online identities tend to mirror offline identities.

Advocacy

Partially SIG, news, education, and social communities, advocacy communities provide resources and other support for people with a particular social change issue. The purpose of an advocacy community is to identify and gather like-minded individuals in large enough numbers to help affect social change at all levels of society—from community initiatives to national and international activities. Relationships tend to be strong for smaller groups and online identities tend to mirror offline identities.

Gaming

Gaming is big business. For many years, video gaming was king, but it was often a solo activity. An offshoot of video gaming is online gaming. In 2004, the most successful online gaming experience to date, *World of Warcraft*, was released to market. It remains the gold standard for creating a gaming community in which users not only play the game, but create identities, form communities, and socialize online apart from the game. Relationships can become strong and online identities do not tend to relate to offline identities.

Socializing

For many people, the Internet provides an opportunity to initiate or to expand a social network. A good example of a currently popular social community would be the virtual world called Second Life. In this venue, members create new identities and most often do not discuss their offline selves, or they do so in an anonymous manner. Depending on the group, relationships can be strong or weak, and identities may or may not be related to offline identities.

Social networking sites

The prevalence of social networking sites continues to grow. In 2010, the most popular social site, Facebook, had over 500 million users who posted over fifty million times a day. Myspace had 120 million members. Scores of other popular sites cater to the needs of culturally diverse people across the globe.

According to the Pew Internet and American Life Project (2009), 35% of adults in the United States now have an online social network profile compared to 8% in 2005. This number is expected to increase further. While the Pew study is US-centric, we see increasing participation in online social communities across the globe. As noted earlier, the average age of users has increased and the age-group most likely to be found on Facebook is thirty-five and older (McIver 2010). Of particular interest is the finding that African-American and Hispanic users make up the majority of those with online social network profiles (48% and 43% respectively) compared to 31% of white adults. In part, this is explained by the increased diversity of the eighteen to twenty-four age-group. The ongoing Pew study also noted that

- Just over half of online teens (55%) used social networking sites in November 2006 and 65% did so in February 2008.
- 47% of online adults use social networking sites, up from 37% in November 2008.
- 72% of eighteen- to twenty-nine-year-olds online use social networking web sites fully, nearly identical to the rate among teens, and significantly higher than the 39% of Internet users aged thirty and above who use these sites.
- Adults are increasingly fragmenting their social networking experience—52% say they have two or more different profiles. That is up from 42% in 2008.
- Teens continue to be avid users of social networking web sites—as of September 2009, 73% of American teenagers, aged twelve to seventeen, online used a social networking web site, a statistic that has continued to climb upwards from 55% in November 2006 and 65% in February 2008.

The percentage of adult users of social networking sites who maintain a profile on multiple sites has grown. In May 2008, 54% of adults with a social networking site profile had a profile on just one site, while 29% had profiles on two sites and 13% had profiles on three or more sites.

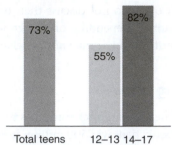

Figure 5.1 Percentage of teens on Social Networking Sites (2009 data)
Source: Lenhart *et al.* 2010, Social Media and Mobile Internet Use Among Teens and Young Adults, Pew internet and American Life Project.

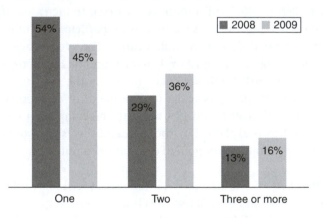

Figure 5.2 Adults increasingly have multiple Social Networking Site profiles
Source: Lenhart *et al.* 2010, Social Media and Mobile Internet Use Among Teens and Young Adults, Pew internet and American Life Project.

Use of virtual worlds to engage in social activities has also grown, though it is more common among teens than among adults.

In September 2009, the Pew study measured virtual-world usage among adults and found that 4% of online adults visit virtual worlds. Usage of virtual worlds is relatively consistent across age cohorts, with 4% of Internet users under age thirty and 4% of those thirty and above visiting virtual worlds. Among adults there are no significant differences in virtual-world use related to gender, race/ethnicity, income, or education.

Differences between online and offline interactions

The reasons that compel people to interact with each other appear to be the same, whether they are offline or online: people need each other for support,

companionship, love, safety, attaining goals, and for some, spiritual fulfillment. They also need each other to affirm a sense of self-view—desire to have
others see value in who one is and what one does (Cabiria 2008a). Sometimes,
the offline world does not provide these values and affirmations and people
turn to online communities in search of fulfillment. But something happens
in the way some people conduct themselves when in the online environment. It is argued that the lack of the sensory cues, so important in offline
interactions, leads to the inability to properly relate to one another (Chayko
2002). Emotional expressions can become misinterpreted, personal boundaries
of social engagement can be crossed (Joinson 2001a), and the sense of the
other as a person can be replaced by a more objectifying perception (Joinson
2001b).

In recent years, research into the psychological effects of media has
increased, especially new media technologies, primarily focused on the
Internet. There is a general consensus that when people associate online, their
behavior differs from their offline interactions, although engaged in similar
activities (Joinson 2003; Suler 2004). Psychologists and sociologists continue
to study the reasons for these differences and propose several possibilities,
including lack of informational cues, deindividuation, disinhibition, uncertainty reduction, anonymity, and trust formation, to name a few.

Informational cues

We are what others perceive us to be. That is, people use their sensory abilities, combined with past experiences, to create an impression of who other
people are. They then relate to the other person based on those impressions,
constantly adjusting perceptions as the other person responds. At some point,
hopefully, the perception of one person merges with the other person's self-
concept to create a relationship that, more or less, functions well. A great deal
of the formation of relationships rests upon each person's ability to "read" the
other person. Using physical nuances, people create meaning out of a wide
variety of cues, such as vocal tone, body posture, hairstyle and clothing, use
of language, and more. With these, people add historical context, cultural
interpretations, and mood. These social cues, as Goffman (1959) called them,
are critical to our ability to understand and relate to each other.

In the online world, people lose many of these cues (Golman 2007) and
attempt to compensate for these losses, sometimes to good effect and sometimes with disastrous results. In a largely text-based world often found in
online social communities, relating to others is largely independent of the
subtleties of social cue generation. Advances have been made in some respects.
Certainly, the creation of avatars, essentially cartoon-like placeholders used

to represent the self in virtual spaces, has returned some of the lost cues. The introduction of voice into formerly text-based spaces also helps improve on relationship building. Current software programming that gives avatars more life-like facial and body gestures is close to mainstream release (Orvalho, Miranda, & Sousa 2009). However, the current state is still primitive, in many ways, even in light of the complexity of the existing programming.

This is not to say that the lack of social cues is always a negative. As creatures prone to stereotyping based on social cues, the lack of normal stereotyping triggers can allow people to approach others from a more neutral place and build an assessment of the other person unclouded by biasing attributes. For some people, crippled by inescapable real-world judgments of them, the online environment can provide respite and the opportunity to be known for something other than their perceived deficits (Joinson 2001a). For others, the lack of cues can cause discomfort and abnormal behavior in an attempt to compensate for the missing elements. Within online social communities, the introduction of sensory cues is hotly debated. Some prefer complete anonymity, while others crave more authenticity.

Deindividuation

Jung (1946) described individuation as "the development of the psychological individual as a differentiated being from the general, collective psychology. Individuation, therefore, is a process of differentiation, having for its goal the development of the individual personality" (561). Conversely, losing one's individuality or uniqueness can be described as deindividuation. We can look at deindividuation as something one experiences within one's self or something one does to another.

Some theorists have noted that the reduction of social cues prevents people from being able to express themselves, and for people to not fully grasp the identities of others. This lack of sense of self, and lack of sense of self in relationship to others, can create intense psychic discomfort as one seeks to resolve identity confusion (Erikson 1968). The ways in which one attempts to resolve this issue can present itself as a form of retaliation against the source of deindividuation, while at the same time expressing some sort of palpable identity. Uniquely identifying one's self through atypical behavior is a way to address a sense of anonymity so often experienced in virtual environments.

The paradox here is that anonymity can also be pleasurable, yet the lack of a rooted identity in the virtual space can lead to extreme responses. Classic theorists such as Jung (1948), Rogers (1954), Allport (1955), and Maslow (1968) all note the drive of people to be regarded as unique individuals, and that the inability to be perceived as such can lead to unusual personality shifts. In fact, these concepts have been tested for decades, noting that deindividuation can lead to impulsive behavior and atypical actions (Festinger, Pepitone, & Newcomb 1952; Zimbardo 1969). Later researchers agree with the proposals that deindividuation can be an explanation for abnormal and uninhibited behavior (Siegal *et al*. 1986).

Jung (1948) proposed that loss of identity releases a violent and primitive response in an attempt to reregulate one's self. In the online environment, we can see this in instances of "flaming" (intense emotional responses directed toward others) (Joinson 1999; Suler 2004), "griefing" (creating annoying, even destructive, situations) (Suler 2004), "overt or hyper-sexuality" (engaging in extreme online sexual behaviors) (Ross 2005), promotion of "extreme views" (voicing societally offensive, even illegal, points of view) (Zimbardo 1969), and "cyber-stalking" (constantly interjecting one's self into the online environment and conversations of another) (Basu & Jones 2007).

Disinhibition

Disinhibition can be described as behavior that shows little concern for one's self-presentation to others or for their judgment (Coleman, Paternite, & Sherman 1999; Joinson 1998). This has also been coined as the "disinhibition effect" when discussing online behaviors (Golman 2007; Suler 2004). Suler (2004) noted that disinhibition in online environments could arise out of several psychological factors, including anonymity, the asynchronous nature of many online communications, and the lack of strong socially constructed boundaries that tell us when we are out of line. This disinhibition effect is in itself a neutral effect that takes on a value depending upon its use. For example, a marginalized person who enters a virtual space might feel free from the shackles of repression and explore relationships in new and positive ways. For them, disinhibition can be used as a means of self-discovery and self-expression that promotes psychic healing (Cabiria 2008b). Other uses can be for reckless, destructive, or inflammatory purposes (e.g., flaming, expressing extreme views) that negatively affect the well-being of the individual and of others (Golman 2007).

Disinhibition can be related to deindividuation, in that, when one feels a loss of uniqueness, she or he is motivated to explore atypical behaviors as a means to recapture a sense of identity (Coleman, Paternite, & Sherman 1999). In a virtual world, often devoid of deep social cues, the attempt at being seen as unique can take on extreme forms. For example, in virtual worlds, avatars are often highly idealized versions of the human operator that engage in behaviors that would be unlikely, and perceived as "against type" in their human operator's offline world.

The online disinhibition effect can be broken down into six primary factors (Suler 2004):

Asynchronicity: because many online social community dialogs do not occur in real time, a person can post a message and then move on, to return at some future point or perhaps never to return. Knowing that they can be spared retribution, they can voice their opinions in whatever manner they wish. For some, this provides an emotional release valve.

Dissociative anonymity: when a person feels that they are anonymous, they feel freed from the constraints of social boundaries and may act in a manner that is atypical in their offline lives.

Dissociative imagination: seeing the online world as a place where rules and regulations do not apply, people may create any number of new identities, engage in role-play scenarios, and change approaches to each other at will. They may knowingly and willingly enable each other's fantasy creations.

Invisibility: similar to anonymity, with the exception that even if some offline identity information is available to online participants, the lack of physical presence (the invisible body) creates a disinhibition effect. For example, people are more likely to be rude on the telephone than they would be with the same person face to face.

Minimizing authority: "On the Internet, nobody knows you're a dog" (Steiner 1993). This cartoon caption from the *New York Times* captures the essence of this factor. Online, people may not know who is a janitor and who is a university chancellor. This serves as a disinhibiting effect in that people do not have informational cues to help determine relationship boundaries. Offline, one might speak differently, and more freely, to a janitor, than to a chancellor; online, one might treat everyone the same.

Solipsistic introjections: in the absence of social cues, we tend to create images and identities of the person with whom we interact online. Our creations may not even be close to the real attributes of the other person, but they serve a psychological purpose within us, allowing us to relate to someone according to our needs.

Self-disclosure

Compelling research indicates that online communications lend themselves to high levels of self-revelatory behavior (Rheingold 1993). There are several theories as to why people are more likely to engage in atypical self-disclosure online when compared to similar offline situations. Part of this discussion is based on the lack of social cues. In offline interactions, people depend upon a more holistic form of communication—words, body, history, and context—to create meaning about the words and the relationship. Online, people must ask more questions (Tourangeau 2004) to help them fill in the gaps of knowledge about the other person that social cues would have normally addressed. In addition, some people feel compelled to disclose more about themselves in order to establish their own identity within the relationship (Tidwell & Walther 2002).

Both actions—increased self-disclosure and increased question-asking—are meant to help each person form a safe environment for the interaction, as well as counteract the anonymity inherent in online activities by establishing some sort of identity (Cabiria 2008a). It was found that there is an inverse relationship between question-asking and self-disclosure, and the provision of informational cues: as more informational cues are provided, then question-asking and self-disclosure decline (Cabiria 2008a; Tidwell & Walther 2002; Weisband & Kiesler 1996). It would appear that people are more likely to use self-disclosure as a means to encourage dialog to gain information about the other person. Once a person is satisfied with the level of information they have about someone, they decrease their own information giving (Joinson & Paine 2007). This all relates to the need for uncertainty reduction: people require a certain level of information about each other in order to create a safe interaction event (Berger & Bradac 1982).

Concerns have been raised that online interactions are often shallow due to limited social cues, asynchronous communications, and the transient nature of group memberships (Chayko 2002). In addition, people may present themselves differently than they do in their offline lives, which can complicate the forming of meaningful relationships. After all, how can a meaningful bond occur if one or more participants in the relationship present themselves in a less than authentic manner? Yet, it would appear, given the high levels of question-asking and self-disclosure, that online relationship formation can, in fact, aid in creating strong relationship bonding. It would be beneficial to explore compensatory information-seeking activities, such as question-asking and self-disclosure, to see if they adequately replace their offline counterparts.

Trust formation

Our ability to form and maintain relationships requires that we can trust others, and that they can trust us (Axelrod 1984). This trust factor can be based on assumptions we make about each other as a result of the information cues we present. We trust that the cues are accurate and that people will behave in a manner that corresponds to how they have presented themselves (Luhmann 1979, 1988).

Offline relationships can be very complex, even with an abundance of informational cues. In any beginning relationship, there is a level of risk (Rousseau *et al*. 1998) while people fill in the information puzzle about each other. At any point, a person may come across an information "puzzle piece" that does not fit some preconception about the other person, causing a shift in perspective or even an end to the relationship (Chiles & McMackin, 1996). Online, the complexities grow. As there are relatively few informational cues, people may engage in heightened question-asking and self-disclosure as a compensatory way to fill in this identity puzzle and to reduce risk. The problem is that some people engage in elaborate dissociative online activities, creating a potential high-risk situation.

The second trust condition, interdependence, notes that a relationship requires the cooperation of each party in the relationship in order to achieve mutual and individual goals (Rousseau *et al*. 1998). People seek out each other for mutual benefit. By helping the other person achieve their goals, we can expect assistance to achieve our own. A level of trust is required to maintain this interdependence. Offline, many informational cues can become apparent to let us know if the relationship is one sided, or can potentially become one sided. Online, it may take longer while people fill in their trust puzzle, since identity plasticity (the ability to change one's identity) and engagement in dissociative behaviors are so easy to accomplish (Donath 1999; Luhmann 1988; Turkle 1995).

The influence and effects of online groups

Social networking sites offer people some very distinct advantages, including the ability to maintain relationships, especially those separated by distance or schedules. For decades, the telephone, and then instant messaging and e-mail, helped people bridge a social gap created by full schedules, transient lifestyles, isolated living circumstances, or other conditions that made frequent face-to-face contact difficult or impractical. However, this meant that each had certain disadvantages, including the need for synchronicity (telephone) and limited ability to discover other people to add to the network. With online social networks, people could create a personal profile and, depending on the services offered, include images, links to favorite sites, video files, and much more. Additionally, all of this information was persistent, in that it appeared in complete form whenever the sites were accessed. These sites had history. One's online personal history and profile equate to offline informational cues, helping people to create identities and to have access to the identity information of others (Tajfel & Turner 1986).

Inherent in these online interactional exchanges is a concept called social capital. Social capital, under various names, has a long history of sociological discourse documented at least 110 years ago when Dewey (1899) suggested that people help other people to create a situation in which others would then feel compelled to return the favor. A formal definition of social capital describes it as a construct that enables benefits as a result of one's relationships with others (Bourdieu & Wacquant 1992; Coleman 1988; Lin 1999). We join social groups, offline and online, to engage in social-capital activities, in which we create goodwill, engage in good deeds, and provide information and support in full expectation of receiving the same from others at some future point.

Psychologically, there appears to be some other benefits incurred from online social networking and social-capital building. For example, people with low self-esteem appeared to benefit more from their online social network activities than did people with high self-esteem, presumably because they had support from others as a result of social-capital gains not found in their real lives (Ellison, Steinfield, & Lampe 2007). We also know that people need safe spaces in which to explore identity issues, especially in the formative adolescent and young adult years (Sullivan 1953). Online social communities offer a variety of groups in which aspects of one's identity can be spotlighted and explored in ways that might not be possible in their offline environments (Cabiria 2008a). However, online social network activities are not always positive and the utility of these sites for beneficial psychological and social development is continually explored and debated (Kraut *et al.* 2002; Shaw & Gant 2002; Valkenburg, Peter, & Schouten 2006). Still, it is apparent that people who create social capital through online engagement are likely to behave in more positive ways that lead to better psychological health and development (Cabiria 2008b; Helliwell & Putnam 2004; Morrow 1999).

A number of studies have investigated the subject of Internet use and psychological and social well-being (e.g., Kraut *et al.* 1998). While the results of these studies are not conclusive, it appears that frequent Internet use is associated with increased measures of depression and loneliness (e.g., Kraut *et al.* 2002; Nie 2001; Valkenburg & Peter 2007). Conversely, studies in which Internet use included frequent participation in online social communities indicated increase in self-esteem and overall well-being (e.g., Shaw & Gant 2002; Valkenburg, Peter, & Schouten 2006). It can be assumed that people with poor offline social networks could see an increase in positive affect once they have found an online community of similar others with whom they could frequently interact (Cabiria 2008b).

Increased self-esteem or identity

Theorist Morris Rosenberg (1965, 1989) proposed that the self is made up of two interrelated components—identity and self-esteem. Identity is that part of the self that performs cognitive functioning and which perceives and interprets meaning, while self-esteem is the affective self that deals with one's feelings and resulting behaviors. We present to the world an image formulated from these two components. In thinking about how social construction influences self-presentation, we can see how one's sense of self is determined by how one perceives the world and interacts with others, interprets and gives meaning to those interactions, and then behaves based on the feelings those interpretations engendered. Our self-esteem and identities emerge from social interactions (Owens, Stryker, & Goodman 2006). We can conclude from this that when people have positive experiences in online social communities, the positive meaning that they give to their experiences can increase their positive feelings about themselves. When people feel positive about their relationships, increased interaction also increases the potential for social-capital gain, which, as was noted, can lead to higher self-esteem.

Reduced social isolation and loneliness

Concern over the perceived shallowness of online relationships was countered by acknowledging that some people tend toward increased question-asking and self-disclosure, leading to potentially stronger relationships. However, this is not to say that weaker relationships don't also have value. In an essay titled "The Strength of Weak Ties," Granovetter (1973, 1983) noted how casual relationships had very powerful social and psychological purposes—giving people access to a wide variety of information, increasing their support networks and increasing perceptions of self-worth. This has been supported by more recent research on the utility of weak ties (Rosen 2007).

For some people, the promise of anonymity is antithetical to their needs. Feeling isolated due to geography, physical limitations, social ostracization, and/or mental health issues, some people may have very few, if any, offline

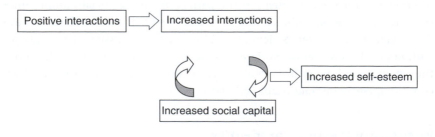

Cabiria 2010

Figure 5.3 Online social group processes

social ties. For those individuals, the goal in joining online social groups is not necessarily to explore identity development or to find some sort of cathartic release from social constraints, but to actively engage in personal interactions and to build a variety of social networks (Cabiria 2010). We can think of a healthy social network as containing a core group of people with whom we closely identify and interact (our strong ties), followed by a middle layer of people with whom we interact in a more casual manner (our support-ing ties), and ending with a layer of people who provide informational and support functions as needed (our weaker ties). By building multilayered social networks, people can actively, and openly, alleviate their offline sense of isolation and loneliness. For some, the benefits gained in online interactions become transferable to their offline lives (Cabiria 2008a).

It is worth noting that research is contradictory on Internet use and loneli-ness. For example, Katz and Aspden (1997) found that Internet use improves one's social network while aiding in building new ones. However, O'Toole (2000) and Sanders *et al.* (2000) noted that increased Internet use led to weaker relationships and sense of isolation (also see Morahan-Martin 1999). It should also be noted that these and other related studies occurred prior to the explosion of more sophisticated online social networking sites. Clearly, more research is needed in this vital area to see if technological improvements in profile-building and relationship-building tools have changed people's sense of belongingness or isolation while engaged in online social activities.

Conclusion

From its earliest beginnings, the Internet was envisioned as a mass communi-cations tool capable of keeping people connected, and providing a platform for the sharing of information. With virtual online interactions come special considerations when attempting to build and maintain relationships. Due to the lack of various cues, people engage in behaviors that can be perceived as dysfunctional in the real world, but which have utility in the virtual world. Increased self-disclosure can serve to quickly establish one's identity and reduce social discomfort, while disinhibition, paired with anonymity, can provide a means of avoiding real-world labeling and establishing a new iden-tity framework. In attempting to relate to others, one might engage in solip-sistic introjections, creating a mental image and identity of the virtual other as a way of establishing a contextual space for interactions to occur.

However, some of these behaviors are not only perceived as dysfunctional in the real world, but in the virtual one as well. With anonymity comes extreme behavior in which people might espouse radical ideas, resist rules and authority, and engage in atypical activities that could be considered psychologically and socially unhealthy. It has been proposed that these more radical activities are a response to the loss of sensory and social cues, and a reaction to the loss of identity and sense of self.

It is clear that research into the psychological effects of engaging in online social communities requires more data. While it is now obvious that the potential for identity redevelopment and beneficial positive effects exists, research into the negative effects captures much of the public attention. Additionally, as these online social communities and related technologies evolve, and our online interactions become more textured and nuanced, we can expect to see stronger online parallels to our real-world behaviors.

Subject in focus

The impact of virtual-world involvement

While we all make daily compromises as we navigate social interactions, the extent of these compromises can potentially lead to psychological distress. We can look at them as a measure of the gap between the public persona and the private persona—what we want the world to believe we are, and what we know ourselves to be. This gap, or dissonance, may lead some people to online communities where they can choose to reveal their hidden selves more fully while still remaining anonymous. In an often anonymous environment, they can attempt to reduce the public-private persona gap, thus reducing their distress. To exemplify this, we will follow the path of one participant in a recent study of the real-world effects of virtual-world involvement.

All of her life, Eleora (pseudonym) said she felt like she did not belong to any one group. Not being able to identity with others in key aspects of her life, including ethnically, racially, and sexually, caused Eleora to exhibit a sense of loneliness, feelings of isolation, low self-esteem, and lack of authenticity as she attempted to hide her feelings and her differences. Eleora became "an other," and this otherness eventually led her to the creation of a virtual self.

In 2007, something amazing happened to Eleora. On a whim, she joined a virtual world known as Second Life. Her real life would never be the same. Soon she began to find other people with similar interests. Within a few days, she actually became part of a lesbian and gay group; she joined poetry groups, a Victorian role-play group, and an educator's group. While her real life remained hidden to her new online friends and theirs to her, what mattered most was the acceptance these online friends gave each other. While the real world was often dark and gloomy in her mind, the virtual world was bright, colorful, and exciting.

After a few months, Eleora noticed a problem—the gap, or dissonance, between her real life and her virtual one became wider, and her discomfort in the real world increased. Eleora began a new adventure, but this time in the real world. She gradually began to do in the real world what she did in the virtual one—she joined special interest groups, volunteered for gay social service organizations, and started to have real-world friends. Slowly, the gap between her real-life identity and her virtual one diminished. At some indeterminate point, Eleora was no longer living unauthentically in the real world, and it was all due to her anonymous but authentic experiences in the digital world. For Eleora, the disinhibition effect and positive dissociate behaviors allowed her to cast aside her damaged identity and, through frequent question-asking and self-disclosure, she was able to build trusting relationships. All of this served to increase her self-esteem and give her the strength (and online support system) to make real-life changes. As of 2008, Eleora was doing great in both her offline and online worlds, having achieved a healthy integration of the two.

Discussion question

Can meaningful relationships develop between anonymous members of a virtual world?

Further sources of information

Baumeister, R. & Tice, D. M. (1990). "Anxiety and social exclusion." *Journal of Social and Clinical Psychology, 9*, 165–195.

Burt, R. S. (2001). "Bandwidth and echo: Trust, information, and gossip in social networks." In J. E. Rauch & A. Casella (eds), *Networks and markets*, (30–74). New York: Russell Sage.

Donath, J. (2007). "Signals in social supernets." *Journal of Computer-Mediated Communication, 13*, 231–251.

Gackenbach, J. (2007). *Psychology and the Internet*. New York: Elsevier.

Gergen, K. (1991). *The saturated self: Dilemmas of identity in contemporary life*. New York: Basic.

Kraut, R., Patterson, M., Lundmark, V., Kiesler, S., Mukhopadhyay, T., & Scherlis, W. (1998). "The Internet paradox: A social technology that reduces social involvement and psychological well-being." *American Psychologist, 53*, 1017–1032.

McKenna, K. Y. A. & Bargh, J. (1998). "Coming out in the age of the Internet: Identity 'demarginalization' through virtual group participation." *Journal of Personality and Social Psychology, 75,* 681–694.

Morahan-Martin, J. & Schumacher, P. (2003, November). "Loneliness and social uses of the Internet." *Computers in Human Behavior, 19, 659–671.*

Postmes, T. & Spears, R. (1998). "Deindividuation and anti-normative behaviour: A meta-analysis." *Psychological Bulletin, 123,* 238–259.

Robinson, J., Kestnbaum, M., Neustadtl, A., & Alvarez, A. (2000). "Mass Media and social life among Internet users." *Social Science Computer Review, 18,* 490–501.

Jo Bryce and Linda K. Kaye

Computer and Video Games 6

Since the latter part of the twentieth century, video games have become a major source of entertainment for a wide range of individuals. Figures show that within the last ten years, over twenty-five million gaming devices and more than 335 million computer and video games have been sold in the UK (ELSPA 2008). The combined video and computer game sales in the US in 2009 was over 10.5 billion dollars in 2009, and 67% of American households own some form of video game entertainment hardware (ESA 2010). Games are played on a range of different platforms, including computers, consoles (Microsoft Xbox 360, Nintendo Wii, Sony PlayStation), handheld consoles (Sony PSP, Nintendo DS), iPods, and mobile phones.

These figures demonstrate that gaming is a popular contemporary leisure activity, as suggested by a recent survey finding that playing video games was ranked the favorite leisure activity for males aged twelve to twenty-four, and third highest for those aged twenty-five to forty-four (Vorhaus 2008). Recent figures also suggest that 97% of American teenagers (twelve to seventeen years) play video games (Lenhart *et al.* 2008) and children have been found to spend at least six hours per week playing video games (Anderson, Gentile, & Buckley 2007; Gentile *et al.* 2004). Concerns have been voiced about the frequency of gaming among young people, as it may displace other activities, such as engagement in physical activity (Ho & Lee 2001) and academic work (Gentile *et al.* 2004). This is of particular concern given recent research suggesting that time spent playing video games predicts poorer school performance and attention problems in adolescents (Gentile 2009).

The popularity of this activity and wide availability of violent video games in the commercial market has led parents, politicians, and the media to raise concerns about the potential negative effects of gaming. Gaming has been widely constructed as a social problem that requires regulation to protect young people from the effects of exposure to violent content, and this has been reinforced by reported links to a number of high-profile school shootings in recent years. The Columbine High School shootings in 1999 (US), the Virginia Tech massacre in 2007 (US), and the more recent case in Winnenden in 2009 (Germany) have all been claimed to involve perpetrators who were frequent players of violent video games, and claims have been made that violent video games are a significant causal factor for such acts (McGraw 2007; Thompson 2007). Such cases have continued to generate debate on this issue, despite the lack of clear evidence that many of the perpetrators were regular gamers (Ferguson 2008).

Concerns about the potential impact of gaming and exposure to game violence have led to a substantial body of research investigating the associated potential for addiction (e.g., Chappell *et al.* 2006; Griffiths 2008), desensitization to real-world violence (e.g., Bartholow, Bushman, & Sestir 2006; Carnagey, Anderson, & Bushman 2007), and increased aggressive attitudes and behavior in both children and adults (e.g., Anderson & Bushman 2001; Carnagey, Anderson, & Bushman 2007). This research has developed from the research tradition on media violence in movies and television (Huesmann *et al.* 2003) and adopted the associated theoretical and methodological frameworks to examine the potential effects of playing violent video games. Many researchers have claimed that exposure to video-game violence has more negative outcomes than exposure to violence in television and movies because the player takes an active role in performing acts of violence rather than being a passive viewer (Anderson & Bushman 2002; Dill & Dill 1998). The active involvement of playing and receiving feedback on performance of violent acts is claimed to reinforce the associated thought processes of players (Swing, Gentile, & Anderson 2009) and lead to stronger reinforcement and modeling of such behavior (Anderson *et al.* 2003).

The short- and long-term influences of violent game content on aggressive attitudes and behavior have been explained using a variety of different theoretical models: Social Learning Theory (Bandura 1977), Cognitive Neo-Association Model (Berkowitz 1989), Script Theory (Huesmann 1986), Excitation Transfer Theory (Zillmann 1983), and the General Aggression Model (Anderson & Carnagey 2004; Anderson & Dill 2000). The majority of research in this area is experimental and attempts to find causal links between exposure to game violence and aggressive thoughts, feelings, and behavior (e.g., Anderson *et al.* 2004; Arriaga *et al.* 2008; Markey & Scherer 2009).

This chapter critically reviews current theoretical and empirical evidence for the link between exposure to violent game content and aggressive attitudes and behaviors, and outlines a number of associated theoretical and methodological criticisms of the existing literature. It argues for the need to take a more holistic approach to understanding this issue, which incorporates an examination of the potential influence of a wider range of factors than is currently included in contemporary research on the psychological and social effects of computer gaming.

Proposed effects of exposure to game violence

Physiological arousal

Exposure to violent game content has been claimed to have a number of physiological effects associated with arousal (e.g., increased heart rate, changes in blood pressure, and hormonal levels), which may lead to aggressive behavior (Anderson, Carnagey, & Eubanks 2003; Anderson & Ford 1986). Violent images have been found to be more arousing compared to those that are neutral or negative but nonviolent, and to increase state hostility in male undergraduate students (Bartholow, Sestir, & Davies 2005; Bushman, 1995).

Aggressive feelings

Numerous experimental studies have demonstrated a link between exposure to violent game content and aggressive feelings (e.g., Anderson & Ford 1986). Participants in violent video-game conditions have been found to be significantly more hostile than those in nonviolent conditions after play (e.g., Carnagey & Anderson 2005), although Unsworth, Devilly and Ward (2007) failed to find similar results.

Aggressive thoughts

Arousal is claimed to cause individuals to think more aggressively through the development and reinforcement of aggressive cognitive and behavioral scripts (Anderson & Morrow 1995; Anderson *et al.* 2003). Scripts are cognitive templates for guiding behavior in different situations (e.g., responding to interpersonal conflict) that develop by learning (Huesmann 1986, 1998). Scripts which suggest that aggression is the correct response to provocation and conflict are hypothesized to be strengthened by repeated exposure to violent game content, and such processes create a hostile attribution bias or a habitual tendency to interpret ambiguous situations as aggressive or provoking (Crick & Dodge 1994). This increases the likelihood of the activation of such scripts in response to both ambiguous and provoking situations, increasing the likelihood of the performance of aggressive behavior (Anderson *et al.* 2003; Berkowitz 1993; Möller & Krahé 2009). Activation of these knowledge structures may become unconscious and automatic as they are strengthened by repeated exposure, and operation of such processes at an early age may increase normalization of aggressive attitudes and behavior (Bushman & Anderson 2002; Todorov & Bargh 2002).

Numerous experimental studies have examined the influence of exposure to violent video games on aggressive cognitions (e.g., Anderson, Carnagey, & Eubanks 2003; Anderson, Gentile, & Buckley 2007). Cues associated with violence (e.g., the presence of weapons) have been found to increase aggressive cognitions measured by faster recognition of aggressive target words in word recognition tasks (e.g., Anderson, Benjamin, & Bartholow 1998). Uhlmann and Swanson (2004) found that participants in the violent game condition responded to aggressive stimuli in the Implicit Association Test (Greenwald *et al.* 2002) faster than those in the nonviolent game condition. Children reporting high levels of exposure to violent game content have also been found to have an increased hostile attribution bias in response to hypothetical, ambiguous scenarios (Anderson, Gentile, & Buckley 2007). These studies provide evidence for the short-term influence of exposure to violent game content on cognitions, but the ability to draw firm conclusions about causal effects requires longitudinal research (Bryce & Rutter 2006; Möller & Krahé 2009).

Desensitization

Desensitization has been identified as a key process by which repeated exposure to game violence is linked to aggressive attitudes and behavior. Gamers are hypothesized to become habituated to the violence depicted within games, which reduces physiological reactivity and sensitivity to the observation of violence in real life (Carnagey, Bushman, & Anderson 2007). Studies have examined this effect using physiological measures of arousal, and found evidence of reduced emotional reactions to violent experimental stimuli (Bartholow, Sestir, & Davis 2005; Staude-Müller, Bliesener, & Luthman 2008). Desensitization has also been claimed to further reinforce aggressive scripts, and increase the likelihood that individuals will respond aggressively to ambiguous or conflict situations (Anderson *et al.* 2003; Huesmann *et al.* 2003).

Modeling aggressive behaviors

The modeling and reinforcement of behaviors is another key process by which exposure to violent game content is claimed to increase aggressive attitudes and behaviors (e.g., Bandura 1973, 1986). Social Learning Theory suggests that children learn and imitate appropriate behaviors through systems of reward and punishment by parents, peers, and the media (Anderson *et al.* 2004; Bandura 1986; Bandura, Ross, & Ross 1963). Frequent exposure to violent game content is claimed to increase the imitation of viewed behaviors, reinforcing the belief that such behavior is justified, and increasing the accessibility of associated cognitive and behavioral scripts (Anderson *et al.* 2003). A number of experimental studies have found higher levels of aggressive behavior in participants who played in violent instead of nonviolent conditions (e.g., Arriaga *et al.* 2008; Bartholow & Anderson 2002). A recent longitudinal study found that violent video games significantly predicted later physical aggression by increasing aggressive norms and the hostile attribution bias (Möller & Krahé 2009). However, another recent experimental study found no evidence of such a link, leading the authors to conclude that there is no predictive relationship between playing violent video games and aggressive behaviors (Ferguson *et al.* 2008a).

The General Aggression Model (GAM) and General Learning Model (GLM)

The General Aggression Model (Anderson & Dill 2000; Anderson & Huesmann 2003) and General Learning Model (Buckley & Anderson 2006) draw together existing socio-cognitive models explaining the effects of game violence on learning, personality, and aggression-related outcomes. These models account for both the person (e.g., individual beliefs, attitudes, previous experiences) and the situation (e.g., provocation or other aggressive cues, exposure to media violence) as input variables for the learning of aggressive behaviors (Buckley & Anderson 2006). The interactions between these input variables influence the individual's internal state and determine the way in which they learn to respond aggressively to external events (Anderson & Bushman 2002).

These models claim that playing violent video games primes aggressive cognitions (e.g., scripts), which produce aggressive affective states (e.g., anger) and increase arousal (Anderson & Bushman 2001, 2002). The long-term effects of such processes leads to the development of knowledge structures through learning, which reinforce a pattern of responses that cause them to respond more aggressively to their environment (Anderson & Bushman 2002; Buckley & Anderson 2006). Support for the GAM has been provided by a number of studies suggesting that exposure to violent game content increases aggression-related thoughts, feelings, and behavior in children and adults (e.g., Anderson & Carnagey 2009; Bushman & Anderson 2002), as well as two meta-analyses of research on the effects of video games (Anderson & Bushman 2001; Anderson *et al.* 2010).

Moderating factors

Despite the claims of a definitive relationship between exposure to violent game content and aggression on the basis of this research, the failure of many other studies to consistently replicate associated results (e.g., Colwell & Kato 2003; Ferguson *et al.* 2008a; Ihori *et al.* 2007) has led to a number of criticisms of the theoretical and methodological assumptions of the literature (e.g., Bryce & Rutter 2006; Ferguson *et al.* 2008b). One criticism of the meta-analyses previously described (Anderson & Bushman 2001; Anderson *et al.* 2010) is that the included studies fail to sufficiently account for "third variables" (e.g., trait aggressiveness, family violence), which may moderate the relationship between exposure to violent game content and aggression (Ferguson *et al.* 2008a). It has been claimed that examining the predisposing influence of individual differences, and exposure to multiple risk factors for aggressive attitudes and behavior, would allow a clearer understanding of the potential causal role of violent game content (Browne & Hamilton-Giachritsis 2005; Bryce & Rutter, 2006).

Individual differences

Individual differences are increasingly being examined as potential moderators of the relationship between violent game exposure and aggression-related outcomes (Krahé & Möller 2004; Markey & Scherer 2009). Adolescents with high trait hostility have been found to be more likely to show aggressive responses than those with lower hostility following exposure to violent game content (Bartholow, Sestir, & Davis 2005; Gentile *et al.* 2004). High trait aggression has been found to increase aggressive cognitions and behavior after exposure to violent game content compared to low trait aggression (Anderson & Dill 2000; Bushman 1995). Participants with higher levels of trait psychoticism have been found to have higher levels of aggressive cognitions and hostility compared to those with lower levels following violent gameplay (Markey & Scherer 2009). These results suggest that violent game content does not have the same effect on aggression-related outcomes for all gamers, and highlights the need to identify factors that may increase the vulnerability of some individuals to the effects of violent game content.

Social and environmental factors

The issue of vulnerability also highlights the importance of expanding the current research focus on the individual to include consideration of the potential influence of other social and environmental factors that may influence aggressive behavior (e.g., exposure to domestic violence, family and peer-group relationships) (Browne & Hamilton-Giachritsis 2005; Bryce & Rutter 2006). A recent longitudinal study examining the influence of a range of risk factors in determining relationships between media violence (including video games) and youth violence found that aggressive personality and parental physical violence were positively correlated with delinquent behavior (Hopf, Huber, & Weiß 2008).

The research reviewed in this section of the chapter suggests that the relationship between exposure to violent game content and aggression-related outcomes is complex, and requires an expanded theoretical framework, which recognizes the potential influence of personal and environmental variables on the outcomes of playing video games. Two additional aspects of gaming also require further consideration as potential moderators of the relationship between exposure to violent game content and aggression.

Motivations

The theoretical frameworks outlined in the earlier sections of this chapter are limited by their failure to consider the potential influence of motivations for gaming on associated psychological and social outcomes. Although gaming is widely constructed as a social problem within contemporary society, it is a popular, intrinsically motivated, and enjoyable leisure activity for many people (Jansz & Tanis 2007). It has been found to provide opportunities for the fulfillment of psychological needs and the experience of fun, excitement, and enjoyment (Choi & Kim 2004; Koo 2009; Wood *et al.* 2004). Research also suggests that "flow" is experienced in gaming. Flow is a positive psychological state of mind, which an individual experiences when they are doing an activity that is highly enjoyable and intrinsically motivating. Research has shown that the experience of flow while playing video games is associated with enjoyment and positive affect (Klimmt, Hartmann, & Frey 2007; Smith 2007). Incorporating a consideration of gaming motivations as an additional factor influencing the potential negative outcomes of this activity is an important direction for future research.

Social contexts

Current research examining the aggression-related outcomes of gaming also provides limited scope for examining the influence of the social contexts in which gaming occurs. Playing video games is stereotypically conceptualized as a solo activity, but it is increasingly a social activity facilitating online and offline interactions (Yee 2006, 2007). Research suggests that many gamers prefer to play with others rather than alone (Durkin & Aisbett 1999; Vorderer & Ritterfield 2003). Social interaction has been identified as both a motivational and experiential factor in gaming (Colwell 2007; Kim & Ross 2006; Sherry & Lucas 2003), and to be a predictor of online game enjoyment (Cole & Griffiths 2007).

Social contexts (online or offline) and types of social play (cooperative or competitive) have also been found to be strong determinants of the gaming experience (Lim & Lee 2009; Lim & Reeves 2010), and are also likely to influence the outcomes of gameplay. Competitive play, for example, may lead to greater experience of frustration and aggression than cooperative gameplay (Deutsch 1993). Recent research has also found that the actions of other players (e.g., poor performance) can influence the nature of the social gaming experience, leading to positive or negative affect (Kaye & Bryce, under review). These studies provide evidence of the potentially positive social value of gaming and the associated influence of gaming contexts on the outcomes of the activity. The experience and influence of violent game content in social gaming situations has yet to be addressed empirically and represents an additional important area for future research.

Methodological criticisms

In addition to the criticisms of the narrow, individual focus of much of the research in this area, a number of methodological issues have been identified that complicate the interpretation and generalizability of research results suggesting a link between game violence and aggressive outcomes (Bryce & Rutter 2006; Ferguson & Kilburn 2010). For example, a recent meta-analysis found evidence of a publication bias in favor of studies supporting the link between violent game content and aggression-related outcomes (Ferguson 2007). If studies that do not find evidence of the proposed effects outlined previously are not frequently published, the literature provides an incomplete picture of the existing evidence base and prevents a full recognition of its potential theoretical and methodological limitations.

Validity of lab-based measures of aggression

The reliability and validity of aggression measures used in cross-sectional and laboratory studies have been criticized by a number of researchers (Bryce & Rutter 2006; Ferguson *et al.* 2008b; Ritter & Eslea 2005). Ferguson (2007) claims that unstandardized measures of aggression are more likely to produce greater effect sizes than standardized and reliable measures. Written measures of aggression have been found to have higher construct validity than physical responses measures (e.g., noise-blast protocols) (Carlson, Marcus-Newhall, & Miller 1989), and to be less susceptible to social conformity or demand characteristics that may influence participants when carrying out physical acts of aggression in laboratory settings (Tedeschi & Quigley 1996). However, the majority of published studies use physical response tasks as proxy measures for aggressive behavior and their validity has been questioned. For example, Ferguson and Rueda (2009) assessed the validity of the Taylor Competitive Reaction Time Test, a common measure of aggressive behavior in experimental studies (e.g., Anderson & Dill 2000; Anderson & Murphy 2003), and found that it did not sufficiently correlate with trait measures or physical acts of aggression in young men (e.g., violent criminal behaviors, domestic violence).

Laboratory aggression paradigms have also been criticized for their lack of consideration of behavioral intentions or motivations for aggression (Tedeschi & Quigley 1996). Many physical laboratory measures require participants to retaliate to unprovoked verbal aggression as a measure of reactive aggression, but do not measure proactive aggression, which is a key theoretical component of the aggression paradigm (Tedeschi & Quigley 1996). As the majority of people are not generally motivated to behave aggressively toward others, the requirement to act this way in laboratory settings is not equivalent to real-life experiences. This suggests the need to include choice of nonaggressive reactions to provocation in experimental designs to more accurately reflect the experience of aggression within everyday contexts (Tedeschi & Quigley 1996). The conclusions that can be drawn from research using proxy measures of aggressive behaviors are limited, and the generalization of results to the dynamics of aggressive behavior in real-world settings problematic.

Gameplay period

Regular gamers often invest long periods of time in gaming sessions in order to experience the full potential of a game. A large proportion of existing experimental studies use relatively short time periods for participants to play selected video games (e.g., fifteen minutes), despite using commercial games, which require greater play periods to adequately progress in the game. The extent to which experimental gaming sessions can approximate the everyday psychological experience of engagement with games is questionable, and short play periods are unlikely to provide sufficient time to adequately test the claimed effects of exposure to violent content. Ferguson et al. (2008a) used a significantly longer time period of forty-five minutes in a recent study, and did not observe any significant differences in aggressive behavior between violent video game and nonviolent conditions using self-report and behavioral measures. This suggests that using extended gameplay periods would increase the realism and ecological validity of the gaming experience in experimental designs.

Control of video games between conditions

The choice of video games for use in experimental designs has also been criticized (Bryce & Rutter 2006). Many video games are complex in structure and dynamics, making the choice of games for experimental studies of vital importance. Previous experimental studies have been methodologically limited as the video games chosen for violent and nonviolent conditions have not adequately controlled for other game characteristics (e.g., complexity, genre, level of challenge, graphics). Bryce and Rutter (2006) suggest that differences in these characteristics between games used in different experimental conditions restrict the ability to isolate the effect of game violence on subsequent measures of aggressive attitudes and behaviors. For example, Bushman and Anderson (2009) experimentally examined the effect of video-game violence on pro-social behavior using games that are qualitatively different in game objectives, graphics, difficulty, and narrative. It is possible that other differences between the two games could account for the differences in measured outcomes between the two conditions, making it difficult to definitively claim that it is the violent content that influences behavior. Future studies should ensure the selection of games with different levels of violence, while ensuring control between them on all other game characteristics.

Sampling

Previous experimental research has typically used undergraduate psychology students (e.g., Anderson *et al.* 2004; Bushman & Anderson 2002). While convenience sampling is common in psychological research, it is not necessarily methodologically suitable for video-game research. For example, undergraduate psychology students tend to be female, while gamers tend to be male (Griffiths, Davies, & Chappell 2003; Williams, Yee, & Caplan 2008). Although this may seem trivial, males and females have been found to have different motivations for playing games and to experience video games differently (Kafia 1996; Yee 2007). Chumbley and Griffiths (2006) claim that females are generally less skillful than males in playing video games, and that lower proficiency may moderate the effect of game violence on frustration. Variations in gaming preferences and experiences by gender could potentially influence the outcomes of exposure to violent game content in experimental studies.

The motivations of gamers and non-gamers for participating in gaming research may also differ. Many studies offer course credit for participation and non-gamers may therefore be largely motivated to participate for extrinsic reasons. While some gamers may also be similarly motivated, they may be more likely to participate for intrinsic purposes (e.g., personal rewards through gaming). As gaming behavior is voluntary and the autonomy of gamers is typically high outside the laboratory (Bartle 2004), using samples of non-gamers is unlikely to replicate the intrinsic motivating factors for gaming, and it is questionable whether the experiences and consequences of gaming will be equivalent between these samples.

Using non-gamers is also problematic as their skill level is likely to be low compared to gamers, and this lack of experience and competency is likely to prevent adequate progression in the game. This could influence experiences and outcomes in experimental studies as suggested by the finding that players with more gameplay experience showed lower feelings of frustration than less experienced gamers (Chumbley & Griffiths 2006). The observed increase in aggressive cognitions, affect, and behaviors found in previous research using inexperienced gamers could result from the frustration experienced due to a lack of intrinsic motivation, experience of gaming, and associated skills. This questions the generalizability of findings from studies using samples of non-gamers to gaming experiences and outcomes outside the lab, and demonstrates the need to use representative samples of gamers in empirical research.

Positive gaming

Although a large majority of theory and research focuses on the negative outcomes of playing violent video games, there is a wide range of associated potential positive experiences. Recent developments in active games technology (e.g., Nintendo Wii, Xbox Kinect) provide players with opportunities to engage in forms of physical activity, and have obvious implications for health and well-being. In addition, games such as *Big Brain Academy* encourage players to develop cognitive skills (e.g., mental arithmetic and memory recall). Although some research has examined such positive outcomes (e.g., Green & Bavelier 2003; Maddison *et al.* 2007), it is a relatively under-established area of inquiry. Future research should examine the influence of active gameplay on gamers' physical and psychological well-being, and the extent to which this differs from more "passive" gaming consoles. There is also a need for greater recognition of the potential positive effects of playing video games, and to further explore the factors that facilitate both positive and negative outcomes associated with engagement.

Conclusion

This chapter has critically reviewed the existing theoretical and empirical evidence for the proposed link between exposure to game violence and a variety of aggression-related outcomes. It has also identified a number of associated theoretical and methodological limitations, and indicated areas requiring further research. The research reviewed here suggests that, despite claims by some researchers, the proposed links between exposure to game violence and aggression-related outcomes are not fully established. A wide variety of factors influence the psychological and social development of individuals, and the relative contribution of media violence to such processes can only be fully understood in conjunction with an assessment of the contribution of other risk factors for violent and aggressive behavior.

Despite the inconsistency and debate within academic research in this area, media and public debate continues to claim a direct causal role for violent game content on aggressive behavior. Researchers have concluded that there is minimal evidence to support the hypothesis that excessive exposure to violent video games played a key role in the instigation of the school shootings outlined at the start of the chapter (e.g., Ferguson 2008). Recent studies of such cases have identified psychopathic, depressive, and suicidal tendencies, as well as peer victimization as key factors leading to such tragic events (Langman 2009; Wike & Fraser 2009). Violent acts rarely occur as a result of a single cause, and multiple factors (e.g., involvement in crime, peer victimization, and parental violence) have all been hypothesized to be higher risk factors for violence than exposure to media violence (Hopf, Huber, & Weiß 2008). It is highly unlikely that exposure to media violence, in the absence of other identified risk factors, determines violent criminal behavior or aggression alone, suggesting a much more complex mechanism behind school shootings and other violent behaviors. Such events, and the critical review of the existing literature provided in this chapter, demonstrates the need to further consider the personality and situational contexts in which such events occur.

The conclusions of this chapter are consistent with the extensive review of the available literature undertaken as part of the Byron Review in the UK (Byron 2008) as a governmental response to concerns over the effects of new technologies, including video games, on young people. It concluded that current evidence for the negative effects of new media is weak and inconclusive, and that consideration of such influences should be located within the wider context of young peoples' lives in contrast to the "cause and effect" tradition of research examining the negative effects of computer gaming (Byron 2008).

Subject in focus

Anderson and Dill (2000)

Anderson and Dill's (2000) research examining the effects of playing violent video games on aggressive thoughts, feelings, and behavior is commonly cited as research that supports the positive link between violent game exposure and both short- and long-term aggressive outcomes. In their first study, the researchers measured participants' exposure to violent game content and time spent playing video games, and correlated these measures with self-reported aggressive behavior and delinquency. They also measured aggressive personality to examine its influence on subsequent behavior. The results showed a positive association between the measured variables, which varied by gender and aggressive personality. Males who scored highly on trait aggression showed the strongest relationships between violent video-gameplay and aggressive behavior. This suggests that third variables such as trait aggression influence the links between exposure to violent video games and aggressive behavior, demonstrating that these relationships are more complex than a large majority of theory and research suggests.

The second study was an experiment in which participants were randomly assigned to play a violent or nonviolent video game. Following gameplay, participants completed questionnaires measuring hostile feelings and thoughts, and also completed a competitive reaction time test in which they could punish an opponent through delivering noise blasts using the Taylor Competitive Reaction Time Test (TCRTT). Their results showed that participants who played the violent video game (*Wolfenstein 3D*) delivered longer noise blasts than those who played the nonviolent video game (*Myst*). From this, Anderson and Dill (2000) concluded that playing violent video games increases aggressive behavior.

The results of these two studies led Anderson and Dill (2000) to suggest that exposure to video game violence increases aggressive behavior both in the short and long term. These claims should be interpreted with caution, however, because there are a number of methodological limitations of the design of the two studies, particularly the experimental study (Study 2). As discussed elsewhere in this chapter, the use of the TCRTT as a measure of aggressive behavior is questionable due to a lack of evidence that frequency or intensity of noise blasts are associated with individuals' real-life aggressive behavior (Ferguson *et al.* 2008b). The short gameplay period of fifteen minutes and the use of non-gamer samples also make it difficult to generalize the findings to real-life gaming experiences, and this raises questions about whether similar results would be found in a sample of gamers. Finally, the use of these games for violent and nonviolent game conditions respectively is problematic as they are different types of games. *Wolfenstein 3D* is a first-person shooter and *Myst* is an adventure-based game. They are very different on a variety of game characteristics (e.g., realism, graphics, immersion), which makes it difficult to conclude that the differential effects on aggressive outcomes between the two experimental conditions are solely due to violent content.

Discussion question

Can experimental researchers measure aggression in an ethical and realistic way?

Further sources of information

Anderson, C. A., Gentile, D. A., & Buckley, K. E. (2007). *Violent video game effects on children and adolescents: Theory, research, and public policy*. New York: Oxford University Press.

Byron, T. (2008). *Safer children in a digital world: The report of the Byron Review*. Department for Children, Schools and Families, and the Department for Culture, Media and Sport: London. Retrieved from: http://www.dcsf.gov.uk/ukccis/userfiles/file/FinalReportBookmarked.pdf.

Ferguson, C. J. (2007b). "The good, the bad and the ugly: A meta-analytic review of positive and negative effects of violent video games." *Psychiatric Quarterly*, *78*, 309–316.

Ferguson, C. J. (2010). "Blazing angels or Resident Evil? Can violent video games be a force for good?" *Review of General Psychology*, *14*, 68–81.

Rutter, J. & Bryce, J. (eds.) (2006). *Understanding digital games*. London: Sage.

Rense Lange, James Houran, and Lynn E. McCutcheon

Celebrity and Parasocial Relationships

7

No academic treatise on the media and psychology would be complete without examining those who are at the crossroads of these two topics, namely celebrities and especially the fans who admire or "worship" them. This chapter revisits our widely cited research published in the *British Journal of Psychology* that introduced the Celebrity Worship Scale (CWS, see McCutcheon, Lange, & Houran 2002), and several related studies that we subsequently conducted. The treatment of these articles in the media dramatically revealed that the study of fandom is vulnerable to the same psycho-social dynamics as celebrity worship itself. The CWS article captured the media and public's attention after its findings, and those of a clinical study we did on the topic a year later (Maltby, Houran, & McCutcheon 2003) were prominently featured in *New Scientist* magazine. Akin to the often extreme reactions to controversial statements by celebrities, our articles elicited an avalanche of reactions and accusations, most of which had no basis in fact and that bore little relation to the text of our articles. One issue stands out, namely: we never intended the "S" in CWS to represent anything other than the word "Scale," nor did we anticipate any confusion in this regard. Yet, to this day journalists and academics alike continue to ask us questions about our expert insights into the "serious epidemic" plaguing our society known as the "Celebrity Worship Syndrome."

The extent of the distortion of the article and the continuing public interest it generates is easily illustrated by referring the reader to the Wikipedia.org (accessed on November 6, 2010) entry on "celebrity worship syndrome." From its denigrating tone it will be obvious that our team had no hand in creating this entry, but its existence illustrates that our research had effectively become a "celebrity" (in this case a negative one) in its own right. Also, Google the phrase "celebrity worship scale" and 103,000 hits are returned; repeat the process on Yahoo and Bing, and 2,310,000 and 7,070,000 entries are available, respectively searched 2 August 2011. Most of these entries do consistently—but wrongly—credit us with coining the term "celebrity worship syndrome," and the various web authors cite our research as proposing that the public now suffers from a new and potentially serious psychiatric disorder. Thus, while the CWS article neither found nor implied the existence of a mental health epidemic, "the Internet" says it did and that we are the ones who said so.

Although the Wikipedia page states the opposite, it is also not true that we claimed that everyone is a hardcore celebrity worshiper. Perhaps we have researched and written so much about celebrity worship that someone might have taken a sentence out of context, twisted it a bit, and concluded that we stated that everyone is infatuated with famous people. But, if so, we do not know where that sentence is located. Rather, we believe that it should be clear to anyone that only individuals who score high on the CWS are to be labeled as "celebrity worshipers." Consider the very first words of this abstract: "In a continuing effort to understand why some people worship celebrities" (McCutcheon 2003: 131). If some people worship celebrities does not that imply that some do not? In another abstract we wrote: "Those who scored as celebrity worshipers" (McCutcheon & Maltby 2002: 325). If some scored as celebrity worshipers does not that imply that there were others who did not? Quoting from what is probably the most famous of our studies: "Table 2 shows that approximately 36% of our combined sample scored at or above the theoretical midpoints on the three subscales of the CAS" (Maltby, Houran, & McCutcheon 2003: 27). In plain language, it means that scores from the other 64% were below the cutoff point used to determine that some-one could reasonably be called a celebrity worshiper.

Although we have consistently tried to rectify these erroneous impressions in media interviews and other forums available to us (including changing the name of the instrument to the "Celebrity Attitude Scale: CAS"), this has had no noticeable effect. We now interpret our experiences with the CWS article and our related research as a vivid and personal illustration that the media has a profound and lasting influence on everyday perceptions, beliefs, and behaviors. Although it appears that few people have actually read the CWS article or the many related articles we wrote later, we believe that the method and contents used there represented a major step forward in the scientific study of fandom and parasocial interactions—a fact that is often lost in the media shuffle. For this reason, this chapter aims to reacquaint readers with the original research, as it provides an introduction to a later discussion of our insights into celebrity worship syndrome as a media-induced disorder.

The concept of celebrity and existence of parasocial relationships

From the foods we eat, the clothes we wear, the cars we drive, the political candidates we vote for, to the idols our children "follow" online, celebrities define increasingly important aspects of our lives. Celebrities rely on "fame" as many of them are not particularly knowledgeable or skilled; instead, as Boorstin (1961) noted half a century ago, celebrities are simply "known for being well-known." The concept of celebrity is thus mainly defined through its sociological and psychological properties rather than through more objectively measurable criteria. This chapter focuses on the psychological aspects of fame.

The study of celebrity and fame has generally followed three main trends. First, there is an interest in characteristics that distinguish eminent people with significant skills, looks, or intelligence from the general population (e.g., Albert 1996; Simonton 1999). Other studies have addressed how celebrity affects public attitudes such as consumer behavior (Till & Shimp 1998; Tripp, Jensen, & Carlson 1994). Thirdly, there are psychological consequences of achieving fame. For instance, Schaller (1997) found that fame sometimes leads to chronic self-consciousness and perhaps self-destructive behavior. Indeed, Giles (2000) has described several problems faced by celebrities, including loneliness, making new friendships that are genuine, and the loss of privacy.

Relative to the aforementioned trends, a fourth aspect of being a celebrity has been studied less extensively, namely, the effect celebrities have on their fans – the celebrity worshipers. Yet, such issues have gained in importance due to the exploding role of *parasocial interaction*, that is, one-sided relationships in which one party (the fan) knows a great deal about the other (the celebrity), but the latter does not know the former. Parasocial interaction is promoted by the increasing penetration of cable television, the Internet, and mobile technologies. Now, in addition to attending contests in which their sports idol participates, or visiting live concerts by musical stars, fans have access to detailed information about their idols' lives with the touch of a button at nearly any desired time and place. Also, many celebrities cater to the public's need for personal information by writing blogs or by issuing Twitter messages, while promoting themselves further by including ostensibly personal and diary-like accounts on their public web pages.

As audiences and viewers increasingly come to "know" persona by interpreting their appearance, gestures, conversation, and conduct, celebrities are not the only ones affected by fame (Rubin & McHugh 1987). The symbolic emotional and cognitive processes (Planalp & Fitness 1999) that occur in normal human interaction also form the basis of the impersonal "parasocial" relationships between fans and celebrities (Alperstein 1991). In fact, initially unknown persons who regularly appear on television will often become celebrities through these very processes.

Of course, parasocial interactions can be part of normal identity development during the maturation process. Yue and Cheung (2000) reported that young people can have both idols and models. Idealism, romanticism, and absolutism seem more important in *idol* selection (someone we aspire to be like in our fantasies), whereas realism, rationalism, and relativism coincide with *model* selection (someone we aspire to behave like in daily life). Children and adolescents often revere celebrities such as sport figures or pop singers (Greene & Adams-Price 1990; Raviv *et al*. 1996), but this "worshiping" of role models and celebrities often decreases in intensity with age (McCutcheon *et al*. 2004; Raviv *et al*. 1996). For some adults, however, celebrity worship apparently becomes a significant behavioral phenomenon that dominates their lives (for discussions, see e.g., Giles 2000; Klapp 1962; McCutcheon *et al*. 2004).

Development of the Celebrity Attitude Scale (The questionnaire formerly known as "Celebrity Worship Scale")

The paper by McCutcheon, Lange, and Houran (2002) presented the results of an empirical study of people who showed varying degrees of celebrity worship, as indicated by their answers to a set of thirty-three questionnaire items. This questionnaire used Wann's (1995) Sport Fan Motivation Scale as a starting point, and further included items addressing entertainment issues ("I enjoy my favorite celebrity because of her/his entertainment value"), social or group affiliation motives ("My friends and I like to discuss what my favorite celebrity has done"), and self-esteem ("The successes of my favorite celebrity are my successes also"). Items addressing escape ("News about my favorite celebrity is a pleasant break from a harsh world") and pathological identification ("When my favorite celebrity dies, I will feel like dying too") were also included. Based on preliminary analyses conducted by the researchers, seventeen questions (items) were retained for more detailed analysis, and these are shown in Table 7.1.

We asked 157 women and 92 men, ranging from 18 to 62 years of age, to complete these questions using a five-point Likert style rating scale with 5 being "strongly agree," 1 being "strongly disagree," and 3 being "uncertain or neutral." To obtain a rigorous measure of celebrity worship, we followed an objective measurement approach as is embodied in Rasch Scaling. The present scope does not allow us to provide a complete introduction to this approach, and for an introduction we refer to Bond and Fox (2007). Instead, we note that Rasch (1960) demonstrated that measurement is possible only if respondents' ratings are determined by just two basic factors. These factors are (a) the trait level of the respondent (in the present case, the intensity of respondents' celebrity worship) and (b) the tendency of questions to elicit positive (i.e., strongly agree or agree) responses. For instance, a statement like "I like celebrity X" is more likely to elicit high agreement than statements like "My life revolves around celebrity X." Analogous to the fact that more difficult mathematics questions (e.g., "What is

Table 7.1 The Rasch Hierarchy of the items in the Celebrity Worship Scale

Item no.	Celebrity Worship Scale Items	"Easier" = Highest endorsement
13	I enjoy watching, reading, or listening to my favorite celebrity because it means a good time.	–2.00
19	Learning the life story of my favorite celebrity is a lot of fun.	–1.36
31	Keeping up with news about my favorite celebrity is an entertaining pastime.	–1.03
17	I love to talk with others who admire my favorite celebrity.	–0.95
29	I like watching and hearing about my favorite celebrity when I am in a large group of people.	–0.77
23	It is enjoyable just to be with others who like my favorite celebrity.	–0.60
5	My friends and I like to discuss what my favorite celebrity has done.	–0.26
21	I often feel compelled to learn the personal habits of my favorite celebrity.	–0.25
14	For me, "following" my favorite celebrity is like daydreaming because it takes me away from life's hassles.	–0.20
9	I have pictures and/or souvenirs of my favorite celebrity, which I always keep in exactly the same place.	0.31
12	The successes of my favorite celebrity are my successes also.	0.58
18	When something bad happens to my favorite celebrity, I feel like it happened to me.	0.65
15	I have frequent thoughts about my favorite celebrity, even when I don't want to.	0.80
16	When my favorite celebrity dies (or died), I will feel (or felt) like dying too.	0.96
24	When my favorite celebrity fails or loses at something, I feel like a failure myself.	1.17
6	When something good happens to my favorite celebrity, I feel like it happened to me.	1.23
3	I am obsessed by details of my favorite celebrity's life.	1.73
		"Harder" = Lowest endorsement

the first derivative of 1/x?") will receive fewer correct responses than, say, "What is 10% of $20?" questionnaire items' that elicit lower rather than higher agreement ratings are said to be of greater "difficulty."

Rasch (1960/1980) showed that true measurement is possible only when respondents' trait levels and items' difficulty contribute in an additive fashion to the probabilities of observing a particular response. In particular, he demonstrated that for some function of the probability P_{ri} of observing response r to item i:

$$P_{ri} = (a) - (b),$$

where (a) and (b) represent respondents' trait levels and items' difficulty, respectively, as defined in the preceding paragraph. While external or demographic factors like as age and sex may contribute as well, such factors can only have indirect effects through respondents' trait levels. Thus, if it were found that women exhibit more intense celebrity worship than men, then this can come about *only* through women and men's differences with respect to (a), and sex differences are not due, say, to men and women's differential understanding and interpretations of the particular questions being asked.

When (a) and (b) are indeed additive, respondents as well as items will form true probabilistic hierarchies. That is, individuals with higher levels of celebrity worship will on an average give more positive (i.e., "strongly agree" or "agree") responses on all questions than respondents with lower trait levels. Also, questions that are less "difficult" will on average receive more positive responses than do more difficult questions. This pattern should be consistent for all conceivable subgroups of respondents, including, say, women versus men, older versus younger respondents, etc. Even if respondents' trait levels differ across subgroups, the item hierarchy (i.e., the relative spacing of the items) should thereby not be affected. In particular—and perhaps surprising to some readers—the item hierarchies should be the same for respondents that exhibit low versus high levels of celebrity worship. This contrast is of particular interest, as the finding of similar hierarchies in these two groups indicates that while worshiping intensity may vary, the "semantics" of the celebrity worship dimension remains stable.

Levels of celebrity worship

The main findings of our research are summarized in Table 7.1, which shows the CAS questions, numbered on the left and sorted in order of their endorsement (high on top, to low on the bottom) according to their Rasch parameters on the right (please note that positive numbers reflect greater "difficulty," that is, a tendency to elicit lower agreement ratings).

It can be seen that the order reflects three basic types (or, arguably, stages) of celebrity worship. First, low worship levels—called the *Entertainment-Social stage*—involve individualistic behaviors such as watching, reading and learning about, keeping up with, or listening to celebrities (Items 13 and 19) for purposes of entertainment (Item 31). Next, slightly higher levels of celebrity worship—termed the *Intense-Personal stage*—are characterized by social activities such as watching, hearing, and talking about the celebrity in the company of other fans (Items 17, 29, and 23) or friends (Item 5). Thirdly, the highest worship level—called the *Borderline-Pathological stage* —presents a rather mixed picture. On the one hand, the items suggest empathy, as highly worshiping individuals identify with their favorite celebrity's successes and failures (Items 12, 24, and 6). However, such empathy is accompanied by overidentification (Item 16), compulsive behaviors related to the keeping of pictures and souvenirs (Item 9), repetitive thought patterns (Item 18), and an obsession with "details of my favorite celebrity's life" (Item 3).

Using the Rasch scaling mentioned earlier, we found that these questions form a true probabilistic item hierarchy. (Note: For a more complete description, we refer to the original paper.) As such, the least endorsed behaviors, which few individuals agreed with (see bottom of table), do not replace the behaviors described by the most endorsed items (top of table). Rather, as a person's level of celebrity worship increases, the chances of any behavior being endorsed increases to a highly predictable extent. Yet, regardless of the level of celebrity worship, the probability that an item near the top of the table is endorsed always remains greater than that of items lower in the table. For instance, respondents who admit feeling like a failure when their favorite celebrity fails (Item 24), most likely also enjoy watching or reading about this celebrity (Item 19) or learning about this celebrity (Item 13). It is interesting to note that the location of Item 6 ("When something good happens to my favorite celebrity ...") significantly exceeds that of Item 18 ("When something bad happens ..."). In other words, higher levels of worship are required to identify with celebrities' successes than with their failures.

An Absorption-Addiction Model of celebrity worship

The original Celebrity Worship Scale article explained the levels of celebrity worship identified in terms of an *Absorption-Addiction Model*. Three main findings set the foundation for this:

1. There do *not* seem to be distinctly non-pathological and pathological dimensions of celebrity worship, as suggested by some earlier authors (e.g., Stever 1991; Wann 1995). Rather, in agreement with other researchers

(e.g., Rubin, Perse, & Powell 1985), celebrity worship appears to exist on a *continuum of severity*.

2. The continuum of celebrity worship comprises three general levels or theoretical stages. First, low worship levels are for purposes of entertainment; next, slightly higher levels of celebrity worship are characterized by social activities such as watching, hearing, and talking about the celebrity in the company of other fans (i.e., Intense-Personal components); finally, the highest worship levels involve empathy and overidentification with celebrities to the extent that addictive or compulsive behaviors come into play.

3. The increasing seriousness of the progression of attitudes and behaviors associated with celebrity worship is robust regardless of an individual's age, gender, or the type of celebrity being worshiped.

Most importantly, individuals who obtain high and low scores of celebrity worship agree on the item hierarchy as it is listed in Table 7.1. This finding is quite important because it demonstrates that people interpret the CWS questions the same way regardless of their own level of celebrity worship. For instance, consider the two questions: "I love to talk with others who admire my favorite celebrity" and "I like watching and hearing about my favorite celebrity when I am in a large group of people." The first question is more "difficult" than the first (see Table 7.1) and this question likely elicits lower ratings than the second. The finding that high and low scorers exhibit the same hierarchy means that despite their trait differences, people continue to recognize that talking with others about their celebrity is an indicator of stronger celebrity worship than a liking to watch and hear about a celebrity. In other words, the questions have the same meaning for low and high worshipers, and we conclude that the semantics of the celebrity worship dimension as defined here are invariant across the intensity of celebrity worship.

In subsequent research we have aimed to refine our findings. In particular, we added questions to those listed in Table 7.1 in order to address the three "stages" of celebrity worship in more detail. This approach also allowed us to include some questions that tapped into possible psychopathology, and this yielded the Entertainment-Social, Intense-Personal, and Borderline-Pathological subscales. Because some of the items are common to both versions of the scale, we view the results of this later research as compatible with our Absorption-Addiction Model.

This model can be easily illustrated using adolescents as an example. Specifically, it appears to us as though many children growing up in affluent Western societies develop an attitude of admiration for celebrities, which extends beyond any respect that most celebrities have earned. This process probably begins in early adolescence and continues gradually for a few years.

For most, the type of admiration can best be described as serving *entertainment* and *social* functions. At the lowest level, this involves the enjoyment of such mundane activities as watching, reading about, and listening to one's favorites. At slightly higher levels, it involves socializing with like-minded individuals. Having a favorite celebrity or two gives an adolescent a bridge that enables him or her to connect with other teens, such as reducing some of the anxiety of learning how to carry on a conversation with teens of the opposite sex. Moreover, a study by Wakefield (1995) showed that people are most likely to become fans of baseball players when they perceive that their family and friends are fans also. It appears that friends and peers are instrumental in absorbing new recruits into the process that leads to celebrity worship.

Many adolescents never go beyond the Entertainment-Social stage, but evidence suggests that an introverted nature, an especially difficult set of social circumstances, and a lack of meaningful relationships with others may cause some teens to become increasingly "absorbed" by the lives of these parasocial friends. "Absorption" is a psychological term to describe an effortless focusing of attention rather than determined concentration, and this results in a heightened sense of reality of the idolized celebrity. We believe that this heightened sense of reality promotes worshipers' unfounded beliefs that they have a special relationship or connection with "their" celebrity, thus motivating them to learn more about the object of their attention. Some progress to a point where they seek out other fans as sources of new information concerning the celebrity. Informal social institutions such as fan clubs, Internet newsgroups, and "conventions" often represent the only socially accepted methods available to acquire additional information and coveted specialized knowledge about celebrities.

If the need or capacity for absorption is high enough, if there is a social void caused by a failure to engage other teens, a young person might move on to a higher level of parasocial interaction. This higher level is characterized by empathy with the celebrity's successes and failures, and overidentification with the celebrity. Compulsive behaviors relating to the object of one's parasocial affection are also present. Finally, on the highest level there is an obsession with the celebrity's life. Those deluded and sometimes dangerous individuals who stalk celebrities almost certainly could be found at this level. At the Borderline-Pathological level the parasocial relationship becomes addictive in the sense that there is a progressively stronger involvement required in order to feel "connected" with the celebrity—similar to a psychological tolerance level. Thus, celebrity worshipers are hypothesized to become interested in celebrities via psychological absorption, while this interest is subsequently maintained by means of psychological addiction.

The Absorption-Addiction Model inherently presents both a positive and negative view of celebrity worship. At its core, it implies that there could be a "stalker" in all of us—that is, given the right circumstances perhaps anyone can become preoccupied with celebrities to the extent that devotion to a celebrity interferes with common sense and sound judgment. On the other hand, the model also suggests that those who have a dysfunctional interest in celebrities likely did not start out that way. Rather, they probably began at the more benign levels and the interest in the celebrity gradually transformed into a clinical problem. For example, the Rasch analyses indicate that a sample of adolescents would score higher on the Entertainment-Social subscale than they would on the Intense-Personal or Borderline-Pathological subscales. We also hypothesized that few people actually reach the Intense-Personal stage, so in any sample there should be more respondents endorsing the Entertainment-Social items than the Intense-Personal items.

To test this prediction, we randomly chose four of our studies in which subscale means were reported, two of which were conducted in the United States (Ashe & McCutcheon 2001; McCutcheon 2002) and two conducted in England (Maltby *et al.* 2005; Maltby, Houran, & McCutcheon 2003). When we compared the mean scores per item for the items that went into the makeup of those two subscales, the results were clear. In all four studies, with a combined total of seven different samples, the mean score per item was higher on the Entertainment-Social items for all seven samples. Whether the participants were adolescents, college students, or adults, they were more likely to endorse items like "My friends and I like to discuss what my favorite celebrity has done," than items like "If I were lucky enough to meet my favorite celebrity, and if he/she asked me to do something illegal as a favor I would probably do it."

Prevalence of celebrity worship

There are many media articles that have attempted to ascertain the number of people that show levels of celebrity worship that would be considered of clinical concern. Approximately, one-fourth of the general population scores at the Intense-Personal stage of celebrity worship or higher. This statistic derives from trends reported in three of our clinically oriented articles (see Maltby *et al.* 2004; Maltby, Houran, & McCutcheon 2003; Maltby *et al.* 2001). However, to date there has not been a large-scale, randomized survey of the general population worldwide and all estimates must be cautious.

It is difficult to determine whether the prevalence of celebrity worship has substantially increased or has become a more serious social issue. This question has a few interpretations. First, there is the issue of whether there is a higher proportion of celebrity worshipers today than there was, say, fifty years ago. On the other hand, one could ponder if the consequences of being a celebrity worshiper are greater today than they were in the past. Answering such questions is difficult without reliable longitudinal research. However, a study of newspaper and media reports might shed some light on the extent to which the media have responded to the public's interest in celebrities as well as how interests in celebrities' careers and personal lives has changed qualitatively over time.

Formal and systematic analysis is required to determine whether modern media and technology have fueled higher levels of celebrity worship, since it is not clear whether the media push the sensationalism surrounding celebrities onto the public or whether the media simply give the public what it wants. Our own unpublished research is looking at the correlation between Internet addiction (time spent on a computer) and levels of celebrity worship. Perhaps not surprisingly, even our preliminary findings suggest that people scoring high on a measure of Internet addiction also score highly on celebrity worship.

Our views on the way in which friends and family should behave when a loved one seems overly preoccupied with a celebrity have been published elsewhere (McCutcheon *et al.* 2004). These opinions and other perspectives on the subject should, however, be explored and tested in depth. This is an area that is ripe for clinical research. However, we note that while there are clear cases of dysfunctional celebrity worship (see e.g., Maltby, Houran, & McCutcheon 2003; Maltby *et al.* 2001), it seems possible to also leverage celebrities in ways to reinforce their potential as idols or role models. In this respect, celebrity worship might be positioned as a positive clinical intervention under the right circumstances. We note that in the US the National Basketball Association and the National Football League have initiated media campaigns featuring star professional athletes shown reading to children, distributing food to the poor, and visiting hospitalized youngsters.

Celebrity worship and personality

The Absorption-Addiction Model is broadly consistent with established theory (Maltby, Houran, & McCutcheon 2003). In particular, the three stages of celebrity worship identified appear to parallel the three dimensions of Eysenckian personality theory (Eysenck & Eysenck 1985). That is, the Entertainment-Social factor of CAS reflects some of the extraversion personality traits (sociable, lively, active, and venturesome). The Intense-Personal factor reflects some of Eysenck's neuroticism traits (tense, emotional, moody), and some of the acts described in the Borderline-Pathological subscale seem to reflect some of Eysenck's psychoticism traits (impulsive, antisocial, egocentric). We tested these hypotheses statistically by examining the relationships between the three stages of celebrity worship and the three dimensions of Eysenck's personality theory.

Table 7.2 outlines other statistically significant correlates of celebrity worship. Rather than point to serious psychiatric deficiencies, increasingly higher levels of celebrity worship show associations with perceptual personality variables and personal well-being that can have a strong effect on attitudes and behaviors related to social bonding, as well as often reinforce or exacerbate the process of psychological addiction.

Conclusion

While the celebrities of the past (such as movie stars, sports figures, musicians, and politicians) continue to draw attention, their status is actively

Table 7.2 Empirical correlates of the three celebrity worship stages

Celebrity worship level
Entertainment-Social
Extraversion
Quest for religiosity (among men)
Depression
Emotional autonomy (among adolescents)
Thin childhood/adolescence/adult boundaries
Thin boundaries re: Child-like ideations
Thick boundaries re: Personal and physical environments
Intense-Personal
Neuroticism
Poorer cognitive flexibility
Low extrinsic-personal religiosity
Low extrinsic-social religiosity (among men)
Anxiety
Depression
Negative body image (female adolescents)
Low security and closeness (among adolescents)
Emotional autonomy (among adolescents)
Thin childhood/adolescence/adult boundaries
Thin organizations/relationships boundaries
Thick boundaries re: Personal and physical environments
Borderline-Pathological
Psychoticism
Poorer cognitive flexibility
Poorer creativity
Thin childhood/adolescence/adult boundaries
Thin boundaries re: Child-like ideations
Thin organizations/relationships boundaries
Thick boundaries re: Personal and physical environments
Thick interpersonal boundaries

being challenged within the celebrity culture. Indeed, increasingly localized and purely accidental "celebrity" appears to be on the rise because media and technology have created greater opportunity for parasocial interaction. For instance, we now have celebrities on reality television shows, daytime talk shows, YouTube, and to some extent on sites like Facebook. Social networking sites like Facebook, Twitter, Hyves, LinkedIn, and Myspace all encourage social competition based on popularity as determined by the number of parasocial contacts people can claim.

Although we believe in the validity of our measure of celebrity worship, we recognize that there have been changes in what defines both celebrities and fans. Firstly we see a continuing trend away from celebrities being defined as possessing skills or traits of potential evolutionary value, and toward people whose main skill it is to gain attention for themselves—even at the expense of their own dignity or personal well-being (what we term "empty celebrities"). It would seem difficult to become preoccupied with such typical short-term "fifteen-minute" famers for a sustained period of time. It remains a research question to delineate exactly what changes the status of those mentioned in the "news du jour" into celebrities with sustained status (staying power). One of our underlying concerns is the possibility that the preoccupation of the media with "empty" celebrities has made it difficult for some celebrity worshipers to tell the difference between those who are "empty" and those who have some merit to be constructive idols or role models. This may not be so problematic when the choice is among singers or movie stars. Does it really make much difference if your favorite singer is less vocally talented than most popular singers? However, there seems to be an alarming trend (at least in the US) to make celebrities out of "empty" persons who promote outrageously false political statements that are accepted as truthful by their gullible admirers. The media created these political celebrities, and their continued presence in the media seems to us to be more indicative of their ability to attract admirers than of their propensity for promoting truth.

If societies originally delineated celebrities as those people who rose in status due to skills and abilities that were desirable from an evolutionary standpoint and thus inspired people to copy them in order to gain similar success, then we hope that sustained celebrities in modern society are those individuals who the public has deemed to have merit beyond immediate or short-term social and market forces. Ideally, the staying power of sustained celebrities derives from the possession of skills, traits, or characteristics that have psychological or evolutionary value to the general population. In this sense, the media could be somewhat limited in its ability to create "empty" celebrities. The entertainment industry and other technological forces can draw attention to specific people, but it is the court of public opinion that seems to evaluate these individuals. Thus, we wish for a sustained celebrity status resulting from the media and a public that is less inclined toward celebrity worshiping working together to explore and subsequently validate the social value of individuals who are "known for being well-known."

After a decade of work (for a review of most of our earlier research, see McCutcheon *et al.* 2004), we know that we have merely scratched the surface of understanding this fascinating subject. Nevertheless, we are convinced that the nature of celebrity worship will likely expand and intensify, although the process by which this occurs will differ from today due to changes in the nature of the media and technology. Perhaps the most daunting and pressing research question has yet to be addressed, namely: "Is parasocial communication destined to become our primary vehicle for interpersonal relations?"

We hope the answer is "no," as replacing genuine and lasting social bonds with one-sided perceptions of highly idealized people or a cache of illusory interpersonal connections is not social progress, in our opinion. No discernible psychological disorder or medical epidemic is operating here—that notion was a media invention. But we are facing a sobering societal issue whereby individuals can and are encouraged to use celebrities as "junk food" to fill a hunger that is fueled, in part, by a paucity of legitimate and deep social bonding. We are uncertain of the direction all of this will take or what interventions will be developed to counteract the negative aspects of celebrity worship and parasocial interactions; however, we strongly suggest that readers look for those insights, answers, and solutions somewhere other than on the television and Internet.

Subject in focus

"Celebrity stalking"

The dysfunctional aspects of celebrity worship (e.g., Maltby, Houran, & McCutcheon 2003; Maltby *et al.* 2001) and its potential as an expression of coping and adaptation (e.g., McCutcheon *et al.* 2003, Maltby *et al.* 2004; Maltby *et al.* 2006; Maltby *et al.* 2002) have led to an interest in what might well be the most dangerous subtype of the celebrity worshiper—the celebrity stalker.

In one study, those who scored high on celebrity worship and those who had formed insecure attachments to their parents during childhood were more likely to condone behaviors indicative of celebrity stalking than those scoring lower on celebrity worship and those who had formed secure attachments to their parents during childhood (McCutcheon *et al.* 2006). Furthermore, the relationship between Intense-Personal subscale scores and the tendency to condone celebrity stalking was stronger than the relationship between Entertainment-Social subscale scores and the tendency to condone celebrity stalking, as the Absorption-Addiction Model predicts. Males were slightly more inclined to condone celebrity stalking and older individuals were slightly less likely to condone celebrity stalking (McCutcheon *et al.* 2006). We wish to make clear that the overlap between persons who score high on the Intense-Personal subscale or the Borderline-Pathological subscale and those who are actual celebrity stalkers is quite small. We believe that real celebrity stalkers would score very high on these subscales, but there are so few of them that we have never knowingly administered the CAS to any.

The indirect measure of celebrity stalking used in a related study has been found to be reliable, valid, free of social desirability bias, and weakly related to a measure of trait anger (McCutcheon *et al.* 2006). We think it might prove useful as attempts to learn more about celebrity stalkers unfold. We would welcome the opportunity to administer both the CAS and the measure of celebrity stalking to a group of celebrity stalkers, if only we could locate such a group.

Discussion question

Do celebrities encourage parasocial relationships and stalking through their posts on Twitter and Facebook?

Further sources of information

In the following, we summarize some recent articles of particular relevance to the (future) development of the CAS, along with brief commentaries:

Bond, T. G. & Fox, C. M. (2007). *Applying the Rasch model: Fundamental measurement in the human sciences* (2nd ed). Mahwah, NJ: Lawrence Erlbaum.
Those interested in the Rasch scaling will find a thorough, yet highly readable introduction here. This book discusses theory as well as application, and it provides an up-to-date summary of the field, together with highly instructive computer exercises. Those interested in learning Rasch scaling also may want to download free of charge the fully functional Bigsteps software that is available at http://www.winsteps.com/bigsteps.htm.

All of the analyses similar to those in McCutcheon, Lange, and Houran (2002) can be done with this software.

McCutcheon, L. E., Aruguete, M., Scott, V. B., & VonWaldner, K. L. (2004). "Preference for solitude and attitude toward one's favorite celebrity." *North American Journal of Psychology, 6,* 499–506.

We compared CAS scores with scores on a measure of preference for solitude across three samples. Since high CAS scores reflect a preference for social (or parasocial) relationships, we hypothesized that those who favored solitude would not tend to be celebrity worshipers. This prediction was supported, though most of the relationships were weak. Of particular interest was the finding that those who enjoy solitude and perceive themselves as productive during periods of solitude were especially unlikely to score high on the Intense-Personal subscale. Do productive people value their productivity too much to get caught up in the fortunes of some celebrity?

McCutcheon, L. E., Ashe, D. D., Houran, J., & Maltby, J. (2003). "A cognitive profile of individuals who tend to worship celebrities." *Journal of Psychology, 137,* 309–322.

This study is listed in the references, but we thought it is important and it has been unjustly ignored. We gave the CAS and six different measures of cognition to a group of American college students. We found a significant inverse relationship between CAS scores and cognitive ability on four of them. In other words, the smarter you are, the less likely you are to be a celebrity worshiper. There are three or four possible explanations for this, and we would like to see further research on this topic. Do people with less intelligence gravitate toward a fantasy world in which they lose themselves in the successes of their favorite celebrities?

Sheridan, L., North, A., Maltby, J., & Gillett, R. (2007). "Celebrity worship, addiction, and criminality." *Psychology, Crime, and Law, 13,* 559–571.

Persons who scored as celebrity worshipers also tended to score high on measures of addiction and criminality. This study is consistent with our Absorption-Addiction Model, especially the higher stages of it. The study is also meritorious because it is the first to match preferences for certain types of celebrities (e.g., actors, athletes, musicians) with CAS subscores.

Swami, V., Taylor, R., & Carvalho, C. (2009). "Acceptance of cosmetic surgery and celebrity worship: Evidence of associations among female undergraduates." *Personality and Individual Differences, 47,* 869–872.

Willingness to undergo cosmetic surgery was studied in a sample of 401 British female undergraduates. In general, high CAS scores, and particularly high scores on the Intense-Personal subscale, predicted a willingness to undergo cosmetic surgery. Their results are consistent with results from one of ours (Maltby *et al.* 2005), in which we studied three large samples of British females. Results suggested that females who had a strong parasocial relationship with celebrities perceived as having a good body shape tended to have poor body images of themselves.

Wong, M., Goodboy, A. K., Murtagh, M. P., Hackney, A. A., & McCutcheon, L. E. (2010). "Are celebrities charged with murder likely to be acquitted?" *North American Journal of Psychology, 12,* 625–636.

Almost 200 college students served as mock jurors in a murder trial involving a movie star in one condition, a televangelist in another and an office worker in a third. Otherwise, the transcript was identical across conditions. Overall, the movie star was more likely to be convicted than the other two defendants when their categories were combined. The movie star was especially likely to be convicted by those who scored low (non-celebrity worshipers) on the CAS. The results suggest that celebrity worshipers might not be able to maintain their objectivity as jurors if a famous person is on trial, even if that celebrity is not a personal favorite of the jurors.

PART III

Representation

Linda Heath

Portrayal of Crime

Mass media's portrayal of crime, both fictional and real, has been blamed for distress and disruption in the real world for as long as there have been mass media. For example, early newspapers, termed the "Penny Press," were blamed for both increased crime levels and fear of crime (Gordon & Heath 1981), while the radio broadcast of Orson Welles' *The War of the Worlds* was notoriously criticized for causing fright and panic (Bryant & Thompson 2002). The criticisms originally leveled at comic books (blaming media exposure for the misbehavior of the youth: Bryant & Thompson 2002) are more recently directed at video games or the Internet, demonstrating that while media technologies continue to develop, the concerns raised by society and relevant agencies remain focused on particular themes. Media coverage of crime has been faulted for scaring people, misinforming people, and actually making people more likely to commit crimes.

The current chapter will first examine the portrayal of crime in the mass media, dividing the discussion into portrayals of actual crimes (i.e., news reporting) versus portrayals of fictional crimes (i.e., drama). This discussion will include the hybrid known as docudramas, wherein a real-world event is expanded and reenacted in a fictionalized treatment. Within each of those subdivisions (real crimes versus fictional crimes) we shall consider various types of media, focusing most on those that have been subjected to the most research: newspapers and television. After exploring what the mass media present as "the crime picture," we shall then examine audience and market factors, many of which directly impact on how crime is presented by the mass media. Once we have considered what the media are presenting and who is consuming the messages, we shall look at theories and concepts from psychology and communication studies that have been used to understand potential effects of exposure to crime through mass media. Finally, we shall summarize the main findings from the thousands of studies in this area, looking primarily at the effects of mass media on perceptions, fear, and actual criminal behavior.

The continued popularity of crime

Traditionally, news and information about actual crimes are primarily presented through newspapers and television news programs. In recent years, however, Internet sites have gained market share at the expense of newsmagazines. (See Figure 8.1 from the Pew Research Center for the People and the Press.)

Although many of the same factors influence the coverage of crime reports by both newspapers and television, there are a few important differences that should be considered.

Gordon and Heath (1981) outline the factors that help make crime a staple of the mass media. These factors include the steady supply of events (either local or available from national distributors), the ease of gathering the information (with many police departments providing space and access for reporters), and the inherent interest among readers and viewers in such information. Whether the audience is driven primarily by a desire to assess their own risks or by a more voyeuristic impulse is not clear from the research, and it is likely that different readers and viewers have different motivations for attending to news about crimes. In addition, it is probable that individuals attend to media coverage of crime for complex reasons. We know most people attend to news about local crimes, which would seem to indicate an interest in personal risk assessment. At the same time, we know media presentations about sensational crimes that occur in distant locations are also attended to, which would indicate some motivation other than personal risk assessment is at play (Heath 1984).

Newspaper Readership Declines; Internet News Increases								
	1993	1996	1998	2000	2002	2004	2006	2008
Listened/read yesterday....	%	%	%	%	%	%	%	%
Newspaper	58*	50	48	47	41	42	40	34
Radio news	47*	44	49	43	41	40	36	35
Regularly watch...								
Cable TV news	--	--	--	--	33	38	34	39
Local TV news	77	65	64	56	57	59	54	52
Nightly network news	60	42	38	30	32	34	28	29
Network morning news	--	--	23	20	22	22	23	22
Online for news three or more days a week	--	2**	13	23	25	29	31	37
*From 1994; **From 1995.								

Figure 8.1   Key news audiences now blend online and traditional sources: Audience segments in a changing news environment.
Soure: http://people-press.org/report/444/news-india

The selection of news material

Not all crime is deemed equally worthy of space in the newspaper or on the newscast, however, so the impression of crime that the audience garners from the mass media is not a pure reflection of crime in their local area or in the country. This selective reporting reflects a choice on the part of the media managers rather than a necessity driven by the volume of crime. If newspapers reported crime information in the same size print and with the same level of detail that they report stock prices, they could fit all the daily crimes from even a major metropolitan area in the paper. But editors and producers have chosen to focus on select crimes rather than catalog all crimes that occur daily. Consequently, although "broom stolen from local recreation center" might make it into the newspaper from a very small community (as it did in one town I lived in), most crime coverage in newspapers and on television follows dictates of "newsworthiness."

And what do editors and producers think makes a crime "newsworthy"? Jamieson and Campbell (1992) identified five factors that guide news selection, including but not limited to news about crimes. First, events that are *personalized* are more newsworthy than events that are more abstract. This explains why the media focus is more often on the actors (e.g., President, Speaker of the House, Judge, etc.) than on the ultimate content (e.g., the statement, bill, or legal issue). This is also why media coverage tends to focus on individual crimes rather than statistical patterns or contextual matters. Second, newsworthy events have *drama and conflict*. The live coverage given in 2010 to the runaway balloon that was thought to contain a child reflected the focus on drama, with the follow-up coverage of the staging of the event reflecting conflict.

A third component of newsworthy events is *action*. The audience can see something happening. A bombing, airplane crash, and shoe flying toward the President all have action. Negotiating a peace accord, inflation, and changes in demographic makeup of the workforce do not have enough immediate action to make them newsworthy on a daily basis. Eventually the signing of the peace accord, precipitous drop in the market with looks of horror on the faces of stock brokers, and demonstrations for worker rights might make the underlying process newsworthy for a day, but the actual "news" needs action to receive coverage.

A fourth component is *novelty and deviance*. Another family argument that turns physical isn't news. A family argument where someone unleashes a pet tarantula to hold family members hostage is. The classic phrase is "dog bites man isn't news; man bites dog is news." By definition, frequently occurring events are not novel, so the thousands of instances of shoplifting, speeding, and assaults that happen every day are not "news." Even some murders are not news, or are, at most, covered in a small article on an inside page of the newspaper. Finally, a story is more newsworthy if it has a *link to an ongoing theme*. A murder of a homeless person in a park in a major city that might not be covered at all under some circumstances could be front-page news if there had been a rash of such murders recently. Similarly, a purse snatching from an elderly woman might not be covered unless the media had discovered (or created) a "crime-wave against the elderly" (Fishman 1978).

Beyond those five basic characteristics of newsworthy events, Harris (2004) added four more secondary characteristics. First, to receive coverage an event must be *inoffensive*. That is, some events are difficult to present without having the media outlet receive volumes of phone calls and e-mails from readers or viewers who are outraged by the coverage. Often such events have a sexual nature, such as the police raid on a bathhouse in a city where I once lived, which resulted in a photo of two police officers carrying a six-foot plastic object out of the building. The local newspaper decided not to run the picture. Other times, the event is offensive to important advertisers. I was curious why local papers in one city I lived in did not report local murders (or buried them on page 25), although the papers gave front-page coverage to gruesome crimes that happened elsewhere. Finally, a reporter told me it was an unspoken agreement between the media and the local government in this city that depended heavily on tourism dollars in the economy. Don't scare the tourists by putting local crimes on the front page!

Another secondary characteristic is *credibility*. Although lots of people think that they have ridden on alien spacecraft, to my knowledge none of those reports have made it into the mainstream media. (There are notable exceptions in specialized media available at grocery checkout lanes.) Again crime news meets this criterion, because the police or prosecutors are deemed credible sources, and they are readily accessible in most media markets.

Events that can be packaged as *sound bites* are also more likely to be considered newsworthy than those that can't, although Harris (2004) argues that sound bites are not a recent development. Slogans and nicknames (e.g., Jack the Ripper) have been used to identify events for decades. In recent years, however, the ability to fit a story into a sound bite is considered to be a necessity rather than an optional extra for news coverage, especially for television coverage of crimes.

Finally, events that have a *local hook* are more likely to be covered. When a major disaster occurs elsewhere, reporters scramble to find out if any of the victims were local or there is any connection to the immediate geographic area.

These criteria align with basic psychological principles concerning attention and memory. We attend to things that have personal relevance, that are vivid, that contain action and conflict. We process information more fully if it is novel or unexpected or thematically related to other things we have recently been thinking about. We try to ignore things that are offensive or not credible (although it is not clear whether we are very good at that). And we remember things better if they are catchy. Editors and producers do not randomly select and focus on these characteristics of newsworthy events; they choose factors that will attract attention and be recalled enough to create more demand for that type of news.

Consequences of selection

Applying these characteristics of newsworthy events to crime news leads to certain predictable and well-documented distortions of actual criminal events as they get transformed into media messages. Most obviously, routine, mundane events are underreported, as typical events that happen all the time are, by definition, not "news." Second, more violent crimes than property crimes are reported, as property crimes generally do not have the action and drama that generally accompany violent crimes. Consequently, bank fraud that results in financial losses of thousands of dollars will not be reported, but a bank robbery that netted $200 will be. White-collar crimes such as insider trading or Ponzi schemes will go unreported even if discovered, whereas the theft of a llama from the zoo will be covered extensively. Similarly, media critics claim that the disappearance of a very photogenic victim is covered much more extensively than the disappearance of a less attractive victim. Critics further claim that victimizations of blond (and therefore European American) women are covered much more extensively than victimizations of women with brown or black hair (who are often of other ethnic backgrounds). Although the many factors that influence coverage make it difficult to prove or disprove this claim, many recent heavily covered disappearances fit this pattern.

Among classes of violent crimes, such as assaults or homicides, crimes committed by strangers are much more likely to be reported by the media than crimes committed by friends or family members, leading people to underestimate the scope of domestic violence and overestimate the rate of stranger violence in society. The image of crime presented by the media is also more random than many crimes actually are (Heath, Gordon, & LeBailly 1981). For example, "missing children" in the US are generally teenagers who have run away from home or children taken by the noncustodial parent, and yet those details are often obscured by the media. Similarly, the vast majority of rapes are committed by someone known to the victim rather than by a total stranger, but this detail is often not reported, leading readers and viewers to assume that the victim was chosen totally at random (Heath, Gordon, & LeBailly

1981). This is not to say that we as a society should not be concerned about children who are abducted by parents or women who are raped by men who are not total strangers, but the impression provided by the media is erroneous in ways that might place children and women at greater risk of victimization. Similarly, actions taken by victims that might have made them more vulnerable to victimization are generally not reported by the media, either because the reporters do not know the details or because they do not want to appear callous. Often criminal victimizations of women who leave a bar willingly with a stranger or teenage runaways who accept shelter from "helpful" strangers from the bus station are presented as victims chosen at random, leading readers and viewers unaware of the danger of such actions.

These factors affect both newspaper and television portrayals of crime, but there are some additional factors that influence television coverage more than print news. Of primary importance is the visual impact of the event. Both newspaper and television crime coverage has been accused of following the "if it bleeds, it leads" mantra, but television news in particular needs videotape to accompany the report. Critics maintain that television news coverage is more about visual impact rather than objective seriousness of the event, with stations competing to achieve the most gripping footage. A piece of unsubstantiated journalism lore is that after a fire destroyed a Catholic church a reporter from one local station boasted to someone from another station that his film had bigger flames, whereupon the other reporter responded, "Yes, but our nun was crying harder than your nun." This interest in the visual sometimes leads to extended live coverage of rather uninteresting events, such as a balloon floating along or a white Bronco being pursued at slow speeds down an LA highway, events which gain interest because they might end dramatically (in the case of the balloon) or because they involve a celebrity (in the case of the O. J. pursuit).

Other sources of news about actual as opposed to fictional crimes include newsmagazines, Internet sites, and reality crime shows, such as *America's Most Wanted*. Newsmagazines generally cover crimes that grip the national attention for extended periods, such as the O. J. Simpson case, the Natalee Holloway disappearance, or any school shooting that result in multiple deaths. Because newsmagazines do not have the immediacy of television and newspaper coverage of these crimes, they often provide more context and analysis of such crimes. The Internet, on the other hand, has the advantage in terms of timely reporting, often reporting the crime within minutes of its occurrence. Frequent updates follow major crime stories, often supplemented by "citizen journalism" reports, video, and pictures. Finally, the genre of television programs such as police news programs, public affairs programs, reenactments, and documentaries provide an additional media source of news about crimes. Content analysis of such programs about real crime shows that the crime presentations are more similar to crime drama than to crime as presented on television news programs (Bryant & Thompson 2002).

Further portrayals of crime: Fiction and docudramas

Although early newspapers ran serialized novels that sometimes dealt with crime, currently most strictly fictional crime presentations in the media occur on television, in movies, and in novels. Most research has focused on the effects of television crime drama or violence in cartoons because young children can be exposed to such media messages and the effects of such messages are thought to be particularly powerful among young viewers. Presentations of fictional crime on television can be further subdivided into presentations that are intended to be realistic depictions of present-day crime and those that are intended to be fantastical or historically distant, such as tales of vampires, zombies, space battles, or Westerns.

What do we know about the amount of fictional crime on American television? The National Television Violence Study (1998) concluded that about 60% of television programs overall contained violence, with that percentage increasing in prime-time network and cable programming. One-third of all programs contain at least ten violent acts, with the average program containing at least six violent acts per hour. The majority of programs (75%) show no punishment for the perpetrator and in over half the instances, no one is shown experiencing pain. Consequently, crime on television is sanitized and trivialized (Bryant & Thompson 2002; Sparks 2006). Minow (1996) documented that the average child spends about three hours per day watching television, and Strasburger and Wilson (2002) documented that the average children's show has fourteen violent acts per hour, though Gerbner claims the rate is thirty-two per hour (Sparks 2006). Fictional crime follows the same pattern as media reports of real-world crimes, with the more violent crimes vastly overrepresented. For example, whereas about 87% of real crimes are nonviolent, only 13% of television crimes are, and murder makes up 50% of television crimes and only .2% of real crimes (Harris 2004).

Straddling the line between real-world crime reports and fictional crimes are docudramas, which are fictionalized accounts of crimes that really happened. The docudramas can vary in significant ways from the details of the actual crime. For example, the Academy Award-winning film *Dead Man Walking* was based on the work of Sister Helen Prejean who served as a spiritual advisor to men on death row for homicides. Although Sister Helen was an advisor to the movie and actually served as a spiritual advisor, the criminal depicted by Sean Penn was actually a composite of two murderers with whom

Sister Helen had worked. There is an undoubtedly wide variation in how closely the docudrama depictions match the actual crime in reality. Harris (2004) reports that when Jennifer Casolo, a peace worker, was approached about collaborating on a movie about her experience being arrested for being a revolutionary in El Salvador, the producers wanted to change the story from her being innocent (the reality) to her being guilty (evidently thought to be more dramatic). The producers also wanted to say that she fell in love with one of her captors, which had not happened. She turned them down, so you never saw that dramatic but untrue depiction of her experience.

Crime media consumption trends

The media landscape is like shifting sands. Although new forms of media have always been evolving, displacing, or significantly altering previous media forms, the rapidity with which new forms spring up is mind-boggling. Whereas television saturation took about twenty years to reach a high enough level to challenge radio and movies (Hennigan *et al*. 1982), the Internet as a provider of news content has challenged daily newspapers and newsmagazines in a fraction of that time. What follows is an overview of current trends in the consumption of media that present depictions of crime.

Newspapers

The number of daily newspapers being published in the US has been declining for decades, with many cities that previously had two independent newspapers currently having only one or having two separate mastheads published by the same editorial board (generally a morning and afternoon version under separate names). One newspaper (*The Chicago Daily News*) actually went out of business when I was in the middle of conducting a content analysis on it in the late 1970s! Readership among adults is also on a downward trajectory, with readership falling from 78% in 1970 to 59% in 1997, with an alarmingly low rate of 31% among young adults (Halimi 1998). As has been the case for decades, the favorite sections or features of newspapers are the sports coverage, the coupons, the comics, and advice columns rather than the hard news. Probably contributing to the decline of the daily newspapers are the many free weekly "shoppers" that have emerged, which present the coupons and some very light content with no hard news.

Newspaper readers tend to be older, male, better educated, and have higher incomes than nonreaders. They tend to watch less television than nonreaders, other than television news, which they watch more than nonreaders (Harris 2004). The decreasing number of newspaper staffs employed by newspapers has resulted in a greater reliance on wire stories, with fewer local reports beyond what is easily available from police blotters. Similarly, there are fewer in-depth investigative reports and more of the news hole devoted to features and light news.

Newsmagazines

Even as we go to print, newsmagazines (e.g., *Newsweek*) are struggling to avoid bankruptcy and to redefine themselves in a way that makes weekly presentations relevant. The effect on media crime coverage will probably not be that great, however, as crimes that have been covered in newsmagazines in the past will continue to be covered in newspapers and on television news reports.

Television

Television reached almost full saturation (98%) by 1980 and has remained constant since then, with the average US household now having over two television sets. The average television set is turned on for seven hours per day, unless the television is hooked up to cable, in which case it is on for eight hours per day. Most American households (75%) now have cable television, with cable programming taking an ever-increasing share of the viewership (Harris 2004). TV viewing is not evenly distributed across the life span, with young children watching TV for about 2.5 hours per day until age eight, then increasing to about four hours per day by age twelve, then falling back down and not rising again until after child rearing is complete. The elderly, women, African-Americans, and people with lower incomes watch the most television (Roberts 2000).

One side effect of the changing patterns of television viewing is that it has become increasingly difficult to research the effects of viewing particular types of programming. The use of video recorders and Digital Video Recorders (DVRs) to record programs allows time shifting and repeat viewing, making it increasingly difficult to determine viewership for various programs. Also, although researchers can still ask respondents how much time they spent "yesterday" or "typically" or "last evening" watching television, a tedious series of follow-up questions are necessary to determine if the person was watching ten hours of home decorating shows or ten hours of crime and mayhem or two hours of news, two of sports, two of crime, two of home decorating, and two of classic comedies. Long gone are the days when people had only three choices (or four, counting "no television" as a choice) corresponding to the three networks. Also long gone are the days when the three networks followed similar patterns, all airing a lot of Westerns one year and a lot of medical drama a few years later. Finally, long gone are the days when people had to walk all the way across the living room to change the channel on the television set, leading most people to stay glued to the same network all evening. Prior to remote channel devices (aka "clickers"), people's viewing resembled rocks. Now viewing resembles ping-pong balls. Determining their exposure to crime news and crime drama has therefore become much more challenging.

Internet

A major contributor to the shifting sands of the current media landscape is the wide saturation of the Internet in people's homes. The Internet has the ability to deliver not only news about crimes within minutes of their occurrence but also television drama, news analysis, and comments by experts, witnesses, and crackpots. The Internet (via blogs, social networking sites, Wikipedia, and e-mail, among other options) has the ability to remove the professional editor, publisher, or producer from the information stream and make available a worldwide audience to anyone who cares to post a video, comment, or analysis. This audience, however, is also available to anyone who cares to post a fake or highly edited video, comment on something that never happened, or analyze a situation using totally falsified data or information. Whether overall the open access will lead to the availability of more or less accurate information about crime (and everything else) remains to be seen.

Theoretical frameworks relevant to media portrayals of crime

The thousands of research studies that have been conducted on the effects of media portrayals of crime have been based primarily on theories and concepts drawn from psychology, sociology, political science, and communication studies. The majority of research, however, has been focused on media effects on aggressive and violent behavior, which is covered in Chapter 1. A smaller but still substantial body of research has looked at the effects of media portrayals of crime on perceptions, anxiety, and views of society. Next we review theories that have supported the research on the effects on perceptions, anxiety, and views of society.

Hypodermic-Needle Model/Magic Bullet Theory/Direct Effects Model

Campbell, Martin, and Fabos (2009) refer to the Hypodermic-Needle Model (also known as the Magic Bullet Theory or Direct Effects Model) as "one of the earliest and least persuasive media theories" (527). This model grew out of the seemingly powerful effects of the media in driving whole nations to war, first evidenced by the US entry into the Spanish-American war in 1898 by the Hearst newspaper's inflammatory coverage of the sinking of the battleship Maine in Havana Harbor, and later with Hitler's use of radio to promote the Holocaust among Germans, leading to World War II. This model posits that great power resides in the media, which can function as a hypodermic needle and inject ideas into the population. By 1940, research findings were beginning to draw that assumption into question, led by research on the H. G. Wells radiocast of *War of the Worlds*, which research showed did not affect all listeners equally and, in fact, affected some listeners not at all. This increasing sophistication led to a more nuanced theory.

Minimal-Effects Theory/Selective Processes

This model emphasized the roles of selective exposure and selective retention in determining the effects of media messages. The guiding idea here is that preexisting attitudes guide what viewers, listeners, or readers attend to and retain, so that media messages serve to reinforce preexisting ideas and attitudes rather than to sway people to new ways of thinking. Klapper (1960) summarized the findings of many studies of media persuasion and concluded that media primarily influence people who do not already have an opinion and those who are poor and have little education, leading to the conclusion that media effects are quite limited and operate primarily among the uninterested and uninformed (Campbell, Martin, & Fabos 2009; Straubhaar & LaRose 2006).

Uses and Gratification Theory

Straubhaar and LaRose claim the uses and gratification perspective "dominates" thinking about media consumption behavior (2006: 400). This theory posits a much more active role for the audience. Far from passively being shot by a hypodermic needle or magic bullet, the audience members select the media messages to serve predetermined purposes. For example, one listener might tune into a conservative talk radio program to hear comments to reinforce his own views on political matters, whereas another person might tune into such a program to be amused at the ludicrous comments, whereas a third person might assiduously avoid hearing such a program because it infuriates her to hear such comments. Consequently, the effect of the same program on three different people can be very different depending on the peoples' motivations of exposing themselves to the message. Regarding crime programming, one audience member might seek out television drama about sexual assaults to help her learn how to avoid such situations, whereas another person might avoid such shows because they are too upsetting and cause her to be fearful. A third person might watch such shows to convince herself that she is very different from the victims in order to increase her feelings of security.

Uses and gratification research is still a productive area of media study, with a fairly recent application being the "friendship" the audience feels with commentators, radio announcers, and television personalities (Harris 2004). The presence of familiar faces and voices has a reassuring effect for many members of the audience, as evidenced by "Uncle Walter" Cronkite being considered the most trusted man in America for a number of years.

Agenda-setting

Although this concept is more commonly found in media studies of political processes, it is also relevant to media studies of crime, as it helps us to understand how people come to believe that crime rates are rising when they are actually falling, or that certain types of crimes are more serious or prevalent than others when in reality the opposite is true. The agenda-setting concept traces its roots back to Lippmann's seminal work in which he explored the ways in which the media creates images of reality that might be at odds with the objective reality. An aphorism in the area is that although the media do not dictate what people think about issues, they do influence what issues people think about. One way media messages set agendas is via framing of issues. Is domestic violence a crime or a marital problem? Is personal safety the responsibility of the individual or the police? This framework is still useful for understanding how media messages influence thoughts and opinions.

Cultivation Hypothesis

George Gerbner and his associates at the University of Pennsylvania (Gerbner *et al.* 1980) have tracked television messages since the 1960s to document what those messages are as well as how those messages affect people's views about the world. The project looks at gender roles, work roles, ethnic differences, and crime and violence presentations, among other topics. The Cultivation Hypothesis posits that television cultivates views of the world. So, for example, people who see only European Americans having professional occupations on television come to think all professionals are European Americans. And people who watch a lot of television crime come to think that similar crime rates (and types of crimes) exist in the real world—with murder being vastly overrepresented compared to actual crime statistics. Or with gun deaths almost always being homicides, instead of the 50% that are suicides in the real world. Gerbner and his associates developed the Mean World Index to measure perceptions of violence in the world. More recent work has found that, as with other theoretical formulations, the effects of media images are not "one size fits all."

Effects of media portrayals of crime

Newspaper and television coverage of actual crimes has been shown to influence perceptions of crime prevalence and details, as well as increasing fear of crime among subsets of the audience. First, the media can create "crime waves" where none actually exist, as evidenced by Fishman's (1978) study of crime waves against the elderly in Philadelphia. The media reported several minor crimes against older residents in close temporal proximity, and then coverage snowballed. Experts were interviewed about the vulnerability of the elderly and the callousness of criminals who would prey on them. Every instance of an older person having her purse snatched was reported. Citizens were alarmed. The elderly felt terrified. Then the media moved on to a different theme. In came the researchers who examined the actual crime data for the period during the "crime wave" and discovered there was no change at all in the victimization rates of the elderly. As had been the case all along, the elderly were crime victims at rates much lower than other age-groups. This had been an entirely media-created event.

Another way in which media coverage of crime can distort perceptions is by emphasizing crime relative to other problems or issues, creating a type of agenda-setting. Lowry, Nio, and Leitner (2003) examined the impact of media reports of crime versus actual crime rates in explaining the high percentage of people who reported crime as the most important problem facing the country and found that network television news coverage accounted for four times as much variance in the responses as did the actual crime statistics. Similarly, Romer, Jamieson, and Aday (2003) found that exposure to local television news was strongly related to respondents' fear and concern about local crime.

The media also can create distorted views about the relative prevalence of crimes and specific aspects of these crimes. People are actually in much greater risk of dying on the toilet or in the bathtub than in gang cross fire, but the media don't report on cases of people dying on the toilet, so most people don't even think about that possibility (Slovic, Fischoff, & Lichtenstein 1982). Similarly, gun deaths that are homicides are reported by the media, while suicides generally are not, leading people to be unaware that half of gun deaths are suicides (Heath, Kavanagh, & Thompson 2001). Of the gun deaths that are actually homicides, most are committed by family and friends. Such crimes receive less coverage than deaths caused by someone being caught in gang crossfire, for example, and again the public's perceptions of risk follow the media picture rather than the objective reality (Heath, Kavanagh, & Thompson 2001).

Beyond general misperceptions about crime patterns and risk, media messages about crime can also influence the fear of crime and self-protective behaviors of the audience. The impact of news reports of crime on the fear of crime is more nuanced than the impact on crime risk assessment, however. Heath (1984) examined fifty-six newspapers nationwide for the degree of randomness, sensationalism, and location of the crimes they reported. Telephone interviews with readers of those newspapers and nonreaders from those cities revealed that the geographic location of the crime that was typically reported played an important role in determining the effect of such coverage. Among readers of newspapers that reported mostly local crime, having high proportions of random or sensational crimes was associated with higher levels of fear of crime among readers than among people from those cities who did not read newspapers. Among readers of newspapers that reported mostly nonlocal crimes, however, high proportions of random or sensational crimes were associated with lower levels of fear than that reported by nonreaders from those cities. Readers appear to be using a social comparison method to process crime reports. Sensational, random crimes that happen in my own backyard are very scary, but when those crimes happen elsewhere, my backyard looks pretty good by comparison. It was not just the case that readers were *not made afraid* by those reports of crimes in distant places; they were significantly *less afraid* than if they had not read about crime at all. This general pattern has been replicated in studies by Liska and Baccaglini (1990) and Chiricos, Eschholz, and Gertz (1997).

Fear and fiction

Do media presentations of fictional crimes frighten us to the same extent that media reports of actual crimes do? Gerbner and his associates, working from a cultivation hypothesis, claim that media exposure results in the perception that the world is a dangerous place (Gerbner *et al.* 1980). Doob and McDonald (1979), however, found that exposure to televised crime and fear of crime in the real world were not related. Heath and Petraitis (1987) separated "fear of crime in the neighborhood where I live" from "fear of crime in the world beyond my neighborhood" and found that fictional televised crime was related to fear of crime "out there" but not fear of crime in the immediate neighborhood. They suggest the Mean World Gerbner and his associates are studying is the world "out there" but not the immediate locale where ample personal experience is available to outweigh media messages.

Do media depictions of crime frighten children as well as adults? A survey of parents by Cantor and Nathanson (1996) found that 37% of children between kindergarten and sixth grade were frightened or upset by news stories on television. Regarding fictional crime, we see a developmental trend, with research by Cantor and associates showing that children at very young ages are frightened by threatening characters and situations, whereas older children are frightened more by threats of realistic or abstract images (Bryant & Thompson 2002). Frightening mass media images can continue to cause anxiety even in young adulthood, according to a study by Harrison and Cantor (1999).

Conclusion

Media messages about crime are abundant in newspapers and on television. In fact, the frequency of such images seems to be increasing. Very violent, scary, and random crimes are overrepresented in media depictions compared with real-world occurrences. Readers and viewers of such presentations are likely to base their understanding of the world "out there" on media images, leading to increased levels of fear of crime and distorted impressions of relative crime frequency and detail. Finally, although media messages about crime produce significant effects on perceptions and emotions, the effects are small relative to those determined by personality, environment, and family experiences.

Subject in focus

Media-generated crime waves

One case of arson is unlikely to make the newspaper or evening news in most major cities. Three cases of arson are a "wave of arsons." Similarly, one mugging of an elderly person is not news. Three muggings in close temporal proximity and there's a "crime wave against the elderly." This pattern is especially evident during slow news times, such as when Congress is in recess and the economy is not gyrating about. As reluctant as the media are to report dry, contextual statistics, they are quick to report "trends" based on just a few vivid instances of kidnappings, muggings, or other crimes, especially when the victims or assailants are of an identifiable (and preferably surprising) group, such as the elderly or the very young. And these "crime waves" can be totally created by the media, even when dry, objective statistics show crimes against or by the crime wave group are actually declining!

Probably the best documented instance of a media-generated crime wave happened in New York City in 1976. Newspapers and television news programs reported on a "rash" of muggings and robberies of elderly victims in the city. This "trend" was evidenced by fifty-five reports about the crime wave against the elderly over a seven-year period, including reports of specific incidents as well as interviews with experts and the general population about what this alarming trend indicated about society in general. This "crime wave against the elderly" was covered by the mass media across the country.

The mayor of New York condemned the juvenile justice system, which was reportedly failing to bring youthful offenders under control, leading to the crime wave against the elderly. The NYPD's Senior Citizens Robbery Unit, which had been formed just the year before, became a source for useful quotes to substantiate the crime wave against the elderly.

The most interesting part of this "crime wave against the elderly" is that it occurred amid a flat or declining rate of actual crime against the elderly in New York. Mark Fishman documented that, according to official New York City police statistics, the rate of most crimes against the elderly was flat, and homicide of elderly victims actually showed a 19% drop from the previous year! Clearly the "crime wave" was a creation of the media, abetted by the availability of the new police department unit devoted to crimes against the elderly.

Discussion question

Should newspapers focus on sensationalist crimes that readers are most interested in or do they have a duty to focus on more common crimes that represent a more realistic threat?

Further sources of information

Harrison, K. & Cantor, J. (1999). "Tales from the screen: Enduring fright reactions to scary media." *Media Psychology*, 1, 97–116.

Heath, L., Kavanagh, J., & Thompson, R. (2001). "Perceived vulnerability and fear of crime: Why fear stays high when crime rates drop." *Journal of Offender Rehabilitation*, 33, 1–14.

Minow, N. (1996). *Abandoned in the wasteland: Children, television, and the first amendment.* New York: Hill and Wang.

Romer, D., Jamieson, K. H., & Aday, S. (2003). "Television news and the cultivation of fear of crime." *Journal of Communication*, 53, 88–104.

Elizabeth Behm-Morawitz and David Ta

Racial and Ethnic Stereotyping

Because of the medium's capacity for fixing an image in the public mind, its responsibility for avoiding stereotypic and demeaning depictions becomes central to its role. The encompassing nature of the medium necessitates that diversity among decisionmakers, newsmakers, and newscasters become an integral aspect of television.

US Commission on Civil Rights 1979

In 1977, the US Commission on Civil Rights published the first of two reports examining the representations of minorities on US entertainment and news television programming as well as the diversity of workers in the television industry. On the heels of the US civil rights movement and rising concerns over racial discrimination, the Commission turned to investigate the frequency with which minorities and women appeared on television, the types of roles they occupied on screen, and the roles they were given beyond the screen in industry jobs. The Commission utilized the help of Communication scholars Nancy Signorielli and Lionel Barrow, Jr to conduct a systematic analysis of television portrayals and the television industry. Their findings indicated that minorities were significantly underrepresented and stereotyped on television. Further, a lack of minority employees in industry positions of power was revealed. It was argued the composition of the television industry contributed to the limited and often stereotypical portrayal of minorities on television.

Over thirty years later, disparities in the frequency and nature of media portrayal based on race/ethnicity persist (see Figure 9.1). Though the rate of depiction of some minority groups has increased since the Commission's report, racial/ethnic minorities are still underrepresented on television and in the media in general. Further, content analytic work suggests that many longstanding racial/ethnic stereotypes endure in the media today despite the changing television landscape.

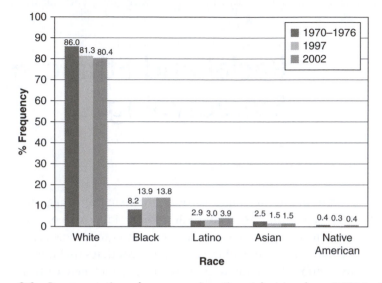

Figure 9.1 Representation of race on prime-time television from 1970 to 2002
Note: Data from 1970 to 1976 are from a research report conducted by Gerbner and Signorielli (1979), 1997 data are from Glascock (2003), and 2002 data are from Mastro and Behm-Morawitz (2005).

As the quote at the start of this chapter indicates, the Commission recognized television as a pervasive and significant influence in American life and as a cultural storyteller that should be studied and held accountable for the messages—and subsequent effects—it produces. Most relevant to the present topic is the idea that the media play an important role in socializing individuals and normalizing race-related attitudes, beliefs, and behaviors.

This chapter provides an overview of the research examining the representations of race and ethnicity in the media (television, in particular) as well as the influence of these representations. In this chapter, we will (1) define race and ethnicity as well as the concept of stereotyping; (2) provide a summary of the research, analyzing the representations of race and ethnicity in the media; (3) identify key theoretical frameworks from which to study the effects of media stereotypes on individuals; and (4) provide a summary of the effects of exposure to racial/ethnic stereotypes in US news and entertainment television programming.

The construction of race and ethnicity

From psychology, we know that people engage in *social categorization* to help make sense of the world they inhabit. This cognitive categorization involves constructing social categories to which we assign people; and it is this practice that aids us in efficiently processing and adapting to our environment. Though efficient, the categorization of people, however meaningless, into groups creates an "us" versus "them" perspective that often results in discrimination (Billig & Tajfel 1973). A considerable amount of research, originating with the 1970s social identity literature, demonstrates that group comparisons are made to favor one's own group (the ingroup), rather than the outgroup (Abrams & Hogg 1990; Billig & Tajfel 1973). One common form of social categorization we practice from a young age is that of categorizing people based on race and ethnicity.

Race and ethnicity are two socially constructed group categories, which reflect cultural values and beliefs and that carry great meaning and power for our lived experiences (Downing & Husband 2005). *Race* can be thought of as "a human group defined by itself or others as distinct by virtue of perceived common physical characteristics that are held to be inherent" (Cornell & Hartmann 1998: 24). Physical characteristics such as skin color and facial features are common markers of categories of race. The development of racial categories is quite political as they are oft used as a basis upon which to discriminate and wield power (Downing & Husband 2005). *Ethnicity*, on the other hand, shares some similarities to race but is generally conceptualized as being positive and a social category that is, more often than race, designated by ingroup rather than outgroup members (Downing & Husband 2005). Schermerhorn (as cited by Cornell & Hartmann 1998) defines ethnicity as "a collectivity within a larger society having real or putative common ancestry, memories of a shared historical past, and a cultural focus on one or more symbolic elements defined as the epitome of their peoplehood" (19). Based on this definition, ethnicity is defined by criteria, or symbols, such as geography, kinship, interactions, religion, and language.

Stereotyping

What naturally follows from the human process of social categorization into racial/ethnic groups is racial/ethnic stereotyping. *Stereotypes* are generally defined as "mental representations of the world" (Stangor & Schallor 1996: 6) that influence how we respond to people and situations we encounter in our lives. We hold stereotypes about the capability, appearance, attitudes, interests, traits, social status, occupation, and behaviors of social groups (Golombok & Fivush 1994). Though stereotypes are typically thought of as negative, stereotyping is not an inherently debased process. Rather, it reflects our ability to organize and process stimuli without having to expend large amounts of cognitive energy and time on making sense of things we encounter in our daily lives. However, racial/ethnic stereotyping is what might be termed *race thinking* (Downing & Husband 2005), typically resulting in the devaluing of and prejudice against individuals and groups based solely on their race and/or ethnicity. Most often people engage in race thinking without consciously realizing that they are employing stereotypes in their thinking about social groups and lived experiences. When stereotypes are shared and become a part of the fabric of a culture, discrimination and the likelihood of one experiencing prejudice increases exponentially (Stangor & Schallor 1996).

Scholars have long recognized that media representations of race and ethnicity are a powerful means of creating, reinforcing, and activating group stereotypes. The "mass media are an important collective repository for group stereotypes" (Stangor & Schallor 1996: 12). Media both reflect and create culture and play a role in determining the way we view ourselves and others in the world around us. More specifically, the media play three roles in contributing to real-world stereotyping. First, media can activate existing stereotypes, making it more likely that individuals will use these stereotypes when judging people in the real world. Second, media can create stereotypes, constructing culturally based meaning of race and ethnicity. Third, media can help to debunk stereotypes and improve race relations. In this chapter, we will discuss all three of these potential impacts of exposure to racial/ethnic media portrayals. Before one can examine the effects of media stereotypes about race and ethnicity, however, one must examine how minority groups are portrayed by the media.

Media representations of race and ethnicity

To better understand how racial/ethnic minorities are treated in the media, Clark (1969) identified four stages of portrayal of minorities on television: (1) nonrecognition, (2) ridicule, (3) regulation, and (4) respect. Indeed, most research examining race and ethnicity in the media centers on the medium of television due to its pervasiveness and the fact that Westerners spend most of their daily media minutes with television. Clark described the first stage of minority representation on television, *nonrecognition*, as the absence of a minority group on television. Minority characters are not mistreated, caricaturized, or regulated; rather, they simply are not there. For example, Asian characters are nearly absent on US prime-time television programming, and Asian characters in films are often played by white actors.

The second stage of minority portrayal is *ridicule*. Here, portrayals of minority characters are satirized, caricaturized, and generally put down for the purpose of bolstering the majority group. Early US television programs like *Amos 'N' Andy* (1951–1953) were notorious for portraying black people as unintelligent buffoons for comedic purposes (Mittell 2010). To reinforce the humor in these acts of buffoonery, producers would play laugh tracks to indicate to the audience that these characters are to be laughed at and ridiculed.

The third stage is *regulation*. Here, minority characters appear as the protectors of social order. Police officers, detectives, and spies, for example, are played by Latino and black characters to signal positive roles being given to minority groups. This was typical in the 1960s for black and today for Latino characters (Harris 2004). And during this stage, other character types are dominated by the majority, and the minority characters are contained to the role of the protector as well as traditional minority stereotypes like those of the criminal and buffoon.

The final stage is *respect* where portrayals of minority characters do not differ from the majority in terms of the range of roles occupied. Minority characters get cast as both good and bad characters and in a diversity of roles matching the dominant group. This does not mean that minority characters are no longer stereotyped or marginalized in some way; however, achieving "respect" indicates considerable presence on television in a wide variety of different portrayals.

As you read through this chapter, consider how the representations of various minority groups in the media do or do not fit this progression as theorized by Clark. In the next section, we consider the idea of *cultural erasure*, which dovetails with Clark's stage of nonrecognition, and then we provide a historical overview of the portrayal of blacks, Latinos, Asians, Native Americans, and Middle Easterners in US media.

Erasure in the media

Overall, racial/ethnic minorities are underrepresented and stereotyped on mainstream US television (Signorielli 2009). Though the negative stereotypes are certainly concerning, minority groups face another problem in media representation in the form of cultural erasure. Mittell (2010) highlights this issue when he talks about the cultural visibility of minority characters. While minorities are starting to occupy more prestigious roles, their cultural identity is not well represented. These characters put on a mainstream performance that is seen as white (Jhally & Lewis 2007; Mittell 2010). The types of roles that have been typically seen on television that were played by white characters embody a white cultural identity. In essence, when minority characters play these roles, the only aspect of the character that changes is the race, while the white cultural identity remains intact. Thus, beyond simply being absent or stereotyped in the media, racial/ethnic minorities have to contend with the potential for cultural erasure by media.

One of the earlier portrayals of cultural integration comes from *The Cosby Show*. Jhally and Lewis (2007) argued that *The Cosby Show* created a necessary illusion for both white and minority audiences. Bill Cosby and his family were treated as an affluent, positive black family, but discussions about cultural heritage were nonexistent. The narrative of the *The Cosby Show* demonstrates blacks achieving the American Dream but only if their attitudes and values aligned with that of the white majority (Jhally & Lewis 2007). In essence, it is communicated that a minority character should act and embrace the values and morals of the typical white character in order to be presented in a positive light.

Stereotypes are worrisome because it creates an "othering" effect by generating mainstream portrayals that downplays racial identity while emphasizing an assimilationist model (Mittell 2010). When groups of people are othered, people disassociate themselves from the othered group by creating reasons why they are better than this social group. Those who do not conform to integration (in this case identifying with white culture) are seen as bad, different, or odd. Indeed, many popular television shows on prime-time networks bolster an integrated setting such as having black and Asian doctors on *Grey's Anatomy*, but how different are they from white characters? It is argued that the media most often work to reproduce white privilege under the guise of diversity, consciously or not.

Content analysis

Beyond this critical/cultural perspective of understanding the politics of race and ethnicity in the media, mass communication research in the US has more commonly taken a social scientific approach to systematically documenting minority portrayals via the method of content analysis. *Content analysis* is defined "as a research technique for making replicable and valid inferences from texts (or other meaningful matter) to the contexts of their use" (Krippendorff 2004: 18). In other words, content analysis is a careful, typically quantitative analysis of the content of communication (e.g., mass media messages), and the connection of the findings to the social and political context in which they appear, thus making meaning of the observations. The term "text" is loosely applied such that any media message may be termed a media text. Historically, most of the research on the portrayal of minority groups in the media has focused on blacks, given their status as the largest minority group in the US However, Latinos have superseded blacks in size and are now the largest and fastest growing minority group in the US. Thus, more recent research is beginning to focus attention on media portrayals of Latinos. In addition to this research on Latinos and blacks, US research has investigated the representations of Asians, and to a lesser degree, Native Americans and Middle Easterners.

Representations of blacks

The minority group appearing with the most frequency on television is blacks (Escholtz, Bufkin, & Long 2002). Blacks constitute 14–17% of the prime-time population while whites comprise 73–80% of characters appearing on prime-time television (Children Now 2001; Children Now 2004; Mastro & Behm-Morawitz 2005; Mastro & Greenberg 2000). Overall, blacks are the only racial/ethnic group that is proportionally represented on television. Despite being proportionally represented and the largest minority presence on television, blacks have a long history of negative portrayals in the media.

Historically, blacks are poorly represented in the media. Early depictions of blacks show black characters as subordinate to white characters. For example, the Black Mammy character plays to the stereotype of being dark, overweight, unattractive, and asexual (Jewell 1993) serving as a "friend, advisor, surrogate mistress of the manor, and mother; she possesses the virtues of a valued domestic servant: faithfulness, obsequiousness, and acquiescence" (Hudson 1998: 224). Research has revealed two other stereotypes for a black woman. First, the Jezebel stands in stark contrast to the Mammy in that she is considered a sexual threat to the white woman. She is exotic looking, erotic, and sensual, "portrayed as a mulatto or fair-complexioned African-American female, who possesses features that are considered European ... The bad-black-girl is depicted as alluring, sexually arousing and seductive" (Jewell 1993: 46). Second, the Sapphire is a newer stereotype that is historically based, but created by television. The Sapphire character emerged not from a misconception of folklore and print media, but as a live television image of character Sapphire Stevens in *Amos 'N' Andy* (White 1985). She is evil, bitchy, loquacious, stubborn, and hateful (Bennett 2000) and is depicted as the Angry Black Woman. For example, Michelle Obama was portrayed as a Sapphire character by conservatives during the election campaign (Kaplan 2008). Conservatives created and distributed media images of Michelle Obama in a militant outfit with an emphasis on the arms and a large Afro. She was depicted in the US by the conservative Right as someone who takes charge and who would be violent if you crossed her path. Modern depictions of black women on television stem from images and historical stereotypes of black women in the United States (Hudson 1998), and based on these historical images, depictions of black women in the media are still overwhelmingly negative (Chideya 1995).

As is typical of most racial/ethnic groups, representations of blacks differ based on gender. Black male characters have traditionally been depicted as buffoons, lazy, and dim-witted for the amusement of mostly white audiences (Mittell 2010). Early on, most of these black characters were played by white "blackface" performers (Mittell 2010). From the early 1950s, portrayals of blacks shifted alongside social influences to better represent them on television. Today, a black American on prime-time television is typically a middle-class character (Mastro 2009) who is a professional or in law enforcement (Children Now 2001; Children Now 2004; Mastro & Behm-Morawitz 2005; Mastro & Greenberg 2000). He enjoys a moderate level of success and social authority (Mastro & Behm-Morawitz 2005) and is the least aggressive character on television (Mastro & Greenberg 2000).

This image of the affluent black American is in direct contrast, however, with how they are seen on television news, particularly local news broadcasts (Dixon, Azocar, & Casas 2003). Overall, blacks are portrayed negatively and embody the stereotype of criminals. Blacks appear in a 2:1 ratio in relation to whites when the topic is crime (Romer, Jamieson, & DeCoteau 1998). Blacks are more likely to be depicted as the perpetrator of a crime (Dixon & Linz 2000) and prejudicial information is more frequently reported when the defendant is black rather than white (Dixon & Linz 2002).

Representations of Latinos

Latinos are the fastest growing minority group in the United States (Keck 2010), and yet remain underrepresented on prime-time television (Mastro & Behm-Morawitz 2005; Poniewozik 2001). According to the US Census (2008), Latinos have surpassed blacks by making up 15.1% of the population compared to blacks who make up 12.3% of Americans.

Overall, the research indicates that the portrayals of Latinos on prime-time television are unfavorable (Greenberg, Mastro, & Brand 2002). While their overall presence on television is limited, there are a few well-known stereotypes that have plagued this community over the years (Greenberg, Mastro, & Brand 2002; Ramirez Berg 1990). Dominant stereotypes of Latinos are that of a Latin lover/harlot stereotype and the criminal stereotype (Mastro & Behm-Morawitz 2005). The Latin lover/harlot stereotype is exemplified by Latin men and women who appear sexualized and primarily interested in sex. They are provocatively dressed, sexualized, and are typically sexual aggressors interested predominantly in sex and romance. The criminal stereotype, on the other hand, portrays Latinos as deviants, such as bandits, gang members, or drug runners for drug cartels (Harris 2004). These characters are more aggressive, less intelligent, poorly groomed, and less attractive than their white counterparts (Mastro & Behm-Morawitz 2005). Other representations of Latinos include the buffoon or clown (Greenberg, Mastro, & Brand 2002).

In the news media, Latinos are likely to appear as criminals; however, unlike blacks, not at a rate that is disproportionate to real-world crime figures (Dixon & Linz 2000; Mastro & Greenberg 2000). Also, recent scholarship recognizes that Latinos are garnering attention by news media because of the issue of illegal immigration in the US. The status of Latinos as the fastest growing minority in the US, in combination with the tough economic climate and national security issues, is drawing attention to the issue of illegal immigration. In recent news, talks about illegal immigrants and illegal immigration have been primarily focused on Latinos crossing the border from Mexico to the United States (Passel 2006). Though little empirical research exists examining the stereotype of the Latino as an illegal immigrant, news patterns suggest this is an area ripe for future research.

Lastly, some potentially positive changes have been observed in the representations of Latinos in entertainment television. Perhaps, due to the growing market of Latino consumers (Martinez 2007; Nielson 2009), Latin-based television shows are being imported via satellite and many programs have Spanish language translation (Martinez 2007). Further, shows such as *George Lopez* and *Ugly Betty* offer American audiences a picture of a Hispanic family.

While these shows are riddled with stereotypes, they are of the few that do have a Latino family represented. *Ugly Betty* in particular is seen as complex because it allows issues of race, gender, and sexual orientation to be discussed in a comedy drama.

Representations of Asians

Asians are one of the fastest growing minorities in the US (NAAPIMHA 2010). Asians currently make up 4.5% of the US population (US Census, 2008), but they only account for 1 to 3% of television characters (Children Now 2001; Children Now 2004; Mastro & Behm-Morawitz 2005; Mastro & Greenberg 2000). Given the infrequency with which Asians appear in US-based entertainment media, little content analytic work is available examining this minority group. Much of what we do know about representations of Asians comes from analysis of Asian characters in film. Additionally, similar to early media casting of blacks, Asian-American characters were typically played by white actors (Iiyama & Kitano 1982). That criticism still resonates today due to white actors being cast over Asian actors to play Asian characters (Aucoin 2010) with the latest criticism directed at movies like *Dragonball: Evolution* (2009), *The Last Airbender* (2010), and *The Weapon* (2012).

Historically, Asians have been portrayed as villains, usually following tensions between the US and Asian countries (Harris 2004). For example, after the 1989 Tiananmen Square massacre, Chinese officials were seen as villains on action-adventure shows. Other common stereotypes depict Asian men as experts in martial arts, asexual, and undesirable (Park, Gabbadon, & Chernin 2006). For Asian women, there is the stereotype of the Dragon Lady who is desirable but dangerous (Ogunnaike 2003: E1). In general, gender analyses reveal that men are usually portrayed as masculine and domineering, while women are passive, emotional, and irrational (Harris 2004). This is consistent with the portrayal of Asian men as they are seen as experts in martial arts. But, unlike their white counterparts, they are deemed to be undesirable to both the audience and other characters on screen (Park, Gabbadon, & Chernin 2006). The stereotypic representations of Asian women, however, are not always in line with traditional gender roles. The stereotype of the Dragon Lady reflects a dominant, aggressive, martial arts persona, which makes her dangerous to the masculine identity but desirable because she is attractive and sexualized. Though the aggressiveness of the Dragon Lady contrasts with gender stereotypic representations, the sexualization of this character is consistent with the treatment of women, generally, by US media.

Other images of Asians include being portrayed in conservative attire in the workplace and being passive in nature (Mastro & Stern 2003), and frequently seen in technology advertisements (Mastro & Stern 2003). While Asians have been historically stereotyped on television like other minority groups, they are probably more positively portrayed than other minorities in US media (Harris 2004). The type of stereotyping that Asians experience is consistent with the image of the model minority. Here the image that the audience sees is that of a group that academically, socially, and commercially succeeds. Having this type of stereotype creates the illusion that problems do not exist within this group. Issues of primary health, housing, employment, education, acculturation, immigration, and legal issues are undermined or misrepresented because of the model minority stereotype (NAAPIMHA 2010). It also can create pressure for those within the group to uphold that idealized image and some might burn out under the pressure.

Representations of Native Americans

Little empirical research exists on Native American representation on television. This group makes up less than 1% of the population in the US (US Census 2008) and less than 1% of US television characters (Mastro & Behm-Morawitz 2005). Because there are so few Native Americans in the population, most people's knowledge about this group comes from the few but memorable media representations in history textbooks, cartoons, and films. Historically, we do know that Native Americans have been negatively stereotyped by the entertainment industry and the news media (Bird 1996, 1999; Merskin 1998; Weston 1996).

Their portrayals on television are usually bounded by history (Merskin 1998) and there are rarely any modern depictions of Native Americans. They are known as bloodthirsty savages from old movies (Harris 2004) or faithful sidekicks to white men (Morris 1982). The stereotype of the savage was brought to life through depictions of the Native American practice of "scalping," which, ironically, was a behavior that some historians now say white men did more often to Native Americans rather than the reverse (Harris 2004). A popular recent depiction of Native Americans can be seen in Stephenie Meyer's *The Twilight Series* in the depiction of the Quileutes as shape-shifters who are animalistic, aggressive, uncontrollable, and closely connected to the forest and animals (Wilson 2010). In other somewhat recent media portrayals, Native Americans have been seen as wise elders or warrior characters (Bird 1999). In terms of television representation, there is little to no representation of this group on television (Mastro & Greenberg 2000). When they are shown, it is usually in the news regarding land claims litigation and Indian-run casinos (Harris 2004).

Representations of Middle Easterners

The last minority group to be discussed in this summary is Middle Eastern people. Arguably, Middle Easterners are one of the most mistreated groups in the media today. One possible reason why they are mistreated in the media is the sociopolitical relationship Middle Eastern countries have with Western countries (Said 1979; Shaheen 2001). Another is because they are one of the smallest minority groups in the US. This group makes up approximately 0.42% of the US population (US Census 2008); therefore, it is important to consider how they are represented in the media, because for many people, that is their only exposure to Middle Eastern peoples. In comparison to other racial/ethnic groups, some argue that this group of people is particularly poorly represented and stereotyped in American popular media (Shaheen 1984, 1997, 2001; Suleiman 1988), and because of recent controversies surrounding America's war in Iraq and Afghanistan, Arabs and Middle Easterners are typically seen as the enemy in the news media.

There is little empirical research examining their portrayals on entertainment television because there are so few Middle Easterners on television. However, when they are seen on television, they are viewed with an oriental lens (Said 1979). Orientalism is a typical stereotype that Middle Easterners have which does not distinguish the average Middle Eastern person from her/ his religion; everyone who is from the Middle East is Arab, and the culture is viewed as primitive compared to Western culture (Said 1979).

Further, researchers have documented the representation of Middle Eastern men as Islamic terrorists (McConnell 2003; Steet 2000; Wilkins 1995). In light of the 9/11 terrorist attacks on the World Trade Center and the Pentagon, the relationship between terrorists, the Middle East, and Islam are salient and most of the time synonymous in the minds of many Americans because of representations by the news media.

The effects of exposure to racial/ethnic media stereotypes

A natural next step to take from studying the content of media is to study the influence of exposure to this media content. Indeed, as media effects scholars, we study the content of media because we are ultimately interested in the impacts mediated stereotypes may have on people. It was not until more recently, however, that scholars made headway in documenting the effects of racial/ethnic media stereotyping. Approximately twenty-five years ago, in the 1980s, scholars began to dedicate efforts to empirically examine the influence of media representations on individuals, yet this research today is arguably still in its early stages.

This relatively small body of media research seeks to illuminate the connection between exposure to media stereotypes of race/ethnicity and people's real-world attitudes, beliefs, identity, self-concept, and behaviors. Consistent with past mass communication research, this research confirms that a relationship exists between exposure to media stereotypes and individuals' propensity for making real-world race-based stereotypic judgments.

Research has shown that there is a significant relationship between exposure to racial/ethnic portrayals in the media and audience evaluations of race/ethnicity in terms of competence (Zuckerman, Singer, & Singer 1980), social roles (Atkin, Greenberg, & McDermont 1983), pro-minority policies (Ramasubramanian 2010), and stereotype-consistent race-related attitudes and beliefs (Dixon 2006a; Dixon & Maddox 2005; Ford 1997; Mastro 2003; Mastro, Behm-Morawitz, & Ortiz 2007; Mastro, Tamborini, & Hullett 2005; Oliver *et al.* 2004).

Guiding this body of research are theoretical frameworks with roots in sociology, psychology, and communication. Taken together, these perspectives suggest that media can have short- as well as long-term effects on how people view themselves and others, and how they experience the world. In this section, key theoretical concepts will be discussed as well as studies that exemplify each approach in studying the influence of media stereotyping on real-world attitudes and judgments.

The construction and activation of racial/ethnic stereotypes

From the psychological tradition, *priming* is the effect of exposure to a stimulus on one's subsequent thoughts and evaluations. This theoretical approach suggests that exposure to media stereotypes activates stereotypes, in the short term, and causes individuals to make stereotyped judgments following exposure. Central to priming is the construct of *salience*. Salience refers to how memorable, meaningful, or readily available a piece of information is to an individual (Scheufele 2000). In the context of media effects, priming explains that exposure to a media stimulus readies individuals to make evaluations based on the constructs that the media have primed and thus made most accessible to individuals. For the present topic, exposure to a stereotype of a minority group in the media may prime individuals to think about members of that group in terms of the stereotype.

The influence of the portrayal of minorities—African-Americans, in particular—on television news as criminals has garnered the attention of scholars. Studies demonstrate that exposure to depictions of African-Americans as perpetrators on US news influences judgments of guilt (Dixon 2006b; Mastro *et al.* 2009), policy beliefs (Dixon 2006a), and stereotyping (Dixon 2006a; Mastro *et al.* 2009). When the race of the perpetrator is African-American rather than white, white viewers are more likely to say that the criminal featured in the news story is guilty. Further, they are more likely to suggest a tougher punishment for a nonwhite than for a white suspect. It is hypothesized that this occurs because the common stereotype of the African-American criminal is triggered, or *primed*, by news broadcasts. Viewers, then, use this stereotype to not only judge the individual suspect depicted in the news story, they use this stereotypic information to judge other members of this same racial/ethnic group.

Dixon and Maddox (2005) conducted an experiment with college students and found that, consistent with priming theory, exposure to a dark-skinned African-American perpetrator in a television news story about the murder of a race-unidentified police officer primed cognitions related to the stereotype of the African-American criminal. The activation of this stereotype resulted in heightened emotional response to and increased retention of the crime story. So, in comparison to the white and light-skinned African-American perpetrators, the dark-skinned African-American primed stereotypic thoughts. This suggests that skin tone in addition to race/ethnicity may be important to understanding stereotype construction and application.

In the previous example, the commonly held stereotype of the African-American criminal had already taken root in the participants' minds, so the media portrayal was thought to simply be activating that stereotype and making it more readily available for use in making real-world judgments. However, the media can also contribute to the formation of new racial/ethnic stereotypes and produce long-term effects.

Mental models provide us with a framework from which to understand this idea of stereotype creation as well as activation. Mental models are cognitive representations of situations, people, places, events, and things (Radvansky & Zacks 1997), and these cognitive structures are flexible and able to adjust to the presentation of new information. The media may help us to create new mental models related to race and ethnicity *or* they can increase the likelihood that we retrieve from memory particular mental models (i.e., those based on the stereotypes presented in the media). This theoretical framework aids in explaining how media teach us to think about racial/ethnic groups. In other words, media may create, not just reflect, racial/ethnic stereotypes.

Mastro, Behm-Morawitz, and Ortiz (2007) proposed the use of mental models to explain the relationship between repeated exposure to stereotypes of Latinos on US television and real-world attitudes and beliefs about Latinos in the US and found support for the application of this framework. The survey-based study indicated that the more television college students consumed and the less real-world contact the students had with Latinos, the more stereotyped their judgments were of Latinos in the real world. Mastro *et al.* (2007) argued that heavier television exposure, and thus, greater exposure to stereotypes of minorities, contributes to the increased creation and retrieval of mental models consistent with stereotypic representations. Thus, repeated media exposure may be both contributing to the creation of stereotypes of minorities, as well as making stereotypic information more accessible. Unlike the Dixon and Maddox (2005) experiment, the phenomenon under study here is the long-term, or cumulative, effects of exposure to media stereotypes on people's attitudes and beliefs.

Cumulative (long-term) impacts of viewing media stereotypes

Like Mastro, Behm-Morawitz, and Ortiz's (2007) study, the majority of the studies examining the influence of media representations of race/ethnicity examine cumulative effects of media exposure and employ a survey design. This means that rather than examining the short-term effects of exposure to a particular media stimulus, these studies investigate the cumulative, or long-term, influence of media exposure on race-based attitudes and beliefs. Though these studies provide a picture of how our media habits affect our real-world, race-based attitudes and beliefs, they are correlational in nature and can only demonstrate a statistically significant relationship between media exposure and racial/ethnic stereotyping, not a causal relationship.

The concept of *chronic accessibility* has been developed to explain these cumulative effects of repeated exposure to primes. From within the priming framework, it is proposed that repeated exposure to media stereotypes, or frequent activation of this stereotypic information, would make this stereotypical content consistently more accessible (Lepore & Brown 1999). Thus, exposure to media stereotypes may have long-term, or persistent, effects on how people view the world. For example, Dixon (2008) found that adults living in Los Angeles, California who had heavier exposure to local television news overrepresenting blacks as criminals were more likely than other residents to perceive blacks to be violent. The frequent exposure to the stereotype of the African-American criminal in the news makes this stereotype more accessible and therefore more likely to be applied when making judgments about blacks.

Cultivation Theory, developed by George Gerbner and colleagues, provides another framework from which to study the cumulative effects of exposure to media representations. Cultivation Theory posits that over time, heavy exposure to media (namely television) results in an individual possessing a view of the world that is more similar to the mediated version of reality (Gerbner *et al.* 2002). In the case of racial/ethnic stereotyping in the media, the frequent, repeated exposure to such media content would increase the likelihood that individuals would adopt race-based attitudes and beliefs in line with these media representations. Mastro, Behm-Morawitz, and Ortiz's (2007) study demonstrates a cultivation effect within a mental models framework, and Lee *et al.* (2009) found additional support for heavy television consumption by college students being linked to the stereotyping of Asian-Americans. Lee *et al.*'s research further suggests that the genre of television consumed may be important to understanding the relationship between media exposure and individuals' real-world racial/ethnic stereotyping.

A Social Identity Approach

The last major area of research related to understanding the effects of racial/ethnic media stereotyping is driven by Tajfel's Social Identity Theory. As discussed earlier in this chapter, people have a tendency to categorize individuals into social groups (e.g., racial and ethnic groups) and to make comparisons based on favorable ingroup characteristics and, typically, negative outgroup characteristics such that the ingroup is benefitted. Interpersonal contact with members of the outgroup is thought to aid breaking down stereotypes and improving group relations (Tajfel & Turner 1986). However, in reality, racial/ethnic segregation often develops and discomfort can arise from attempting to interact with outgroups with whom you have had very little experience and with whom relations have been strained. In the case of media stereotyping, it is thought that *mediated contact* with members of racial/ethnic minorities may produce both negative and positive results.

First, for example, Mastro (2003) applied Social Identity Theory to understand the negative effects of short-term exposure to negative stereotypes of Latinos on college students' real-world attitudes and beliefs about Latinos. Here, Social Identity Theory was used as a framework to explain how the stereotypic information was used by dominant ingroup members (i.e., white students) to make unfavorable judgments about outgroup members (i.e., Latinos).

Second, Ortiz and Harwood (2007) demonstrated a potentially positive effect of exposure to a minority group in the media. As previously mentioned, though US television clearly relies on racial/ethnic stereotypes, there is the potential for television to provide representations that challenge stereotypes and model an equitable social order. Ortiz and Harwood found that exposure to a black-white televised friendship (on MTV's *Real World: Austin*) and a gay-straight televised friendship (on NBC's *Will & Grace*) was related to less reported social distance between majority (i.e., white, straight) and minority (i.e., black, gay) group members. This cautiously suggests that positive interactions between racial/ethnic majority (ingroup) and minority (outgroup) group members in the media may have the potential to improve real-world race relations and reduce ethnocentrism.

Conclusion

In summary, the past thirty-five years of mass communication research on race and ethnicity and the media has demonstrated a consistent underrepresentation and stereotyping of minority groups on television. The most progress in equal representation in the US media has been observed with portrayals of blacks in US entertainment television programming. Asians, Latinos, Native Americans, and Middle Easterners are still underrepresented. Though the television offerings have increased dramatically since the Commission's 1977 and 1979 reports on minorities in US television programming, the range of roles has not significantly increased for many minority groups. Rather, they are still presented in a narrow set of roles that serve to reinforce racial/ethnic stereotypes.

Additionally, mass communication research demonstrates a link between media consumption—television viewing, in particular—with real-world racial/ethnic stereotyping. The majority of this research, however, is correlational in nature and focuses on news, rather than entertainment, portrayals. Future research should examine entertainment television exposure as well as exposure to other entertainment media, such as video games and films. Future studies should also examine the intersection of race and other demographic variables, such as class, age, and sexual orientation. Presently, only the intersection of race/ethnicity and gender is commonly examined.

Subject in focus

Influence of perpetrator race

Part of the typical American daily ritual is to view television news in the morning and/or evening. Crime and violence stories are thematic portrayals in television news, and the portrayal of race and ethnicity in these stories may affect not only what we think about the suspect pictured in the news but also what we think about minority groups, in general.

Mastro *et al.* (2009) conducted two experiments to examine the influence of a perpetrator's race in a television news broadcast on white college students' judgments of guilt of the suspect, recommended sentencing, and general race-based attitudes and beliefs. These two studies help to shed light on the causal relationship between exposure to the media stereotype of the minority criminal in television news and real-world race-based attitudes and beliefs. In both studies, college students viewed one of four professionally produced five-minute television news broadcasts (containing three news stories) wherein only the race (white, black, Latino, and race-unidentified) of the perpetrator in the crime story varied across the broadcasts. In addition to examining the effects of the news broadcasts on the students' judgments, the researchers also investigated the role that the gender of the participant would play in the hypothesized relationships. They found some support for the idea that male students engaged in self-protection of their gender (and racial) identity by assigning a lighter sentence to a white male perpetrator than a race-unidentified perpetrator. In the case of a race-unidentified perpetrator, it is hypothesized that white participants often "fill in" the race of the suspect and presume them to be a minority because of the longstanding, strongly held stereotype of the minority criminal. However, unlike in the case of a clearly identified black or Latino perpetrator in the news, a race-unidentified perpetrator offers up the opportunity for white participants to avoid feeling prejudiced when making judgments about this ambiguous suspect. They are not, after all, suggesting a heavier sentence for black or Latino males outright, but may be doing so when their biased judgments are not as blatant in the case of the race-unidentified suspect.

Additionally, both studies suggest that exposure to the news story featuring the black suspect results in the most negative judgments of blacks, and the most favorable attitudes toward blacks were revealed after viewing the story depicting the white suspect. One unique contribution Mastro *et al.*'s work makes to the literature is the use of an implicit measurement of stereotyping. In study two, the researchers utilized the Implicit Association Test (IAT) to measure implicit attitudes toward blacks and Latinos. The test is a computer-based, timed response task where participants attempt to quickly match good and bad adjectives with images (i.e., in this case, images that vary based on race/ethnicity). Data are analyzed by assessing how long it takes for individuals to match up "good" or "bad" words with images of African-Americans, for example. While surveys are plagued by issues of social desirability, the IAT is thought to be impervious to such biases and to measure cognitive connections we have in our brains that we might not be aware of but that affect how we judge others. To take a sample IAT test, visit https://implicit.harvard.edu/implicit/.

Discussion question

If the portrayal of perpetrator race encourages the development of racial stereotypes, should the media censor their content?

Further sources of information

Givens, S. M. B. & Monahan, J. L. (2005). "Priming mammies, jezebels, and other controlling images: An examination of the influence of mediated stereotypes on perceptions of an African American woman." *Media Psychology, 7,* 87–106.

Hudson, S. V. (1998). "Re-creational television: The paradox of change and continuity within stereotypical iconography." *Sociological Inquiry, 68,* 242–257.

Oliver, M. B. (2003). "African American men as "criminal and dangerous": Implications of media portrayals of crime on the 'criminalization' of African American men." *Journal of African American Studies, 7,* 3–18.

Power, J., Murphy, S., & Coover, G. (1996). "Priming prejudice: How stereotypes and counterstereotypes influence attribution of responsibility and credibility among ingroups and outgroups." *Human Communication Research, 23,* 36–58.

Rome, D. (2004). *Black demons: The media's depiction of the African American male criminal stereotype.* Wesport, CT: Praeger.

Signorielli, N. (2009). "Race and sex in prime time: A look at occupations and occupational prestige." *Mass Communication and Society, 12,* 332–352.

Williams, D., Martins, N., Consalvo, M., & Ivory, J. D. (2009). "The virtual census: Representations of gender, race and age in video games." *New Media & Society, 11,* 815–834.

10 Gender Stereotyping on Television

Research on gender-role images and stereotypes began in the mid-1950s when Head (1954) and Smythe (1954) found that men outnumbered women by three to one in prime-time programs broadcast in New York City. During the mid- to late 1960s numerous studies examined images of women in the media, establishing baseline measures. This body of research has continued, with concern about the media's—particularly television's—influence on gender-role stereotypes as high on the research agenda today as it was during the early1970s.

This chapter will begin with a discussion of the theoretical orientations of research on gender roles. It will summarize the findings of past and ongoing research, with emphasis on studies conducted during the first decade of the twenty-first century, looking, in particular, at the author's ongoing study of fall prime-time programming broadcast between 2000 and 2009.[1]

Theoretical orientations

Socialization is the way people learn about their culture and acquire its values, beliefs, perspectives, and social norms. It is an ongoing process; we are socialized and resocialized throughout the life cycle. Traditionally, parents, peers, teachers, and the clergy have had the major responsibility for socialization. Numerous studies have found, however, that the mass media play a very important role in the socialization process (Berry & Mitchell-Kerman 1982; Roberts & Bachen 1981; Roberts & Maccoby 1985). The actual processes of media socialization, however, are different from those used by more traditional agents. Media socialization does not permit face-to-face social interaction and may lack some of the seductive or coercive powers of traditional agents who have the tools of interpersonal communication at their disposal (Wright 1986). Nevertheless, the media have their own brand of seductiveness and much of the socialization through the media may involve observational and/or social learning.

Social or Observational Learning Theory (Bandura & Walters 1963) examines the role of modeling in a child's social development. It posits that viewers, especially children, imitate the behavior of television characters in much the same way that they learn social and cognitive skills by imitating their parents, siblings, and peers (Lefkowitz & Huesmann 1980). Bandura's (1986) extension of cognitive processing to Social Learning Theory added rules and strategies to the traditional why, what, and when of behavior change. Television provides not only specific responses but the strategies and rules that viewers may use to copy what they observe (Comstock 1989). Television's stereotypes are particularly suited to the processes of Social Learning/Cognitive Theory because they provide simplistic, often one-dimensional models of behaviors, strategies, and rules that appear regularly in many different genres of programs (Bandura 2009).

A second relevant theoretical orientation is Cultivation Theory (Morgan, Shanahan, & Signorielli 2009). This theory explores the general hypothesis that the more time viewers spend with television, the more likely it is that their conceptions about the world and its people will reflect what they see on television. Thus, in order to understand the effects of television on attitudes, beliefs, and behavior, television must be studied as a collective symbolic environment of messages with an underlying pattern or formulaic structure. Due to commercial constraints, television presents a common worldview and common stereotypes through a relatively restrictive set of images and messages that cut across all programs in all delivery systems. The term cultivation refers to "the specific independent (though not isolated) contribution that a particular consistent and compelling symbolic stream makes to the complex process of socialization and enculturalization" (Gerbner 1990: 249). Studies conducted in the tradition of Cultivation Theory continually show that television content has little diversity with frequently recurring features and thematic elements (Morgan, Shanahan, & Signorielli 2009; Signorielli & Bacue 1999).

Images on television

The world of television drama with its numerous channels and ongoing schedule changes gives the illusion of constant change. Yet, the hundreds of content analyses of television content present a very different picture. In short, the world of television, its themes, characterizations, and stereotypes exhibits considerable and remarkable stability.

Certain key aspects of television's portrayals have undergone little change in the past sixty years. The underrepresentation of women is one of these elements. In study after study, men outnumber women in prime-time dramatic programming (Greenberg & Worrell 2007; Signorielli 1985, 1989,

1993; Signorielli & Bacue 1999). The earliest studies of network television broadcast during the early 1950s (Head 1954; Smythe 1954) found three men for every woman. Most of the studies conducted during the 1970s and early 1980s found a similar male-female distribution and a high degree of consistency in other elements of character demography (see Signorielli 1985). Change in representation began in the mid-1980s and by the end of the eighties the proportion of females in samples of prime-time broadcast programs increased to about one-third of the major characters. Since the mid-1990s, the percentage of females has remained steady at 40% of the major characters (Signorielli & Bacue 1999). Moreover, the author's ongoing research also shows that between 1967 and 2009 there has been a statistically significant linear trend in the number of female characters. The proportion of women increased significantly and steadily between 1967 and 2009—moving from 24% of the characters in 1967 to a high of 44% in 2004 and 41% in the fall of 2009.

Greenberg and Worrell (2007) examined the demography in television's new programs using *TV Guide*'s fall preview issues for network broadcast programming published between 1993 and 2004. This analysis found that women made up 39% of the new characters each season and that there was never a season in which the characters were equally distributed between men and women.

Past research has also shown that program genre often determines the male-female distribution. Action-adventure programs broadcast from the late 1960s until the end of the twentieth century had the fewest female characters while situation comedies had the most equal distribution of men and women. Dramas overrepresented male characters until the 1990s, when the distribution became 54% male and 46% female (Signorielli & Bacue 1999). These patterns have continued during the first decade of the twenty-first century. The author's ongoing analysis finds representation still dependent upon program genre, but given the constraints on the economics of broadcasting that have emerged since 2000, the distribution of programs by genre has changed. Today, there are fewer situation comedies while there are more action programs and low-cost reality programs. The most recent gender distributions show that by genre, situation comedies are 56% male and 44% female, action programs are 67% male and 33% female, while dramas are 55% male and 45% female, and reality programs have a 60% to 40% male-female distribution.

Similar patterns are found in cable programming even though cable, because of its numerous channels, has been heralded for its likelihood to provide greater diversity in programming. Gerbner (1993) comparing the demography of network and cable programming found that the patterns of underrepresentation in broadcast programming were also prevalent in samples of cable television. Kubey *et al.* (1995) found, in an analysis of 1035 randomly selected ten-second intervals of programming on thirty-two different cable channels throughout the day, that males outnumber females by about 2.5 to one across all channels. Moreover, the distribution was most skewed in programming seen during the prime-time hours.

Age and occupations

In addition to underrepresentation of women, the world of television has consistently presented gender-stereotyped images of both men and women. A meta-analysis, a statistical technique that consolidates the results of several studies on the same topic, of eight content analyses (Herrett-Skjellum & Allen 1996) found strong evidence of gender stereotypes on television. In particular, studies consistently found that women in prime-time programs are likely to be younger than men (Signorielli 2004), cast in traditional and stereotypical roles (Signorielli 1989), and more likely to have blond or red/auburn rather than black or brown hair (Davis 1990). This is not to say that nontraditional women do not appear on television; it is just that these images are not found consistently. Most of us can easily cite many examples of women who are not stereotyped and much of the research examining non-stereotyped roles has focused upon small samples of programs (see, Atkin 1991; Reep & Dambrot 1987). Moreover, in fairly recent programs (e.g., *Providence, Law & Order*), many of the female characters who break with the stereotypes on one dimension (e.g., occupation) fall back upon traditional stereotypes when involved in or dealing with a romantic relationship (Signorielli & Kahlenberg 2001).

Television places great value on youth—with the greatest emphasis on the youthfulness of women. At the end of the first decade of the twenty-first century, the message is still that a woman's value is in her youthfulness. Study after study shows that the world of prime-time network broadcast television overrepresents young adult and middle-aged characters while underrepresenting children, adolescents, and the elderly. Moreover, from the earliest analyses, women have been cast as younger than men. Signorielli (2004) found less than one in ten male and female characters were children or adolescents. Young adults and middle-aged characters appeared most frequently and more females than males were classified as young adults while more males than females were portrayed as middle-aged.

At the same time, prime time continues to underrepresent and undervalue older people. Signorielli (2004) found that in samples of prime-time programs broadcast between 1993 and 2002, the proportion of older characters on television remained very small and that women aged faster than men.

The analysis found very negative messages of aging, particularly for women fifty or older. Men between fifty and sixty-four were often seen as vibrant, categorized as middle-aged, and eight out of ten were still seen in the work environment. Women of this age were more likely to be categorized as elderly and only half had jobs outside the home.

Character portrayals in the first decade of the twenty-first century show that children, adolescents, and the elderly continue to be underrepresented while young adults and middle-aged characters are overrepresented. Women are still more likely than men to be cast as young adults (40% of the females compared to 32% of the males) while men are still more likely to be cast as middle-aged (59% of the males compared to 51% of the females). Moreover, women, on average, tend to be about four years younger than the men. Turning fifty also has different repercussions for male and female characters. Once again, women over fifty are seen in diminished roles. They are more likely than men to be cast as elderly (30% of the females compared to 16% of the males) and while three-quarters of the men over fifty have a job; less than half of the women are shown working outside the home. Consequently, at the end of the first decade of the twenty-first century, television programs are still populated by age-groups advertisers most want to reach—young adults and the middle-aged.

Another set of gender stereotypes are found in occupational portrayals and provide the most evidence for stereotypes (Herrett-Skjellum & Allen 1996). Early studies of prime-time programming found that women's employment possibilities were limited, with clerical work being the most common job (Signorielli 1993). Today, more women on television are presented as employed outside the home and their jobs more prestigious than forty years ago (Signorielli & Bacue 1999). Whereas in the 1970s, women were often depicted in traditional female occupations such as teachers, nurses, secretaries, and clerks, during the 1980s and 1990s fewer women were cast in these jobs and more found in traditional male or gender-neutral jobs. Men, on the other hand, appear most frequently in traditional male occupations and very few are found in traditional female jobs.

Signorielli and Kahlenberg (2001) found that the world of work on television is determined by dramatic rather than educational considerations. Television programs revolve around those jobs that help tell a good story. The work of doctors, lawyers, police, and forensic specialists is more interesting and exciting than the everyday work of laborers and bus or truck drivers. Therefore, more mundane jobs in which most people spend their work life are rarely found. Moreover, the world of work on television does not present work or occupations very realistically, because while we know that characters have jobs, we rarely see them actually working. For example, recent and very popular crime-scene programs (*CSI*, *Law and Order*) present these jobs as more glamorous and exciting than they actually are; the mundane day-to-day, but important, tasks are often overlooked (Houck 2006). Overall, content studies show that work on television typically appears to be easy and exciting and characters are almost always successful.

Overall, fewer women than men were categorized as having an occupation—only six out of ten females compared to three-quarters of the male characters. But women were not always cast in traditional female jobs. By the end of the twentieth century, women were just as likely as men to be cast as professionals (doctors, lawyers, teachers, etc.) and in white-collar (managers, clerical) jobs. Race and gender were also intertwined in occupational portrayals such that women of color were more likely than white women to be cast in blue-collar (service) jobs or in law enforcement.

Since the turn of the century, the author's ongoing analysis shows that fewer women than men are still seen as having a specific job: three-quarters of the men but only six out of ten women are portrayed in an occupation. At the same time, only one in five women is cast in a traditional female job while about one-third have traditional male jobs and another third have gender-neutral jobs. Half of the males, on the other hand, have traditional male jobs and one in three has a gender-neutral job. Less than 5% of the male characters had traditional female jobs. Women were as likely as men to be cast as professionals but while one in five men were cast in law enforcement-related jobs, only one in ten of the women was so employed.

Content analyses of Japanese television show similarities with images in the US and other countries. Women have consistently been underrepresented and presented as younger than men (Saito 2007). Similarly, occupational portrayals are gender dependent with men in "male" jobs (police, soldier) and women in "female" jobs (entertainers). At the same time, although not seen very frequently, women were more likely than men to be found in nontraditional jobs.

Children's programming and movies

Female characters are especially shortchanged and underrepresented in children's programs. In cartoons, studies consistently find that males outnumber females by four or five to one with differences by cartoon type (Signorielli 1985, 2008). The fewest female lead characters were found in chase-and-pratfall cartoons (*Tom and Jerry*), followed by continuing adventure cartoons (*Teenage Mutant Ninja Turtles*), and teachy-preachy cartoons (*The Smurfs*).

Thompson and Zerbinos (1995) found that female cartoon characters of the 1990s were more assertive, intelligent, independent, and more likely to show leadership qualities than the characters of the 1970s and 1980s. Nevertheless, female characters were also more likely than male characters to be portrayed in traditional stereotypes (emotional, romantic, affectionate, and domestic). Male cartoon characters of the 1990s were presented as more intelligent, more technical, more aggressive, and they asked and answered more questions. Finally, in the cartoons of the 1990s, male characters typically had recognizable jobs while the females were often cast as caregivers.

Cartoons broadcast at the start of the twenty-first century continued to be stereotyped. Leaper *et al.* (2002) found that male characters outnumbered female characters by four to one in traditional adventure cartoons (*Spider-Man)*, two to one in comedy cartoons (*Animaniacs*), and 1.5 to one in educational/family cartoons (*Carmen Sandiego, The Magic School Bus*). There was, however, an almost equal representation of males and females in nontraditional adventure cartoons (*Sailor Moon, Gargoyles)*. At the same time males were more physically aggressive, particularly in the traditional adventure cartoons, than the females. Overall, females were more fearful, more supportive, more polite, and more interested in romance. Similarly, an analysis of children's programs on network, public stations, and cable outlets seen in 2005 (Smith & Cook 2008) found that male characters appeared more often than female characters, particularly in programs rated TV-Y or TV-Y7. Finally, males outnumbered females in all types of children's programs particularly adventure cartoons (*Teenage Mutant Ninja Turtles*) seen on Saturday mornings during February 2007, except those geared toward teens (*Hannah Montana, That's so Raven)* (Signorielli 2008).

Cartoons stereotype aging. Robinson and Anderson (2006) examined 121 different episodes of forty-one different animated children's programs on ABC, Fox, WB, Nickelodeon, and the Cartoon Network in October 2003, focusing on characters who appeared to be over fifty-five years of age. This sample of 1356 characters had 107 (8%) older characters (eighty-two when duplicates were eliminated). About three-quarters (77%) were male. Most of the older characters were seen in minor roles and these older characters were shown with negative physical stereotypes; they were ugly, overweight, toothless, and often needed a walker or cane.

Superheroes are particularly stereotyped. Baker and Raney (2007) found that two-thirds of the superheroes were very muscular males and one-third were average sized females. Female superheroes were more emotional, attractive, concerned about their personal appearance, and asked questions while the male superheroes were more likely to exhibit angry behaviors. Although all of the superheroes were physically aggressive and powerful, female superheroes were more stereotyped because they often worked under a mentor while the male superheroes had positions of leadership and operated independently.

Gender stereotypes are also found in educational and informational (E/I) programming. Barner's (1999) analysis of social/emotional E/I programs (e.g., *Bobby's World*, *Ghostwriter*) aired in the summer of 1997 found that most programs had males as central characters and included a boy's name in the title. Moreover, no programs had a female in the central role or a girl's name in the program's title. Males outnumbered females 58% to 42% among major characters. Males exhibited 2.1 behaviors per scene compared to 1.5 behaviors per scene for females. These behaviors, moreover, were often gender stereotyped. Males made and carried out plans and sought attention, were more aggressive, dominant, and active—behaviors that elicited consequences. Female behaviors, on the other hand, were deferential, nurturing, and dependent—behaviors that typically did not result in consequences for the character.

Images in movies

Movies consistently underrepresent female characters and perpetuate gender stereotypes. Lauzen and Dozier's (2005) analysis of the top films of 2002 found that three-quarters of the characters were male to one-quarter female, and that men were cast as older (in their thirties and forties) than the women (usually in their twenties and thirties). Males, particularly those older than forty, were often seen in powerful and leadership roles while older women were largely invisible, very negatively stereotyped, and perceived as less attractive, less friendly, and less intelligent (Bazzini *et al.* 1997).

Similarly, the top teen movies distributed between 1995 and 2005 (e.g., *Clueless*, *Mean Girls*, *She's All That*) had more female than male characters— 55% female to 45% male. There were few, if any, adult characters; 99% of the characters were high school or college students (Behm-Morawitz & Mastro 2008). Although socially cooperative behaviors appeared more often than socially aggressive behaviors and were not gender-related, female characters were significantly more likely than male characters to engage in socially aggressive behaviors. The socially aggressive behaviors were typically not punished and often rewarded.

Smith and Cook's (2008) analyses of films released between 1990 and 2006 found in the hundred top-grossing G-rated movies that only 28% of the speaking characters were females and more than eight in ten narrators were males. Similarly, the analysis of 400 G, PG, PG-13, and R[3] rated films found that only one-quarter of the characters were women with no change in male-female distributions during this sixteen-year time span. Finally, females were portrayed either traditionally (parents, nurturing, etc.) or as hypersexualized (very attractive, thin, alluring attire, etc.).

Disney movies, a staple of children's viewing repertoire, are very gender stereotyped. Dundes (2001) notes that one modern Disney heroine, *Pocahontas*, is defined both by her romantic relationship and her nurturing role. Similarly, Ariel in *The Little Mermaid* shows both her romanticism and her willingness to embrace life as a human in order to marry the prince. Finally, Tanner *et al.* (2003) note that Disney films typically stereotype male-female relationships by presenting couples (e.g., mothers and fathers) in traditional gender stereotypes.

Impact of stereotyping on viewers

The description of television images is an important and necessary first step in understanding the role of television in society. Effects cannot be assessed without knowing what people see. Interestingly, except for research on body image and sexuality, less attention has been paid to the overall effects of gender-stereotyped content in recent years than to the nature of the content itself.

Viewers, particularly children, are aware of and expect to find stereotyped images on television. Thompson and Zerbinos (1997), in structured interviews with eighty-nine children between the ages of four and nine asking about boys and girls in cartoons, found that children perceived stereotyped cartoon characters—boys were active and violent, while girls were concerned with appearances and seen more often in domestic settings. Moreover, children as young as of kindergarten age are aware of television's gender stereotypes and are able to predict whether men or women, boys or girls would be found in these activities on television (Durkin & Nugent 1998). More recently, however, Ogletree *et al.* (2001), looking at two cartoons produced during the late 1990s, found that elementary school children perceived *The Powerpuff Girls* as more aggressive than *Johnny Bravo*. At the same time, even though *The Powerpuff Girls* were seen as more androgynous, they often giggled and sometimes resorted to typically stereotypical female behaviors (e.g., kisses) to achieve their goals. Although viewers, particularly children, perceive the existence of gender stereotypes on television, the more important question is how these stereotypes influence attitudes and behaviors, looking specifically at identification with television characters and the cultivation of gender-role attitudes.

Identification

Identification with characters in the media is influenced by gender-role stereotypes. Children consistently identify with television characters with boys still more likely to name only a male as their favorite character, while girls are equally likely to name both males and females as favorite characters.

Hoffner (1996) examines wishful identification—wanting to be like characters, particularly those characters perceived as successful or attractive. This line of research finds that girls select female characters when they are physically attractive and select male characters who are intelligent and/or exhibit masculine traits such as physical strength. Hoffner's interviews with seven- to twelve-year-old children show that wishful identification is more pronounced with same-sex characters and more pronounced for boys than girls. Interestingly, girls who choose males as favorite characters see them as "pseudo friends" rather than role models and perceive them as intelligent. At the same time, the girls show more parasocial interaction with same-sex favorite characters, usually selected because they are attractive (see Chapter 7 for an in-depth review of Celebrity and Parasocial Relationships).

Aubrey and Harrison's (2004) study of first- and second-grade children found that the boys who preferred stereotyped content and male cartoon characters said that they valued the traits of humor and hard work. Girls who indicated that they preferred male characters (in both stereotyped or counter-stereotyped roles) did not identify with or were not attracted to female characters. On the other hand, those girls who said that they preferred female characters cast in gender-neutral roles were attracted to and identified with female characters.

Identification continues into young adulthood. Undergraduates who watched more teen movies (e.g., *Mean Girls, 10 Things I Hate About You*) expressed greater identification with the characters in these movies (Behm-Morawitz & Mastro 2008). Moreover, college women who said they identified with female action heroes (e.g., *Buffy the Vampire Slayer*) believed that they possessed traits, such as confidence and assertiveness, in common with these female action heroes. These women also perceived that female action heroes were smart, confident, powerful, and attractive (Greenwood 2007). In addition, Hoffner, Levine, and Toohey (2008) found that while male college freshmen's favorite characters were males, only half of the freshmen women chose a female television character as their favorite. These students said that they liked characters portrayed with good paying and higher status jobs but did not particularly identify with characters whose jobs required a higher level of intelligence or skill.

Cultivation of gender role images

The influence of the mass media, especially television, upon conceptions relating to gender roles is an important area of investigation. This research differs from research relating to perceptions of gender roles (stereotyping) in programming or identification with specific characters because it examines how the media may shape an individual's, and especially children's, views of what it means to be a man or a woman. This, in turn, may aid or abet those goals (occupational, educational, personal) that a person may set out to achieve. Clearly, the evidence points to the fact that society's notions of appropriate roles for men and women have changed (Signorielli 1989). We still must determine whether the media, notably television, has helped or hindered this process.

Studies of television's impact or effects are generally hampered because it is almost impossible to find control groups who are not exposed to television. Moreover, those who do not watch television tend to be a small but quite eclectic group (Jackson-Beeck 1977). Finally, nontraditional or nonsexist portrayals of male and female roles have only recently appeared with some regularity. Consequently, the overall effects of these studies are small because even light viewers watch several hours of television a day and experience many of the same things as those who watch more television (Morgan, Shanahan, & Signorielli 2009).

The research generally points to the existence of a relationship between television viewing and having more stereotypic conceptions about gender roles. Meta-analyses have found support for this relationship. Herrett-Skjellum and Allen (1996) examined thirty studies dealing with television and gender-role stereotypes and concluded that these studies, particularly those using nonexperimental designs, show that television viewing is particularly related to conceptions about occupations. Morgan and Shanahan's (1997) meta-analysis of all published studies relating to Cultivation Theory found similar effects in the analysis of fourteen studies relating to gender roles. Hearold's (1986) meta-analysis of 230 studies found that television viewing had a strong effect on role stereotyping. Finally, Oppliger (2007) examined thirty-one primarily nonexperimental studies, finding a positive and statistically significant relationship between exposure to gender-role stereotypes and gender-typed behaviors and/or attitudes. Moreover, the correlations were similar for both males and females and were somewhat stronger for measures of behavior than attitudes. Overall, then, meta-analyses show considerable support for the idea that media images influence people's, particularly children's, conceptions about gender roles.

Several studies have examined the cultivation of gender-role messages among children. Morgan (1982) in a three-year panel study of sixth through eighth grade children found that levels of sexism were higher among all boys and lower class girls and that television cultivates notions such as "women are happiest at home raising children" and "men are born with more ambition than women." Among girls, the amount of television viewing was significantly associated with scores on an index of gender-role stereotypes one year later, over and above the influence of demographics and earlier scores on this same index; there was no evidence that gender-role stereotyping leads to more television viewing. For boys, the patterns were reversed: there was no relationship between viewing and gender-role attitudes, but greater sexism was related to more viewing one year later. Overall, this study reveals that television viewing is most likely to make a difference among those who are otherwise least likely to hold traditional views of gender roles—a concept cultivation theory refers to as "mainstreaming."

In a second study of 287 adolescents using measures taken at two points in time, Morgan (1987) found that television viewing made an independent contribution to adolescents' gender-role attitudes over time, but that television viewing was not related to specific behaviors in relation to seven chores. Signorielli and Lears (1992), in a cross-sectional replication with a sample of children in the 4th and 5th grades, also found statistically significant relationships between viewing and having gender-typed attitudes toward chores but no relationship between viewing and actually doing gender-stereotyped chores. Children, particularly those who said they watched more television and had more stereotyped ideas about who should do which chores, were more likely to do those chores traditionally associated with their gender.

One area in which we continue to find relationships between viewing and conceptions about sex roles is in relation to occupations. While family and friends play a large role in children's socialization about work, television's images have consistently made important contributions, because television characters are seen frequently and are attractive role models. As noted earlier, however, television presents a rather limited picture of occupations that over-represents exciting jobs and shows few characters actually working.

Watching other media is also related to having more gender-role stereotyped views. Behm-Morawitz and Mastro (2008) found that undergraduates who watched and enjoyed teen movies (e.g., *Mean Girls*) saw female friendships in more stereotyped ways and did not have very favorable attitudes toward women. Moreover, watching and liking these movies led to the perception that being more socially aggressive may increase popularity with peers. Studies have also found relationships between watching music videos, especially rap videos, and conceptions about gender roles. Music videos tend to present very gender stereotypical behaviors with rap videos often presenting women as sex objects (Arnett 2001). Bryant (2008) found that greater exposure to rap videos was related to black adolescents having more adversarial ideas about male-female relationships and agreeing with the negative images of men and women in these videos. Interestingly, those youngsters who expressed higher levels of spirituality were less likely to accept the negative images of women, men, and male-female relationships portrayed in these videos. Pike and Jennings (2005) found that gender-role stereotypes may be influenced by commercials. Using an experimental paradigm, 1st and 2nd grade students were placed in one of three conditions: (1) *traditional* who saw toy commercials in which boys played with gender-neutral toys (e.g., Harry Potter Lego and Playmobil Airport Set), (2) *nontraditional* who saw the same commercials with the boys' faces digitally replaced by very feminine girls' faces, and (3) a *control group* who saw nontoy commercials (e.g., Chuck E. Cheese Restaurants and Lucky Charms). The results indicated that those children, particularly boys, in the nontraditional group were likely to say both boys and girls could play with gender-neutral toys while those in the traditional group said that only boys should play with the gender-neutral toys. Finally, one of the very few studies having natural control groups of children with very little, if any, exposure to television (Williams 1986) found changes in conceptions about gender roles after television became available to the control groups. In this study, girls in Notel (town without television) and girls in Unitel (town with very limited television) had weaker gender-typed views than girls in Multitel (town with greater television availability). Two years after the introduction of television into Notel and an increase of television's availability in Unitel, the girls in Notel had become significantly more sex-typed and the views of both these girls and the girls in Unitel were similar to the views of the girls in Multitel. Similar results were found for boys in these towns (Kimball 1986).

There are relatively few studies looking at the relationship between conceptions about gender roles and television viewing among adults. For example, Signorielli (1989), In an analysis of the NORC General Social Surveys (GSS) fielded between 1975 and 1986, Signorielli (1989) found support for a general hypothesis that those who watch more television have more sexist views. Signorielli also found support for a mainstreaming hypothesis; groups of respondents espousing different views when light viewers hold more similar views (with regard to women's role in society) as heavy viewers. This analysis found that even though there was a decrease in the number of respondents who agreed with sexist statements between the 1970s and 1980s, television viewing was related to the maintenance of notions of more limited roles for women in society, particularly in regard to politically oriented issues.

A recent reexamination of this hypothesis using data from the GSS fielded between 2000 and 2006 (Shanahan, Signorielli, & Morgan 2008) found that this relationship had diminished. The authors suggest several reasons for this finding. First, and maybe most important, the GSS questions used to create the dependent measure in the two analyses were different because the questions asked between 1975 and 1986 in the GSS were no longer part of the questionnaire fielded between 2000 and 2006. Hence, the second analysis used different questions relating to gender roles. Second, people's conceptions about gender roles may show little differentiation between men and women because most people today are cognizant of real-life demographics that have pushed more women into jobs, choosing smaller families, lower marriage rates, and so on. While television is slowly catching up to social reality, it is not surprising that cultivation relationships have diminished or disappeared in all but a few groups. Moreover, there is also some evidence that television may cultivate acceptance of nontraditional families such as unmarried women having children (Morgan & Shanahan 1997).

Similarly in many subgroups (women, more educated, and politically moderate) television viewing was related to giving more traditional and gender-stereotyped responses in a November 2005 survey of 417 residents (twenty to sixty-nine years of age) in Tokyo. At the same time, these findings were not found among men or those with less education. Overall, in this sample, conservatives who watched the most television tended to give more moderate responses—indeed, television viewing was more liberating for this group (Saito 2007).

Conclusion

This chapter has explored gender-role socialization from a communication research perspective. Overall, research examining the presentation of gender roles on television reveals a stable image with men generally outnumbering women on television. While occupational portrayals have exhibited some change, those women most likely to work outside the home are single or formerly married. Thus, the consistent image is that the woman who is married cannot mix marriage, child rearing, and working outside the home. Moreover, women who do not fit stereotypical molds on one dimension of their characterization, such as their occupation, often revert to very traditional gender-role stereotypes in relation to their interpersonal relationships with men. These images serve to support the notion that women should not outshine men, particularly those to whom they are married and/or have an ongoing romantic relationship (IMHI 1997).

Research on the impact of such images in regard to conceptions about sex roles points to the existence of a relationship between television viewing and having more stereotypic conceptions about gender roles. These relationships exist at all stages of the life cycle. There is evidence from samples of middle and high school students, college students, as well as adults. In essence, television may be contributing to the maintenance of notions of more limited roles for women in society because the images seen on television typically foster the maintenance of the status quo vis-à-vis men's and women's roles in society.

Continued research in this area is crucial. Future research, however, must be grounded in the content-effects-institutional analysis paradigm noted at the beginning of this chapter. We need up-to-date content studies to assess if there is change in character portrayals and the nature of that change. Then these findings can provide the background data needed to design studies of television effects. We know where the deficiencies lie and we have some idea of how to eliminate them. Continued research can only facilitate this process and prevent us from becoming complacent about what we see on television. Finally, our research on effects is just beginning to make inroads in understanding the powerful impact of this medium on our lives. This research, however, must be driven by specific information on what people see when they watch television, not what we think they see. We have come a long way in the past fifty years. We cannot forget, nevertheless, that we still have a long way to go.

Subject in focus

Gender stereotyping in commercials

Commercials are also sex-typed and stereotyped on numerous dimensions. Strong links are made between attractiveness and the presentation of women (Downs & Harrison 1985; Lin 1997) as well as placing women in domestic settings advertising products for the home (Bretl & Cantor 1988; Craig 1992a). Males outnumber females in all but commercials for beauty or health and household domestic products (Bartsch *et al.* 2000; Ganahl, Prinsen, & Netzley 2003). Women are more likely than men to be seen in commercials for over-the-counter medications and typically presented as the experts in home health care (Craig 1992b). Research consistently shows that a woman's voice is rarely used as a voice-over and that men are presented as authoritative, even for products used primarily by women (Allan & Coltrane 1996; Bretl & Cantor 1988; Lovdal 1989).

A study of US commercials portraying domestic chores in prime-time network broadcast programming found that almost two-thirds of those seen doing domestic chores were women, typically mothers, who performed child care-related activities, cooked, or cleaned (Scharrer *et al.* 2006). Men's performance of domestic chores was often presented humorously sending the message that men are not capable of helping around the house. Overall, most of the chores were stereotyped in terms of who did them. In addition, Stern and Mastro (2004) found that females were most underrepresented as children and in middle age and least underrepresented as teenagers.

Similarly, a study of commercials from Hong Kong and Indonesia indicated similar parameters. Voice-overs were largely male. Men were typically seen in authoritative roles, while women were seen in the home (Furnham, Mak, & Tanidjojo,2000). Similarly, a comparison of studies conducted in the US, Europe, Asia, and South America (Furnham & Mak 1999) found remarkable similarity in portrayals. Males were credible and often the voice of authority, while women were seen primarily as those who use products. Moreover, women were most often seen indoors while men were most often seen outdoors. A review of studies conducted from 2000 to 2008 in five continents found relatively little change from previous studies. Women are still seen in relation to the home, food, and appearance products, while men are found in commercials for cars, sports, and alcohol. Overall, men are heard (i.e., provide the voice-overs) while women, typically young and attractive, are seen (Furnham & Paltzer 2010).

Commercials in children's cartoons are also gender stereotyped (Browne 1998). Boys are more likely to illustrate how to use the product, even when products are gender-neutral. Adult women and men are seen in very gender-typed roles with the women as homemakers and the men working outside the home. Interestingly, a study of images on cereal boxes (Black *et al.* 2009) found evidence of considerable gender-role typing. Males outnumbered females by two to one and were more often portrayed as animals (e.g., Tony the Tiger) or adults, while females were children or adolescents.

Discussion question

If women are more likely to be homemakers than men, are commercials that feature women doing domestic chores representative of the population, or are they stereotyped and sexist?

Further sources of information

Arnett, J. J. (2007). *Encyclopedia of children, adolescents, and the media* (1 & 2). Thousand Oaks, CA: Sage.

Kaiser Family Foundation web site. Available at kff.org.

Mazzarella, S. R. (ed.) (2007). *20 questions about youth & the media*. New York: Peter Lang.

Singer, D. G. & Singer, J. L. (eds) (2011). *Handbook of children and the media* (2nd ed). Thousand Oaks, CA: Sage.

Strasburger, V. C., Wilson, B. J., & Jordan, A. B. (2009). *Children, adolescents and the Media* (2nd edn). Thousand Oaks, CA: Sage.

Van Evra, J. (2004). *Television and child development*. Mahway, NJ: Lawrence Erlbaum.

Notes

1. Data were collected in each fall between 2000 and 2009 except for the fall of 2007 when the author was on sabbatical. The methods used in these recent analyses are the same as those used in Signorielli and Bacue 1999 and Signorielli and Kahlenberg 2003.
2. TV-Y and TV-Y7 are two of the TV parental guidelines currently assigned to television programs in the United States. Modeled after movie ratings, these TV program ratings give information about the age and content appropriateness of the program. TV-Y programs are appropriate for children of all ages while TV-Y7 are appropriate for children aged seven and older.
3. Age- and content-based ratings for movies in the United States. G: general audience. All ages admitted; PG: Parental Guidance, some content is not appropriate for children under age ten; PG-13: parents cautioned, some content not appropriate for children under age thirteen; R: restricted, minor must be accompanied by an adult twenty-one or older; NC-17: no one age seventeen or younger admitted.

Gregory G. Holyk

Politics 11

Communication media and news industries are vital parts of democracies, which, according to democratic theory, need politically informed citizens. News industries selectively gather information about the political world, frame it into news stories, and distribute it through print and broadcast media. This chapter reviews the political impact of the media and describes how recent changes in communication technologies affect political communication and the news media. The chapter begins by outlining the main political functions performed by news industries and the activities and major behaviors of the news media. The chapter also details the degree to which political campaigns involve the media and specifically addresses the role of television as a political communication medium. The prevalence of negative advertising, extensive use of polling, and voter apathy are also discussed. The chapter includes special sections that go into more detail on experimental research on media priming and agenda-setting, the 1960 Kennedy-Nixon televised debates, and the use of new communication technology by the Obama campaign during the 2008 presidential campaign.

Functions of the news media[1]

In many ways it is difficult to separate politics from the media. Indeed, Graber (2010: 229) notes that "Media do more than depict the political environment; *they are the political environment* [italics added]. Because direct contact with political actors and situations is limited, media images define people and situations for nearly all participants in the political process." The mass media's vital political functions in the United States include (1) providing information for citizens, (2) serving as political tools for public and private elites, and (3) alerting citizens when government malfunctions or misbehaves.

Informing citizens

Most people agree that the news media's primary function is presenting citizens with a broad array of information. Through spoken and printed words, sounds, and pictures, news stories allow citizens to observe the unfolding of election contests from afar and scrutinize them from varied perspectives. They focus on freshly breaking events or provide retrospective judgments about past happenings. The stream of news topics is endless, with reporters and editors acting as gatekeepers who decide what events constitute "news" (see later section on actions and major behaviors of the media for more information on this process). The ability to influence the political views of large audiences makes the media extraordinarily important for the individuals and groups whose stories and causes receive publicity or are denied attention.

The media also play a crucial role in political socialization. Young people lack established attitudes and behaviors. Apart from their families and immediate experiences, most information that they acquire about their political world comes directly or indirectly from the mass media. It becomes one of the bases for developing their opinions. Likewise, most of the new opinions that adults form during their lifetime are constructed from information drawn from the mass media. That makes the mass media major contributors to adult political socialization.

Supporting political actors

Successful political actors are able to present persuasive stories to their target audience and create a political environment that is sympathetic to their interests. This is why political actors devote a goodly portion of their resources to gaining favorable attention from reporters. Major tactics include framing press releases tailored to media needs and conducting news briefings. If these tactics are well-executed, the news media are likely to create a political reality that favors political actors. For example, racial segregation in the American South persisted for many decades, with most people in other parts of the country unaware of its ugly manifestations. The situation changed when the Civil Rights Movement finally managed to attract nation-wide media attention.

The fates of the news industry and political actors are linked because political actors generate much of the information that news media need to report, which is about important political developments, while political actors are dependent on the media to reach mass audiences. Media dependence on information known to government officials and other elites leaves reporters open to manipulation. Political actors are well aware of the power that they hold as the most legitimate sources for news reports. Officials also know that reporters must meet deadlines, especially for stories that will also be covered by their competitors. The need for rapid publication makes it likely that reporters will transmit the carefully prepared messages of government officials very much in their original formats.

Acting as a watchdog

Acting as a watchdog on government, and the powerful in general, is considered a major professional obligation by journalists and the public. Media in the United States are quite free to oppose incumbent government officials, weaken them, and occasionally even drive them from office. This power is protected by the First Amendment to the Constitution because unfettered criticism is essential in fighting government corruption and misbehavior. When *The Washington Post* journalists Bob Woodward and Carl Bernstein uncovered and reported the Watergate political corruption scandal that led to the downfall of the Nixon administration in 1974, their work became the stuff of legend. However, toppling a president is an extreme example. The extent to which journalists have acted as watchdogs has varied over time, but there is generally a strong support for this role, which has become a journalistic norm in the United States.

Actions and major behaviors of the media

Media behavior is a complex phenomenon that includes many processes that affect what political information the public receives and how that information is portrayed. Mass communication mediums are therefore important political institutions and vital to the ability of regular citizens to effectively form opinions, vote, and attend to the political process. There are three major behaviors and roles of the mass media: (1) gatekeeping, (2) agenda-setting, and (3) framing.

Gatekeeping

It is not possible for a newspaper, television, or radio news program, or an Internet site to gather and report on all the possible relevant happenings that occur in the world. Therefore, just like any person selects what to attend to in his or her environment, so too must news organizations select certain events and stories out of the constant flow of events and information. In this process, inevitably some events are highlighted and others are not. In this way the media act as gatekeepers of information, letting some through to the mass public and relegating others to obscurity due to inattention.

Agenda-setting

In their role as gatekeepers, the media also act as political agenda-setters, which is a critical aspect of politics. As Cohen (1963: 13) aptly stated, the media "may not be successful much of the time in telling people what to think, but it is stunningly successful in telling its readers what to think about." Those with the power to define which political issues are worthy of attention are able to determine what is considered a problem and whether or not resources will be allocated to that issue. Politicians constantly jockey with each other, interest groups, corporations, and lobbyists, and other interested members of society to get their issues onto the political agenda—an agenda which only has a limited amount of space—and must compete with other issues for limited attention and resources. Through their ability to bring issues to the forefront of public awareness and elicit attention, the media serve as important political agenda-setters. Some events demand attention (e.g., humanitarian disaster, war, presidential campaign) and the media will undoubtedly cover them and therefore put them higher on the agenda. However, there are many other issues and events where the decision is not so clear (e.g., long-term social processes, detailed legislation) where the media may or may not allocate attention and coverage, and thus end up promoting it on the political agenda or deemphasizing it. Not every issue or "condition" becomes defined as a "problem," and the mass media is crucial to promoting various conditions to the status of agenda-level problems worthy of attention (Baumgartner & Jones 1993). In this way, the mass media affect both the public agenda and the policy agenda of political elites (Graber, McQuail, & Norris 1998).

Framing

Once events and issues are chosen for attention by the media, news organizations also need to make decisions about how to frame the event or issue. Few things in this world are purely objective, and this is especially so for politics. The media frame issues by "reporting the news from a particular perspective so that some aspects of the situation come into close focus and others fade into the background" (Graber 2010: 140–1). Framing of issues is integral to politics and politicians make sure they are very careful in how they contextualize an issue so that the description benefits their preferred point of view. The news media are usually not interested in intentionally framing issues to benefit a particular position, which is the case with political figures (although, as noted in a later section, this has arguably changed in today's hyper-partisan cable news environment). In fact, one of the main norms of journalists is a commitment to objectivity and telling "both sides of the story." However, journalists must still make decisions about how to describe an event, how to place a story within historical and societal context, which sources to rely on in telling the story, and what parts of the event or issue to choose and emphasize. All of these decisions result in an overall frame for any issue or story and these frames have consequences in the political environment. Media framing of issues has been shown to have significant effects on opinions and evaluations of the public (Druckman 2001; Entman 2004; Gitlin 1980; Iyengar 1991; Jacobs & Shapiro 2000; McCombs & Shaw 1993; Nelson, Clawson, & Oxley, 1997; Page, Shapiro, & Dempsey 2000).

Classic research: Experimental evidence of media priming

As mentioned, much of the early research found little to no effect of the content of the mass media on the public. However, much of this research was limited by the fact that various long-term and short-term factors contribute to a person's political attitudes. One way to alleviate the lack of control that exists in normal life is to restrict research on media effects to the laboratory and conduct experiments. Classic experimental research on media psychology effects was conducted by Iyengar and Kinder (1987). Instead of attempting to measure the effects of media exposure in the unstructured environment of normal life, they used controlled experimental manipulation of political video messages to measure the effects of these messages on attitudes and perceptions while controlling for other possible influences. The experimental lab situation does not perfectly reproduce the natural process of exposure to media messages that people experience in their daily lives. However, the increased ability to control the message and the environment provide powerful incentives and advantages for researchers examining media effects.

Research participants were first asked about their political views, attitudes, and preferences before the experiment, which provided a baseline for each individual. Next, participants watched carefully constructed "news stories" that systematically varied in their content and messages. For example, news stories varied in what political issues were highlighted as important. Some highlighted foreign policy, others the economy, and others different topics in politics. News stories also systematically varied in terms of whether the president was depicted as responsible or not responsible for the positively or negatively framed political issues. As opposed to uncontrolled studies of media effects, the experiments by Iyengar and Kinder showed definite effects of media agenda-setting and framing. The news videos had an effect on what issues participants considered most important and who was considered deserving of praise or blame for the conditions of a political issue. This research strongly contributed to a movement in the media psychology literature from the view that the media had limited to no effects on the public to the contemporary view that media messages have identifiable effects that depend on context.

The evolution of research on media effects on politics

Research on the effects of the mass media on political processes, public attitudes and preferences has gone through two phases of extremity—from the idea that the media has substantial effects to the notion that it has no effects at all—and has settled somewhere in between as research methodology and understanding have become more sophisticated. Before proceeding onto the specific role of media in political campaigns, it is helpful to give an overview of the longstanding debate over mass media effects on politics in general.

Early theory: Propaganda and substantial effects

Following World War II, there was a heightened sensitivity to the effectiveness of mass political communication and propaganda. People were amazed at how political messages could effectively mobilize whole nations to support war efforts and specifically how Nazi propaganda was able to facilitate the Holocaust. With the advent of television in the 1950s, researchers expected to find pervasive effects of mass media on political attitudes, beliefs, and behaviors.

New research techniques: Limited to no effects

Despite the dire predictions based on anecdotal use of propaganda, most early research was unable to find any media effects. Prominent research studies by Lazerfeld, Berelson, and Gaudet (1944), Berelson, Lazerfeld, and McPhee (1954), Campbell, Gurin, and Miller (1954), and Campbell *et al.* (1960) all concluded that media messages had little to no effects on voter behavior, and that party identification, the state of the economy, and other stable characteristics were the only major predictors of voting. However, these studies partly failed to find any effects due to narrow research questions that focused on voting. These findings are also consistent with established psychological theories indicating that people resist information that does not fit with their previously held notions (cognitive consistency and avoiding cognitive dissonance) and selectively expose themselves to media and information that conforms with their perspective (selectivity bias).

Contemporary understanding: Moderate effects within context

Despite the lack of evidence of media effects accrued in the 1940s and 1950s, researchers refined their research methodologies and began to build a solid body of evidence for moderate media effects. Researchers understood that a lack of evidence for large media effects does not necessarily mean that the media do not have an effect. Media researchers have now reliably demonstrated that the media have a moderate effect on attitudes and behaviors in a variety of political contexts (e.g., Iyengar & Kinder 1987).

Political campaigns and the media

Campaigning and governing by political elites are tailored to the functioning and format of various mass media communication mediums. Even as early as 1976, Patterson (1976: 3) stated that "today's presidential campaign is essentially a mass media campaign ... for the large majority of voters; the campaign has little reality apart from its media version." This holds true today and could be said not only of campaigns, but public knowledge and information about politics in general.

Politicians made use of newspapers and print media when they became available to a wide array of the public and still make use of them today. After radio was introduced in the 1930s, Franklin Delano Roosevelt effectively used this medium to communicate with voters with his classic "fireside chats." The game of politics and campaigning was revolutionized by the widespread introduction of television in the 1950s and today campaigns are largely geared toward generating positive media coverage on television. In the last ten years, new technologies such as the Internet and wireless phones and computers have changed campaigning, providing a way for campaigns to directly communicate with voters and for voters themselves to communicate and participate in the process of campaigning.

Media coverage of campaigns is highly useful for the public. It allows members of the public to learn a great deal about the candidates (personal character, which is used by many voters to assess leadership capability), their policy positions, and various important events that occur during the campaign (debates, press conferences, visits, meetings, and speeches). Research shows that voters do learn a good deal of information from campaign advertising and media coverage of campaigns.

However, campaign coverage has other aspects that are not unanimously positive for the public. Norris (2000a: 6) notes three major developments of the postmodern campaign: (1) fragmentation of audiences and outlets (e.g., the shift from network TV to cable, local TV news, talk radio, and the Internet), (2) tabloidization of news due to commercial pressure, and (3) permanent campaigns informed by constant polling, focus groups, and electronic town hall meetings. Consequently, the mass media, especially television campaign coverage, tends to be candidate-centered not issue-centered, plays up conflicts larger than they might be, and focuses excessively on the "horse race" (who is ahead in the polls) at the expense of substantive issues.

Deliberate use of media by campaigns

Although campaigners have always recognized the importance of the media, their effective harnessing of the media has steadily progressed. The modern media campaign has therefore been called the "mass media campaign." Most voters are not able to directly interact with candidates during a campaign and their only images and communication with candidates is through mass media such as newspapers, radio, television, and now, the Internet. Critics of the modern campaign blame the media partly for the lack of issues in campaigns and the excessive focus on candidates and images of candidates, which are largely carefully constructed for media exposure. As Levine (1995: xvii) points out, "there is a strong belief … that issues do not count in the presidential race, that politics has been stolen from the people by a cadre of professional image-makers, pollsters, and spin doctors."

The sometimes contentious and conflictual relationship between campaigns and traditional mass media channels (e.g., television) has led campaigns to actively seek out "unfiltered media" to get their messages out to the public. New communication technologies such as cell phones, smart phones, e-mail, and the Internet are very attractive to campaigns because they are able to communicate directly with voters without the possibility that their messages may be altered, interpreted, or changed by traditional media forums. According to Gulati (2010: 193), "Today, the World Wide Web is the single best medium for allowing candidates to communicate directly, without any filter, to a multitude of constituencies simultaneously while maintaining a great deal of control over their own message."

This is also the reason for the popularity of television advertising among campaigns. The lion's share of campaign spending goes toward television advertisements that are able to reach a large number of people with effective audiovisuals. Campaigns do not need to rely on the news media to communicate these messages and therefore there is no chance for them to be altered or interpreted for voters directly before, during, or after the message.

In the modern mass media campaign, most campaign events are staged "pseudo events" where candidates attempt to obtain controlled positive media exposure. Campaigns create campaign "events" that lure media and try to control message, setting, and content as much as possible. The prevalence and importance of image, scripting, control over information, and media has resulted in large campaign staffs of image brokers/spin doctors/professional campaign consultants.

Political public relations consulting began with the founding of Campaigns Incorporated in 1933 (Sanders 2009), so professional campaign management is not a new phenomenon. However, the modern focus on message control and image, partly due to the importance of television and the advent of 24/7 campaign coverage by the media, has led campaigns to hire a cadre of campaign, polling, and marketing professionals to run modern campaigns. According to Newman (1999: 18), the important role political consultants play in media-dominated campaigns is so great that the various marketing, strategy, and polling consultants are now the "coaches and managers who determine the outcome, with the media serving as umpires." These political consultants use many of the same techniques gleaned from marketing and social and cognitive psychology research to "sell" candidates in much the same manner as they would sell any product.

The role of television and the Internet

Television

Television emerged in the 1950s as a major source for campaign information and quickly surpassed newspapers and radio as the number one source for political information by the early 1960s. The advantage of television is that members of the public can observe political events quickly, in real time, with both visual and auditory information. Television has become the major mode of campaign communication on the part of campaigns and is the preferred medium to access campaign information for the public.

The ability to bring the intimacy and drama of political events right to each citizen is a central part of television's popularity. Television was able to bring the 1950s McCarthy's House on Un-American Activities Committee hearings into the homes of Americans. Similarly, the famous reporting by Walter Cronkite of the 1963 assassination of President John F. Kennedy brought that important breaking political event into reality for the average person. The intimacy continued to increase in the 1960s as television broadcasted the Vietnam War across the world to the American public, and is credited by some for turning public opinion against the war effort. We saw the Berlin Wall fall before our very eyes. In 1990, the Gulf War was the first war to be televised live and vaulted CNN to international prominence, as citizens were able to observe bombs falling on Baghdad in real time. And no one will ever forget watching the planes crash into the World Trade Center towers and watching them crash to the ground on September 11, 2001.

Television changed the importance and functioning of debates, campaign events, and even the party conventions. Televised party conventions changed the presentation, layout, length, speeches, spending, scripting, entertainment value, and choreography (Panagopoulos 2007). Conventions went from semi-private, unscripted, and contentious elite gatherings to highly scripted and stylized events with unified themes and messages.

Classic research: The Kennedy-Nixon televised debates

Current televised debates attract large audiences, are highly scrutinized by the news media, and affect the voting decisions of undecided and independent voters (Delli Carpini, Keeter, & Webb 2000, in Norris 2000a). However, as television made its way into the political fray in the 1950s, no one quite knew just how much the visuals, closeness, and drama television provides would affect voter perceptions and thus the conduct of political campaigns. That was until the 1960 televised debates between John F. Kennedy (the Democratic nominee) and Richard M. Nixon (the Republican nominee).

During the presidential campaign the candidates agreed to a series of four sixty-minute televised debates. Of the voting public, 55% watched or listened to at least some of all four debates and 80% watched or listened to at least one of the debates. Kennedy and Nixon reacted very differently to the visual format of the televised debate. Nixon seemed quite worn down by the intense travel schedule of the campaign and also opted not to take advantage of makeup (Pfau, Houston, & Semmler 2007: 19). Nixon also suffered from intense sweating on his upper lip during the debates and failed to look at and smile into the camera. Voters also reacted differently to the debate depending on whether they listened to the debate on the radio or watched on television. Voters who watched the debates on television thought Kennedy won the debate, while those who listened to the debate on the radio thought Nixon won the debate. Those who watched the debate thought that Nixon did not "look" as presidential as Kennedy who was young, handsome, charismatic, and comfortable in the visual format that television provided (Berry 1987; Reinsch 1998).

The debates also changed the content of the messages and information communicated to voters. In studying the 1960 Kennedy-Nixon debates, Ellsworth (1965) found that the candidates used more detailed evidence and analysis than at other points in the campaign. Ever since those first televised debates, candidates and their campaigns have paid special attention to the factors that might make a candidate "look and act" more presidential. The debate organizers are careful to even out the height of the podiums so that neither candidate stands above the other giving the visual impression of domination. Candidates are trained to look into the camera and avoid visual behaviors that might suggest nervousness or unease.

The Internet

The development of the Internet and the wireless technology that allows users to access online information anywhere and anytime has resulted in another shift in the way that citizens access campaign information, providing a greater role for the public in the dissemination of political messages and greater control over the consumption of campaign messages.

One of the major consequences of personal control over online consumption of information and the ability of campaigns to directly contact individual technology users is the fragmentation of the campaign audience (this is also true of cable television). According to Pfau, Houston, and Semmler (2007), we are undergoing a fundamental shift away from mass audience campaign communication with common information and news sources to a series of smaller specialized voter audiences that are much more homogeneous (Chaffee & Metzger 2001; Hill & Hughes 1998; Norris 2000a).

For many citizens, the greater fragmentation and tailoring of campaign information is a welcome development. People are able to act as their own news filters and select information that is more in line with their views and campaigns are able to better target specific voter segments with information and messages that are relevant to those voters. The Internet provides a great deal of control and autonomy for voters to access the kind of information that they consider important. Campaign web sites now allow citizens to gather a great deal of information about the policy stances of the candidates and even offer many opportunities for participation in the campaign on the part of individual voters. Individuals can participate in the campaign by texting campaign messages to their friends, Tweeting, or posting statements and links to videos and other web sites on their social networking pages. Blogging, which is writing online web logs that are available to all, is another way that average citizens can use the Internet to participate in politics and campaigns. As you might expect, the shift from traditional mass media for campaign information to the Internet is not even across the age spectrum. Younger voters are gravitating toward the online world of politics much more than older voters.

The two-way flow of information on the Internet allows citizens to participate in the creation and dissemination of campaign messages. In this sense, the

Internet has had the effect of democratizing the campaign process and providing citizens with an array of options for direct participation in campaigning
that was previously unavailable. The downside to this technology is a greater
ability on the part of campaigns for manipulation of voters, unregulated
propaganda, data mining, masking political interest, and misleading people
(Howard 2006). The ability to misrepresent is high with such an unregulated
format and this lack of standards hurts the credibility of much of the information available online.

Television: Spectacle or real added value?[2]

Television, despite its popularity, has a poor reputation as a medium for
political communication and learning. Critics of television often claim that
audiovisual presentation deters viewers from logical thinking about politics,
while encouraging them to make political decisions based on emotional
reactions to irrelevant personality characteristics of political leaders. Indeed,
early research seemed to show that television discouraged political learning
(Becker & Whitney 1980; Gunter 1987). By contrast, newspapers are praised
for their ability to inform the public and enhance public debate, and therefore enhance democracy (Habermas 1989; McLuhan 1964; Postman 1986;
Putnam 2000; Schudson 1998). When television's critics content-analyze
televised news, they focus almost exclusively on the verbal content rather
than adding the visual content that is also an important part of audiovisual
information presentation.

Misgivings about the contributions of audiovisuals to political learning
are understandable. Television is, indeed, inferior to newspapers in terms of
providing a broad array of diverse factual details and abstract information. For
example, if the subject is global warming, words are superior in discussing the
chemistry of the atmosphere, but graphic audiovisuals showing a shrinking
glacier are far more likely to make the problem come alive for ordinary citizens. Television excels in providing a holistic overall impression and a "feel"
for specific political situations.

New research exonerates television news and visual learning from their repu-
tations as inferior mediums for conveying political information. New studies
show that television news viewing is positively related to understanding politics
(Chaffee & Frank 1996; Chaffee, Xinshu, & Leshner 1994; Kleinnijenhuis 1991;
Norris 2000b; Sotirovic & McLeod 2004; Weaver & Drew 2006). Despite the
ambiguities inherent in visual images, people generally understand and agree
upon the meanings conveyed by television pictures (Messaris 1994; Philo 1990;
Sullivan & Masters 1993). Audiovisuals are better able to convey the complex

interactions of real situations and can do so quickly and relatively painlessly. The reality of what is involved in torturing prisoners is grasped instantaneously and seared into memory when one sees the pictures of the Abu Ghraib abuses. Verbal descriptions cannot convey this reality instantly, if ever.

The prevalence of negative advertising

Although political scientists and members of the public criticize the use of negative advertising in modern political campaigns, it remains a large part of campaign advertising in the United States and is becoming more widespread in other democratic countries. Today, one-third of political campaign advertisements are negative and their proportion is only increasing. The increase in negative campaign advertisements is not directly due to the candidate's political campaigns themselves, however. Most of the increase in negative advertising is due to political action committees (PACs), which are political groups that spend money supporting one candidate or another and are not directly tied to the actual candidate's campaign.

Despite the fact that most voters do not like negative advertising, they effectively discourage voters from voting for an opponent and encourage them to vote for your candidate. Classic examples of effective negative campaign advertisements abound. For example, in the 1988 presidential election between George H. W. Bush (Republican nominee) and Michael Dukakis (Democratic nominee), there was an advertisement that blamed Dukakis for letting convicted felon Willy Horton out of jail, who went on to commit further violent crimes. The advertisement was effective in painting Dukakis as soft on crime and is credited with damaging his campaign and contributing to his loss in the election. In the 2004 presidential election between George W. Bush (Republican nominee) and John Kerry (Democratic nominee), a PAC called "Swiftboat Veterans for Truth" ran many negative advertisements questioning Kerry's service medals he won in Vietnam and painted him as an unpatriotic, antimilitary person. These advertisements severely disrupted the Kerry campaign and required a great deal of time and effort to deal with the accusations while Kerry could have been concentrating on other more positive messages (note that although these two examples involve the use of negative advertising on the part of Republican candidates, both parties actively use a large amount of negative advertising).

Of course, it is important to point out that negative advertisements can serve a positive function in politics. They point out the contrasts between candidates on issues and bring important information to the attention of voters that could be helpful to them in making a voting decision.

Polling

The public opinion polling apparatus that operates within politics and the news media have grown tremendously from the time when reliable scientific polling was introduced in the 1940s and 1950s. Now every news organization either has an in-house polling staff or has a permanent partnership with a polling organization that provides continual polling numbers regarding what "the public thinks." The heavy use of polling by the media and political actors has changed the way politics is conducted and reported. Indeed, according to Frankovic (1998: 150), "Polls are not only part of the news today, they are the news. They not only sample public opinion, they define it."

The use of public opinion polling has many democratic benefits. Opinion polling allows the public to have a voice in the democratic process between elections that differs from voting. Political leaders are able to learn what the public thinks about certain issues and the polling enhances democratic responsiveness if elected officials heed the wishes of public majorities while they are in office. However, the pervasiveness of polling in today's politics may have a number of negative consequences. Bruce Newman (1999: 16) neatly summarizes these fears:

> Our electoral system originally was set up to give candidates the opportunity to let voters know who they are and what they stand for during the course of a primary campaign. However, an interesting twist has taken place in politics today. Through the use of scientific polling, candidates now use marketing research to do just the opposite, that is, to find out who the voters are and what they want the candidates to stand for. Candidates can then feed back to the voters the ideas that they know will sell in the marketplace.

Thus, instead of using public opinion polls to inform their policy decisions and campaign platforms, knowledge of public attitudes can also be used to manipulate the public and frame issues for purely political purposes. Indeed, campaigns make extensive use of professional campaign consultants with backgrounds in marketing, and many of these consultants collect demographic and polling data to direct campaign activities, platforms, and messages. Every message and theme is carefully vetted to see how certain groups of voters will respond and adjusted as necessary to have the greatest positive impact on attitudes and behavior. The pervasiveness of polling is not restricted to campaigns. The government also runs a continuous flow of polls and focus groups while in office in order to gain information on how best to "sell" or "frame" policy and public communication.

During the 2008 presidential campaign, reliable polls were available on a daily basis from all the major newspapers and television news organizations, and most of these polls were aggregated and available on political Internet sites such as RealClearPolitics. Every day the public is inundated with numbers representing who is ahead in popular support and how the candidates fare in terms of specific personal attributes (trustworthiness, leadership, likeability, etc.) and policy areas (perceptions of how the candidates would handle the economy, war, crisis, health care, etc.). One notable problem with such a focus by the media on poll results during campaigns is an excessive focus on the "horse race" at the expense of reporting on issues and substance. It is much easier and more concrete for the media to cover who is leading in the polls than it is to delve into complex policy and campaign issues, but it results in an inferior level of reporting and a possible heightened focus by the public on momentum.

Media-induced cynicism and apathy

The mass media has been cited as a primary factor in voter cynicism and apathy. This criticism is not wholly unfounded and is influenced by several common behaviors of the media in terms of its overall content and presentation of political news. In fact, an edited book by Pippa Norris (2000a) focused on three questions highly related to this topic. These topics included: (1) whether traditional standards of journalism have been undermined by technological developments, increased economic competition, and cultural pluralism, (2) whether the process of political communication during election campaigns has produced a more cynical and disengaged public, and (3) whether commercial pressures and "tabloidization" has led to a decline in serious, responsible, and informed coverage of public policy debates. Although Norris points out that some of these worries are exaggerated, she feels that there is a good deal of truth to these claims.

First and foremost, the news media tend to concentrate on negativity, conflict, disaster, and entertainment. In terms of politics, the news media also tend to focus on negativity, scandal, and conflict. In the United States, with the advent of 24/7 cable news and political web sites on the Internet, there has also been a marked increase in punditry, partisanship, and "soft news" or "infotainment." The increase in punditry and partisanship has led to less objective coverage and more focus on partisan bickering, blame, and conflict. Talk radio shows are primarily conservative (e.g., Rush Limbaugh, Sean Hannity), while Internet blogging and reporting has tended more toward the liberal end of the political spectrum. Fox News, CNN, and MSNBC have many programs that are not traditional news formats, but rather host-driven punditry that is nearly all commentary that has a political slant (e.g., Bill O'Reilly, Sean Hannity, and Glen Beck on Fox News and Rachel Maddow on MSNBC).

Shows filled with biased punditry are extremely popular in comparison to traditional news formats. This makes sense considering our knowledge of human behavior (e.g., consistency bias, cognitive dissonance, and selectivity bias). Partisan news formats and the Internet allow people to filter out the information with which they are likely to disagree and expose themselves to information that is consistent with their preexisting beliefs. This may make news consumers happier, but there are possible negative effects of this for politics and the functioning of democracy. This fragmentation of the news audience that is occurring because of cable news and the Internet results in people getting entirely different information from entirely different sources. As Norris (2000a: 7) correctly points out, the era where Walter Cronkite could say "And that's the way it is" is over and has been replaced by the "multiple realities" of the various media outlets and sources. The public no longer has a common, relatively objective source of information for public discussion and to inform their voting choices.

Partisan punditry also gives the impression that there is much more political conflict than actually might exist in society (Fiorina 2004). Focusing on political conflict and scandal in the media may contribute to increased public apathy over the political system and their representatives. Public approval of both presidents George W. Bush and Barack Obama has been highly negative and highly partisan. Public approval of Congress and politicians in general is at a near all-time low and many politicians campaign as "anti-politicians" who are not connected to Washington, DC. Combined with a negative and conflictual news environment, citizen participation in politics has waned (despite an upturn in the 2008 presidential election) and a sense of apathy that all politicians are "crooks," "all government is bad," and the "system is broken" has set in.

The continuing role of media in politics

It should be clear from this chapter that the role of the media in politics has increased tremendously over time with the addition of new and more pervasive communication mediums. The future should be no different. The proliferation of political news on cable television and the Internet show that wherever the ever-changing communication environment goes, politics is sure to follow. The media is integral to politics, and politics is the bread and butter of the mass media. The 2008 US presidential campaign is yet another demonstration of the complex back-and-forth interplay between the media, politicians, and the public that will continue to evolve simultaneously.

Conclusion

This chapter examines the role of the mass media and the news industry in the political environment. The news media and politics are integral to each other. Each cannot survive without the other. The chapter covers the major functions of the news media in politics such as informing citizens, supporting political actors, and acting as a watchdog of the government and the powerful. The news media perform such functions through agenda-setting, gatekeeping, and framing.

The chapter chronicles the evolution of research on media effects, from worries of outright propaganda, to claims of very limited influence, and finally, to the present view of moderate effects within certain contexts. It also examines the major role of the media in modern political campaigns and the significant recent moves toward interactive multimedia campaigns that make extensive use of the Internet and social media, paying special attention to the Obama campaign in 2008. Special sections cover the role of television (with a subsection on the televised Kennedy-Nixon debates), the Internet, polling, and negative advertising in the political process. Overall, the chapter makes it clear that modern politics is heavily intertwined with the modern media environment, and changes in media use and technology will continue to change the way politics is conducted and experienced.

Subject in focus

The 2008 US presidential campaign and new media technologies

In the 2008 presidential campaign, spending reached record heights that would have seemed unfathomable from the point of view of past campaigns. Overall, the 2008 campaign spending across all candidates and parties reached $2.4 billion dollars. The two major campaigns reached a combined spending total of US$1,099.4 million, far outpacing the previous record combined spending level of George W. Bush (Republican) and John Kerry (Democrat) in 2004 of $717.9 million. Barack Obama wisely refused public financing for his campaign, allowing him to raise far more money than John McCain. Obama's record setting campaign spending total of $747.8 million surpassed the total money spent by both candidates in 2004 and was more than double that of McCain's $351.6 million. A large proportion of this campaign money went toward traditional political television advertising.

What the Obama campaign accomplished was to compliment traditional campaign television communication with an array of new communication efforts never before used to such an extent. This was the first time where candidates used new media widely and effectively.

In the past, campaign web sites were static forums where a campaign would post a candidate's policy stances and platform. In 2008, campaign web sites became interactive environments capable of so much more. The Obama campaign web site organized 150,000 events, created over 35,000 groups, registered 1.5 million accounts, and raised $600 million dollars from three million separate donors (from Hendricks & Denton 2010: xvii). In addition to highly sophisticated campaign web sites, 2008 also saw the rise of other communication technology and social media as important factors. Again, the Obama campaign far outpaced the McCain campaign in the use of these new technologies for campaigning. The Obama campaign used new media technology to stay in touch with supporters and have a constant campaign presence 24/7.

On YouTube, a free online site for posting digital videos, voters watched Obama videos fifty-two million times (about 14.5 million hours of video) that would have cost $47 million to broadcast as television advertisements. The Obama campaign posted 1,820 free videos itself on YouTube, and this was supplemented by a host of other supportive videos created by Obama supporters independent of the campaign. Many of the pro-Obama videos on YouTube went "viral," meaning that they were forwarded continuously from friend to friend online and spread quickly like a virus. For example, the "Obama Girl" video, featuring a young and attractive Obama supporter, had thirteen million views by the end of the campaign, more than double any official campaign videos (Powell 2010, in Hendricks & Denton 2010).

In terms of social networking media, by the end of the campaign Obama's Facebook site has 3,176,886 supporters and his Myspace site had 987,923 friends. Obama's number of "friends" online was nearly four times that of McCain (Baumgartner & Morris 2010, in Hendricks & Denton 2010). This type of social networking presence is not inconsequential, especially for the youth vote, because 75% of 18 to 24 year olds have a social networking account. The Obama campaign also facilitated social networking on its own web site by creating myBO, a social networking web site that attracted two million followers, planned 200,000 offline events, created 400,000 blog posts, posted 400,000 pro-Obama videos on YouTube through the web site, created 35,000 volunteer groups, raised $30 million with the independent fundraising pages of 70,000 people, and hosted a "virtual phone bank" that made three million calls in the final four days of the campaign (Baumgartner & Morris 2010, in Hendricks & Denton 2010).

Obama had 100,000 followers on the social networking site Twitter, which allows people to post quick 140 character statements. The Obama campaign used Twitter to keep supporters abreast of Obama's appearances, major announcements, and campaign videos. The use of Twitter by the Obama campaign evolved over time. At first, the campaign used Twitter to briefly post policy positions, but later in the campaign it was used to let people know where Obama was on the campaign trail, to direct people to his web site, and to announce campaign events (Solop 2010, in Hendricks & Denton 2010).

The Obama campaign also made extensive use of text messaging and pseudo-personal e-mails to stay in touch with supporters. They even announced Obama's selection of Joe Biden as his running mate by e-mail and text to his supporters instead of going through the usual mass media channels. The growth of smart phones (e.g., Blackberrys and iPhones), which are capable of connecting with the Internet, is immense, and the Obama campaign used this new technology to keep in touch with support-ers. With this wireless technology, the campaign could reach supporters literally anytime and anywhere.

One other major benefit for organizing and fundraising was the ability to create massive lists of supporters complete with all kinds of demographic information based on e-mail addresses, phone numbers, and web site profiles. All of this information was used to strategically tailor messages that would resonate with individual voters, connect supporters together, and motivate individual voters to volunteer, donate money, and go to the polls. Kenski, Hardy, and Jamieson (2010) call this individualized campaign messaging "microtargeting," and the growth of its use was facilitated greatly by such a large proportion of data gathered by the campaigns through these new communication mediums.

E-mail lists were critical to campaign and volunteer organization for the Obama campaign. By the end of the campaign, the Obama campaign had an e-mail list of thirteen million addresses that they used effectively for organizing, fundraising, and targeting messages. According to Waite (2010: 108, in Hendricks & Denton 2010), the Obama campaign constructed and sent out e-mails constantly to "make everyone on their e-mail list feel like a valued asset, and reward them as such." Whether or not these e-mails had this desired effect remains to be seen, but the technique is certainly novel and the campaign retains the ability to communicate with these supporters post-campaign.

Discussion question

Do recent technological advances provide important information about political candidates or distract voters with slick marketing?

Further sources of information

Glasser, T. L. & Salmon, C. T. (eds). (1995). *Public opinion and the communication of consent.* New York: The Guilford Press.

Graber, D. A. (2010). *Mass media and American politics* (8th ed). Washington, DC: CQ Press.

Kenski, K., Hardy, B. W., & Jamieson, K. H. (2010). *The Obama victory: How media, money, and message shaped the 2008 election.* New York: Oxford University Press.

Notes

1. Note significant portions of this section on functions of the news media appear in Graber & Holyk (2011).
2. Portions of this section on television appear in Graber & Holyk (forthcoming).

Sarita Robinson

Research Methodology 12

In each of the previous chapters, we have seen how the media can impact on individuals, groups of individuals, and on society as a whole. With the media having a more prevalent place in our lives, the need to understand and monitor its impact grows. This chapter outlines some of the key methodologies that have been used to study the impact of the media and considers the strengths and weaknesses of each methodological approach.

Choosing a qualitative or a quantitative approach

Two major methodological approaches exist within psychology, with both qualitative and quantitative approaches being used extensively in media research. Although both approaches are highly valued for the insight they bring to our understanding of human behavior, both approaches have different strengths and weaknesses, which mean that some methodologies are better suited to answering particular research questions than others. Quantitative methodologies tend to be used to test a specific hypothesis using a large sample, with data analysis being completed via statistical analysis. Several methods fall under the banner of quantitative methods, including laboratory or field experiments, forced choice interviews, and questionnaires. Quantitative methods are best suited to occasions where researchers want to find out the answer to a well-defined question: for example, "Do preschool children have better language development if they are exposed to more than ten hours of preschool television during a week?" or "Does watching horror movies lead to an increase in anxiety disorders in teenagers?" The larger sample size and control of other variables mean that the results of quantitative studies are considered more generalizable to the wider population than other approaches.

On the other hand, the qualitative approach, such as open-ended questionnaires or interviews, focus groups, and observational studies, focus on gathering evidence that is not analyzed using statistics but is interpreted by the researcher (Brown & Lloyd 2001). Qualitative methods offer researchers the opportunity to examine in depth the behavior being studied and may be more appropriate when examining sensitive topics. For example, if researching the impact of horror films on mental health, one-to-one interviews or small focus groups would be a more sensitive research methodology than the large-scale administration of questionnaires in a more public forum. However, the major disadvantages of qualitative research methods are that large samples are not normally possible due to time and resource constraints; therefore, the results are open to criticisms of lack of generalizability.

Both methodological approaches have benefits as well as drawbacks and the decision regarding which approach you adopt should be based on the research question you wish to answer. Quantitative methods are best suited to research topics that are open to large-scale participation and have a clear and concise research question, which needs to be answered. Qualitative methods, on the other hand, are best suited to sensitive research areas or to research that has not yet been fully formed. In addition, qualitative methods can be used following quantitative research to help interpret or explore further the initial findings. In the next section of this chapter, research methods commonly used by quantitative and qualitative researchers are outlined and the advantages and disadvantages of each method considered.

Quantitative research methods

The following section will identify the advantages and disadvantages of several quantitative research methods, which have been used extensively within media psychology.

Surveys

Surveys have been effectively used to gather data about a topic by using a number of standard questions and asking participants to answer them with a series of preset responses. The survey can either be administered by the researcher in person with the participant answering the questions verbally (closed-question interview) or the participant can fill in their responses to questions in written form (closed-question questionnaire). Using surveys to collect data has a number of advantages. First, researchers can gather information in a time and cost-efficient manner as a large number of people can be sampled in a short amount of time. This means that an adequate sample can be obtained and therefore statistical inferences about populations can be made. Second, high reliability can be obtained as all participants are presented with the same standardized questions and response choices and so responses cannot be distorted by the researchers' interpretation of the participant's answers.

Reiss and Wiltz (2004) completed a survey using a series of closed questions to investigate why people watch reality television. Participants were asked to fill in a series of questionnaires rating how much they enjoyed various activities such as travel, sport, music, and reality television. Next, participants completed a questionnaire that asked them to rate their motives and motivations toward various behaviors. Statistical analysis of the data from the questionnaires revealed that people who liked two or more reality television shows tended to be more motivated by social life and romance than those who did not watch any reality television.

The second type of survey is the closed-question interview, where the participant is asked a number of predefined questions by an interviewer and asked to reply using a standard set of responses. Dohnt and Tiggemann (2006) used closed-question interviews to investigate the effect of the media on body satisfaction expressed by young girls aged between five and eight years. The advantage of the closed-question interview for this study was that the researchers were able to obtain information from girls who were too young to read the questions themselves. Therefore, the closed-question interview is a good research method to use with people who may struggle to fill in a written questionnaire. The results of Dohnt and Tiggemann's (2006) study suggested that girls who watched more appearance-focused television programs had lower appearance satisfaction. However, one of the major problems with data collected via surveys is the tendency to analyze the data using correlation. With correlations, it can be difficult to know the direction of a relationship. For example, the study by Dohnt and Tiggemann (2006) shows a relationship between body image and the type of television programs young girls watch. However, we do not know if it is watching certain television programs that are leading to poor body image or if poor body image is leading to these young girls seeking out certain television programs.

Further, as correlational analysis looks to identify relationships, sometimes those relationships found can be spurious. For example, many Internet sites point to the relationship between presidents who die in office and the year of election having a zero in it such as Abraham Lincoln (1860) and Franklin D. Roosevelt (1940). Although some astrologers suggest that this relationship is caused by the conjunction between Saturn and Jupiter, it is more likely to be a chance occurrence. Therefore, researchers should be very careful before concluding that the media causes certain behavior, as the relationship could be spurious or the tendency to select a certain type of media may be the effect rather than the cause of a particular behavior.

Laboratory experiments

Laboratory experiments have been used extensively within psychology to gather quantitative data that answer clear and concise research questions. In order to run an experiment, the researcher must decide on the factors they wish to study, identifying the variable(s) to be manipulated (independent variables) and the variables in which the change is to be measured (dependent variables). For example, a researcher might be interested in the effect of playing computer games (independent variable) on children's levels of aggression (dependent variable). As well as deciding on the factors to include in the experiment, the researcher must also decide on the experimental design. Three types of design are commonly used: between, repeated measures, or a mixed design. When using a between design, the researcher will look between two or more groups and compare behaviors. In a repeated measures design experiment, the same participants complete the experiment under different conditions and their performance is compared. And as the name suggests, with a mixed design, the experimenter will use a mixture of both between and repeated measures methodologies.

One of the key advantages of laboratory experiments is that they allow the researcher to control for extraneous variables. Extraneous variables are factors, which—in addition to the independent variable(s) that the researcher is interested in—may have an effect on the dependent variable(s). By using an experimental approach, in a laboratory setting, the researcher hopes to control extraneous variables. Once extraneous variables have been controlled the researcher can be (reasonably) confident that it is the independent variable(s) that are influencing the behavior being studied. For example, in a lab-based study to look at the impact of reading newspapers on happiness, the participant's environment should be controlled. The control of other variables, which may increase happiness, such as chocolate consumption, means that the experimenter can be confident that it is the newspaper and not other factors that are influencing happiness.

However, laboratory-based experiments do have a number of disadvantages. First, experiments tend only to last a short amount of time because participants generally have only a limited amount of time to take part in a study. Short experimental designs can be problematic as people can be quite good at buffering the effects of stimuli for a short space of time. For example, girls may not develop eating disorders as the result of one exposure to images of supermodels. However, in the real world, girls might be exposed to many images of supermodels over the course of a week, month, or year and it might be this cumulative exposure that can lead to eating disorders in a small minority of girls. Further, the duration of some media experiences may last longer than can be examined in a laboratory. Harrison (1999) noted that watching films can have a long-lasting effect on some people. For example, being so frightened by a film that they avoiding seeing the film again or being inspired to become a marine biologist. Therefore, laboratory experiments are not good for looking at the cumulative or the long-term effects of the media.

A second problem with laboratory experiments is that the intensity of stimuli presented may not be as intense as those experienced in the real world. Simons and Silveira (1994) reported the case of two ten-year-old boys who developed persistent anxiety as a result of watching a television program (*Ghostwatch*) in their own home. Although children's reactions to horror movies may be an interesting topic of research, it would be unethical to present children with stimuli strong enough to induce anxiety. Therefore, researchers examining the effects of the media in a laboratory setting may miss some of the effects seen in the real world, as they are unable to replicate the intensity of those media experiences.

A final weakness of laboratory studies is the artificial way in which the effects of the media are examined. Often people will watch television or listen to the radio with other people and are likely to discuss shows or articles in newspapers with others. So, for example, watching a horror movie is generally a social event with friends who are perhaps going to the cinema to watch the film together. Watching a film on your own in a lab is likely to be a very different experience from how you would watch a film in real life, so laboratory experiments can lack what is called ecological validity. That is to say the experimental situation is not realistic and this means that some of the effects of the media may not be replicable in the experimental setting. Further, the factors that may affect people's reaction to the media can be wide ranging and it is difficult to control for this wide range of factors in the lab. This was highlighted by Reeves *et al.*'s (1999) study, which observed that even just altering the television screen size can change the way in which the media message is processed. This emphasizes the large array of variables, which can influence the impact of the media and the difficulty in replicating realistic environments when carrying out laboratory experiments.

Physiological measurements in laboratory experiments

Recent advances mean that psychologists are now able to collect data about people's physiological responses to the media in a noninvasive manner. For example, measuring sIgA concentration in saliva allowed McClelland and Cheriff (1997) to observe a link between watching humorous films and enhancements in immune functioning. Other techniques, such as neuroimaging, mean that we can even look at which areas of the brain are activated when people are exposed to different media stimuli. Techniques, including functional magnetic resonance imaging (fMRI), allow researchers such as Weber, Ritterfeld, and Mathiak (2006) to gain a better understanding of the effect of media violence by looking at the areas of the brain that were activated when males played violent video games.

Field experiments

Field experiments can get round some of the problems of laboratory experiments, as the more naturalistic setting can help researchers look at more realistic behaviors. For example, Savage (2004) notes that it is difficult to monitor the effect of television aggression on violence in the lab as there is a big psychological difference between pressing a button and actually going out and hitting someone. Field experiments may overcome these problems of ecological validity by monitoring behaviors that occur in real-life situations. The increase in the ecological validity of field studies means that the results can be considered to be more generalizable. Gerber, Karlan, and Bergan (2007), for instance, wanted to examine the effects of reading a newspaper on voting behavior and political opinions. By using a field experiment where participants received a daily newspaper, Gerber and colleagues were able to show that even a short exposure to a newspaper influenced voting behavior and some public opinions. As the experiment was completed in the real world instead of a laboratory and the experimental design was closer to a real-world experience, the results were likely to be more reflective of what really happens.

Other researchers have completed field experiments that closely mimic real-world experiences. Paluck (2009) completed a yearlong field experiment in Rwanda to look at the impact of a radio soap opera on reducing levels of intergroup conflict between different ethnic groups. Participants listened either to a radio program aimed at reducing conflict or to a control (health) radio soap opera. As this study aimed to have good ecological validity, the participants were encouraged to listen to the radio program as they normally would—as a group on a communal radio. Although the study used a variety of outcome measures, which asked about changes in participants' beliefs in individual interviews and focus groups, more ecologically valid measures of cooperation were also used. At the end of the study, participants were given a new radio by the researcher and asked to decide how the radio should be shared. This allowed Paluck to look for any differences in interpersonal interactions, which may have occurred as a result of exposure to the different types of radio exposure while participants undertook a real-world task.

Cross-sectional studies

Another form of data collection that avoids some of the problems of laboratory studies is cross-sectional studies. In order to complete a cross-sectional study, a researcher would need to identify two populations or two time points, which differ with regard to the issue being studied. For instance, if we were interested in the impact of the media on eating disorders, we might look at two populations: one population where there is a high degree of media exposure and another population with a lower degree of media exposure. Researchers would then examine whether the population exposed to a certain type of media content also had a higher level of eating disorders. Eddy, Hennessey, and Thompson-Brenner (2007) did just this and looked at the impact of the media on young Tanzanian girls. The study concluded that eating pathologies were more common in subpopulations in Tanzania that had more exposure to Western culture. Cross-sectional studies can also be done across time points if data exists for a population at two or more time points. For example, Crespo and colleagues' (2001) study looked at the increase in obesity between 1988 and 1994 and the possible connection to increased television viewing.

Longitudinal studies

Longitudinal research monitors a group of people over a period of time and looks for any behavioral changes that have occurred. For instance, in 2009, Anderson *et al.* undertook a review of longitudinal studies, which looked at the impact of adverts on alcohol intake. The studies in the review had looked at people's drinking behavior and then monitored their exposure to advertising over a number of months or in some cases years. The advantage of the longitudinal design is that by looking at changes in behavior over time, the studies are able to observe the cumulative effects of advertising, which may not have been evident during a shorter study. Further, longitudinal research can help you monitor how changes in the media, such as the development of new technologies can impact on people as the changes occur. The main disadvantage of longitudinal designs is that it can take a long time to collect data. For example, Hancox, Milne, and Poulton (2004) published data showing a relationship between television viewing habits in children and long-term health problems such as raised cholesterol in adulthood. The study had followed children born in 1972–73 in New Zealand for twenty-six years and the study is still ongoing. Although longitudinal studies help you to gain a more in-depth insight into your participant population, the length of time that some studies can take mean that your sample size can shrink as people drop out.

Content analysis

Content analysis offers media researchers an objective and systematic way of examining certain themes or concepts within either written text or film. Therefore, content analysis allows you to quantify (in a way that can be replicated) a behavior or theme present within a media presentation. For example, Coyne and Whitehead (2008) used content analysis to monitor the level of aggression present in Disney movies. Using this technique they were able to conclude that on average Disney films had 9.3 acts of indirect aggression per hour, but the aggressive behavior levels were low and aggressive acts were usually portrayed in ways that would not facilitate imitation. Although content analysis may be time-consuming to perform, the analysis can be checked for reliability by checking for agreement between two observers.

Qualitative methods

Qualitative methods are generally seen as going beyond the *what*, *when*, and *where* of a behavior and trying to focus on the *why* and *how*. A number of different qualitative methods can be used, the most popular of which include interviews, focus groups, and observations.

Interviews

Interviews can simply be used to describe any method by which the interviewer finds out the thoughts and feelings of the interviewee regarding a topic. The interview can be carried out face to face, or can be carried out over the telephone, or via videoconferencing. Unlike closed question interviews, which are generally considered to be a form of quantitative analysis, open-ended interviews consist of a number of open-ended questions with lots of opportunities for the interviewee to explain their experiences, ideas, feelings, and beliefs regarding the question asked. The interviewer may have a list of interview prompts, but the interviewer is free to follow up on any questions that they think might be important to explore in more detail. As a result, open-ended interviews give the interviewer the flexibility to follow up areas of especial interest.

Open-ended interviews are particularly useful when investigating new phenomenon where there has been limited previous research. For example, Livingstone (2008) used open-ended interviews to look at the influence of social networking sites on teenagers. The interviews in this study lasted around one hour, and comprised a free-flowing, open-ended discussion in front of the computer, while simultaneously going online to visit the interviewee's personal profile and those of others. This helped the researcher to tap into information, which might not have been considered in a questionnaire or an experimental design.

However, researchers should be aware of a number of issues when carrying out open-ended interviews. First, the medium in which the interview takes place can actually affect the relationship between the interviewer and interviewee and could potentially lead to differences in responses given. For example, differences in interpersonal interactions between interviews conducted in person as opposed to over the phone can affect the responses given to the interviewer. Second, even the interviewer's physical characteristics, such as ethnic group or gender, can influence the responses given by the interviewee. Finally, researchers should be aware of interviewer bias: this is where the interviewer can either consciously or unconsciously lead the interviewee to answer questions in a certain way. For example, an interviewer might ask a biased question such as "do you always feel fat when you view supermodels in magazines?" whereas a better non-leading question would be "how do you feel when you view supermodels in magazines?"

In addition to just reading the responses from the interviewees, psychologists have developed techniques that allow the analysis of interviews in a more objective manner. One of these techniques is thematic analysis, which Braun and Clarke (2006: 79) state is "a method for identifying, analyzing and reporting patterns (themes) with data." The researcher aims to look for patterns in the data by first generating codes that describe the data. The second stage is to search for themes that appear frequently in the data (e.g., topics or ideas that appear in more than one interview). The final stage involves the researcher examining the themes that emerge from the data and writing them up in the form of a report.

An example of a study that uses thematic analysis is the work of King and Delfabbro (2009), who interviewed teenagers to try and discover why only a minority of video game players play excessively. The researchers noted that open-ended interviews allowed them to develop a good rapport with the interviewees and to have the flexibility to follow up on points of interest that arose during the interview. The analysis of the interviews revealed that several of the interviewees reported that computer game play gave young people a sense of empowerment, which might have been missing in the real world. By identifying themes in the interviews, the researchers were able to identify causes of excessive game play, which may have not been considered previously and so could lead to more effective interventions to help excessive game players.

Focus groups

According to Kitzinger (1995), a focus group is a form of group interview and should not just be seen as a quick and easy way of collecting data from several people as group interactions are explicitly used in order to enhance the data gathered. In a focus-group discussion, the researcher acts as a facilitator, encouraging participants to talk to each other, ask questions and build on each other's comments, while keeping the discussion on topic. Focus groups are an especially useful research tool when researching sensitive topics as the mutual support provided by the group can break the taboo of sensitive topics as bolder members can bring out shyer members. Further, focus groups can encourage participation from participants who are reluctant to be interviewed on their own (such as those intimidated by the formality and isolation of a one-to-one interview) and can encourage contributions from more reluctant participants or from people who feel they have nothing to say. Another advantage of this research technique is that it does not depend on the literature skills of the participants, as might be the case in a diary or a questionnaire-based study.

Rivadeneyra's (2006) study into Latino high school students made good use of focus groups when looking at the sensitive topic of negative stereotyping of Latinos in English and Spanish language television. After showing students television clips, Rivadeneyra was able to use focus-group discussions to explore how students actually felt after viewing negative portrayals of Latinos, detail which may have been lost if a less flexible approach, such as a questionnaire, had been used.

Before undertaking a focus-group study, a number of decisions need to be made based on both theoretical and practical considerations. Focus-group responses can be affected by many factors; therefore, it is important that the researcher makes informed decisions about how participants for the focus group are selected and how the focus-group discussion is carried out. When selecting members for a focus group, the researcher will have to decide whether to use strangers or people who know each other prior to taking part in the study. It is also important when selecting members of a focus group to decide whether it would be better to question people with similar backgrounds, such as the same level of educational background or socioeconomic status, or whether to question a more diverse group of people. Other factors to be considered regarding the way in which the focus-group study is carried out include the location of the group interview, the group size, and the way in which the ideas generated at the meeting are recorded. For example, if a video recording of the focus-group meeting is to be made, the researcher should be aware that this may make some people feel uncomfortable and so be unwilling to contribute to the discussion.

Although focus groups have many advantages, researchers should also be aware of the disadvantages. The main disadvantage is that focus-group data cannot be checked for reliability. That is to say, the researcher cannot be certain that if the same focus-group study was to be carried out on the same topic with the same people that the same themes would emerge. If a focus group was to be repeated with the same participants, it is likely that changes in group dynamics and opinions just as a result of the first focus-group discussion would lead to different comments and themes. A further disadvantage is that due to the time and expense involved in running focus groups, only a small number of people can take part and so focus groups run the risk of not being representative of the whole population.

Observational methods

One of the best methods for increasing the ecological validity of a study is to observe what people do in real life. Studies that have used observational methods include Bandura's "Bobo doll experiments" of the 1950s, which looked at children's levels of aggression after they had watched adults acting aggressively toward an inflatable doll. Bandura found that young children observing an adult acting aggressively toward a weighted inflatable doll were likely to repeat the same behavior themselves. More recently Brody, Stoneman, and Sanders (1980) used observation to monitor child-parent interactions while the family was watching television. By looking at a number of preselected observational measures such as talking, positive facial expressions, and touching, the researchers were able to show that father-child interactions but not mother-child interactions decreased during television viewing.

There are two ways of carrying out observational research. The first method is overt observation, where the people know that their behavior is being monitored. However, this method of observation can lead to problems as the observee may change their behavior when they know that they are being watched. In the case of overt observation, researchers may record behaviors as they are carried out or may choose to video-record the participants and code the behaviors at a later date. Both methods can be extremely labor intensive and time-consuming. In addition, direct observation can lead to people changing their viewing habits. For example, adults would choose not to watch pornographic material if they knew that these viewing habits were being recorded. Therefore, the researcher should bear in mind that the behaviors observed via overt observations may not be the real everyday behaviors, which people undertake.

The second method is covert observation in which people are unaware that they are being observed. Although this type of observation avoids the problem of participants not acting naturally, covert analysis does have some difficult ethical considerations to overcome. Participants in a covert observational study are unable to give their informed consent to take part in a study as they are unaware that they are taking part in a study. Another problem of observational research is that although ecological validity is increased, so are the number of extranous variables, which the researcher must consider when interpreting the results.

In both forms of observational analysis, it is important that when the behaviors are encoded the researcher maintains a good degree of objectivity. Observer bias may occur when researchers are coding data and inter-rater reliability checks should be carried out to avoid this happening. One of the simplest ways to do this is to get two people to rate the same behaviors and see to what extent they agree with each other. If there is a high correlation between the two rater's scores, it is possible to conclude that their ratings are reliable.

Mixed methods

Alan Bryman (2006) notes that the combination of qualitative and quantitative analysis in recent years has become increasingly common and can have a number of advantages for the researcher. Researchers may, for instance, use qualitative methods, such as focus groups to suggest new lines of inquiry, which the researcher may not have previously thought of. The new variables suggested by the qualitative analysis could then be used in a quantitative study in order to fully explore the previously unconsidered variable. A joint methodological approach that looks for corroboration between quantitative and qualitative data collected can offer more evidence to support the results of a study.

Ethics

As with all psychological studies, any research looking at the effects of the media must safeguard the health and mental well-being of participants. The ethical guidelines produced by the British Psychological Society (BPS) state that participants should not be exposed to any more risk than they would experience in everyday life. In addition, the BPS advises that participants have a right to know exactly what will happen to them and why so that they can give their informed consent to take part in the study (BPS, 2009).

Researchers may want to withhold information about a study, however, because if the participant was aware of the true nature of the study, they might change their responses. For example, studies looking at computer game responses have often deceived participants into believing that they are playing against a human co-player when in fact they are playing against a computer (e.g., McClure *et al*. 2007). In the study by McClure and colleagues, participants were told after they had completed the study about the deception and told why the deception was needed. The researchers also checked to make sure that none of the participants felt distressed after the deception. Finally, the participants were then given the chance to remove their data from the study if they wanted to. The BPS is very clear that deception should not be undertaken lightly. The guidelines suggest that deception is not appropriate if the experimenter deliberately falsely informs the participant regarding the purpose of the research, especially when the information given makes the study seem more benign than it actually is. Deception should also be avoided if the deception leaves the participant feeling uncomfortable or angry when later revealed.

Conclusion

In summary, just like other disciplines within psychology, the psychology of the media can employ many different research methodologies to explore the impact of the media on people. When selecting the most appropriate method for your study, it is important not to go for the method with which you are most familiar or the method that appears to be the easiest. You need to select the methodology that is most likely to comprehensively and ethically answer the research question, which you have posed.

Further sources of information

Berge, A. A. (2011). *Media and communication research methods: An introduction to qualitative and quantitative approaches*. London: Sage.

Clark-Carter, D. (2009). *Quantitative psychological research*. Hove, UK: Psychology Press.

Davies, M. B. (2007). *Doing a successful research project: Using qualitative or quantitative methods*. Basingstoke: Palgrave Macmillan.

Smith, J. A. (2007). *Qualitative psychology: A practical guide to research methods*. London: Sage.

Glossary

Agenda-setting: Indicating to audience members which topics are of most importance.

Anorexia: An eating disorder characterized by extreme dieting behavior and a fear of gaining body weight.

Asynchronicity: Online communications between two or more people that do not occur in real time.

Atypical actions: When a person engages in behaviors that are not considered usual for them to engage in.

Audiovisuals: Communication that involves both vision and hearing (e.g., television).

Avatars: Cartoon-like placeholders used to represent the self, and manipulated by a person using a keyboard so that the avatar moves and interacts in virtual spaces.

Behavior legitimization: Using anonymity in virtual spaces to justify atypical actions, typically of a negative nature.

Black Mammy: The stereotypical portrayal of the overweight, unattractive, and asexual black nanny.

Blackface: The portrayal of African-American/black people by mostly white people in media.

Body image: An internalized and evaluative (positive or negative) concept about one's own body shape.

Body Image Detection Device: A research technique in which individuals manipulate three bands of light to represent their chest, waist, and hip measurements.

Bulimia: An eating disorder characterized by alternate periods of restrained eating and binging on food, which then can cause guilt, resulting in self-triggered vomiting.

Citizen journalism: Media reports filed by people who are not media professionals but are witnesses or participants in newsworthy events.

Closed question: A question that attempts to elicit a short response, such as yes or no.

Cognitive consistency: The desire to hold compatible beliefs and maintain a consistent ideology (set of beliefs).

Cognitive dissonance: Anxiety that results from simultaneously holding contradictory or incompatible beliefs or attitudes.

Collectivistic culture: A culture in which identity is based on the social system to which people belong.

Construct validity: The extent to which a particular scientific measure/scale actually measures the construct it is supposed to (e.g., intelligence).

Content analysis: An objective and systematic research method for examining certain themes or concepts within either written text or film.

Correlational analysis: A technique used to look at the statistical association between two or more factors.

Covert observation: A type of observational research in which the participants are unaware that they are being observed.

Cross-sectional research: Research studies in which the researcher examines differences between two or more populations or between two or more time points.

Cultivation Theory: A theory that posits that individuals' social reality perceptions can become distorted from regular exposure to stereotyped media representations of social phenomena (e.g., social groups, institutions, and events).

Cultural erasure: The poor representation of minority cultural identity within the media, despite increased numbers of minority characters.

Cyberstalking: Interjecting one's self into the online environment and conversations of another.

Deception: The deliberate misleading or withholding of information to participants.

Decidability: The extent to which the audience requires mental effort to process the media message.

Demand characteristics: A cue that may influence the way participants in a scientific study behave. It specifically refers to participants behaving in accordance with the experimenter's expectations of how he/she wants them to behave.

Demography: Vital and social statistics such as sex, age, race, marital status, occupation, etc.

Deindividuation: Usually preceded by anonymity, it is a state in which a person behaves without self-regard or awareness.

Desensitization: The tendency to become less aroused by stimuli (such as violent programs) after repeated exposure.

Direct learning: Learning based on the consequences (reward and punishment) of an act.

Disinhibition effects: Usually preceded by anonymity, it is a state in which a person behaves in an atypical manner and may espouse atypically extreme points of view.

Dissociative anonymity: Usually preceded by anonymity, it is a state when a person feels freed from the constraints of social boundaries and may act in a manner that is atypical in their offline lives.

Dissociative imagination: Viewing the online world as a place where rules and regulations do not apply, people may create any number of new identities, engage in role-play scenarios, and change behavioral approaches to each other at will.

Dragon Lady: The stereotypical portrayal of a strong East Asian woman.

Eating disorders: Unusual eating patterns and attitudes toward food that often result in extreme dieting behavior resulting in significant weight loss (anorexia) or a propensity after eating to engage in deliberate regurgitation of food (bulimia).

Ecological validity: A measure of how closely the study mimics a real-world setting.

Ethical guidelines: A code of ethics, which provides guidelines for ethical practice and decision-making for research.

Effect size: A measure of the magnitude of the relationship.

Elaboration Likelihood Model: A theory focusing on persuasion and the formation and development of attitudes.

Ethnicity: A group distinguishable by common social characteristics, typically designated by ingroup rather than outgroup members.

Extraneous variable: A factor that, in addition to the experimental manipulation, may influence the outcome of the study.

Extreme views: Points of view that go beyond mainstream norms or are atypical for a person to hold.

Fear appeals: Messages intended to elicit fear in an attempt to persuade the consumer to think or behave in a particular manner.

Field experiment: A research study that examines an intervention within a real-world setting.

First-person shooter: A game genre in which gameplay is centered around a weapon-based combat through the first-person perspective. That is, players experience the game through the eyes of the protagonist.

Flaming: Intense emotional responses directed toward others in virtual environments.

Flow: A positive subjective state experienced by an individual when they are undertaking an enjoyable activity.

Focus group: A form of group interview in which several people take part in a moderated discussion to give insight into a predetermined topic.

Framing: Giving audience members a way to conceptualize an issue or a context for a topic.

Gatekeeping: The selection of certain events and stories out of the innumerable events and possible topics ignoring others, allowing some information to make its way through the media funnel and reach the public, while other information does not.

Griefing: Creating annoying, even destructive, situations in virtual spaces.

Health promotion: Educational, political, regulatory, or organizational support for actions, supporting the health of individuals, groups, or communities.

Hierarchy of Effects Model: A theory proposing that consumers respond to advertising in a predictable and ordered way.

Horse race: The tendency of media and others to focus simply on who is ahead in public opinion polls during a political campaign.

Ideal body image: An internalized conception of the body shape the individual aspires to attain.

Identification: Being like another person; adopting the behaviors, attitudes, likes and dislikes, etc. of another person.

Identity: A set of personal characteristics that remain relatively the same over a period of time and by which one can be recognized by others.

Identity plasticity: The ability to change one's identity.

Implicit Association Test: A test that measures the strength of participants' automatic associations between mental concepts.

Impulsive behavior: Acting upon an idea with little or no forethought to its consequences.

Increased question-asking: A means of reducing uncertainty when informational cues about someone or something are absent.

Indirect aggression: Harmful behavior such as spreading rumors that does not involve physically attacking the victim.

Indirect learning: Learning based on observation and imitation.

Individualistic culture: A culture where people look after themselves and their immediate family only.

Infotainment: Mass media news programs that treat factual material in an entertaining manner, often by dramatizing events.

Internet: The Internet is a series of interconnected computers and related hardware and wiring. The Internet is often confused with the World Wide Web, which refers to documents and other files stored on these computers.

Inter-rater reliability: The level of agreement between two or more raters who are using the same measure to observe a behavior.

Interviewer bias: When the interviewer either consciously or unconsciously leads the interviewee to answer questions in a certain way.

Intrusiveness: The extent to which the media creates exposure without initiation by the consumer.

Invisibility: Being anonymous in virtual spaces allows people to be invisible, in that they can remain unknown and unknowable to others.

Jezebel: The portrayal of a black woman as hypersexualized and in competition with the white woman for the white man's affection.

Longitudinal research: Research that monitors a group of people over a period of time.

Marketing mix: The common marketing strategy of considering the 4Ps: product, price, place, and promotion, while planning a campaign.

Mediated reality: A skewed perception of the real world.

Mental models: Cognitive representations of situations, groups, etc.

Meta-analysis: A statistical technique that simultaneously analyzes the results of many different studies about the same topic. The data used in meta-analysis are the findings from each of the studies included in the analysis.

Minimizing authority: The notion that due to anonymity, real-world rankings of people disappear and there is a tendency to treat all other online people the same.

Moderators: Variables that alter the relationship between the independent and dependent variable.

Morbidity: The presence of ill health or disease.

Mortality: Death; a fatal outcome of an illness or injury.

Myst: An adventure videogame developed by Cyan Worlds and released in 1993. Players adopt the role of the Stranger and travel to different worlds to discover the history of the game's characters.

Negative advertising: Political advertisements that attack a political opponent or present him/her in a negative light.

Negativity bias: The tendency to give more weight to negative than to positive messages.

Neuroimaging: Various techniques that aim to either directly or indirectly image the structure of the brain.

Observational methods: Research techniques in which a number of predetermined behaviors are observed.

Open-ended question: A question that attempts to elicit a longer, more detailed answer, including experiences, ideas, feelings, and beliefs relating to the question asked.

Orientalism: The stereotypical depiction of Eastern culture. It is a Eurocentric approach to viewing and romanticizing the Arab and Islamic culture.

Othering: An exclusionary and discriminatory tactic that seeks to create a positive identity with the subject through the stigmatization of the object.

Overt observation: A type of observational research in which the participants are aware that they are being observed.

Parasocial relationship: A one-sided interpersonal relationship with a television character or celebrity.

Partisanship: An adherent or supporter of a person, group, party, or cause, especially someone who shows a biased or emotional allegiance.

Pay per click agreements: Payment based on the number of users actively clicking through to a site.

Pester power: The way in which a child attempts to persuade a parent to purchase a product.

Polling: Surveys that systematically measure the attitudes of the general public, usually involving a standardized questionnaire administered to a representative sample.

Pornography: Sexually explicit material intended to sexually arouse the viewer.

Primary audience: Those that the media seek to inform or influence.

Priming: The presentation of information that causes a readiness or predisposition in the process of processing subsequent information.

Pro-ana sites: Web sites produced for and often by sufferers of anorexia that encourage extreme eating behaviors and reinforce the idea of extreme thinness as beautiful.

Product integration: The extent to which a product is incorporated within the media.

Product placement: The inclusion of branded goods or services into media that is not recognized as an advertisement.

Profile: An individual's information file that contains as much or as little of a person's background as the person wants to reveal to others.

Propaganda: Spreading and propagating particular doctrines or principles through an organized movement or organization.

Psychographics: Characteristics such as personality, attitudes, and interests.

Public health: Organized efforts to prevent illness or disease and prolong life for members of the public.

Publication bias: The tendency to not publish research that does not find a significant effect or that finds a result contrary to existing findings.

Punditry: The giving of opinions, comments, or judgments usually by an expert or author-ity on a subject.

Qualitative methods: A research approach that uses methods, such as open-ended questionnaires or interviews, focus groups, or observational studies in order to gain a more in-depth understanding of human behavior.

Quantitative methods: A research approach that uses methods, such as experiments or forced-choice interviews and questionnaires to test a specific research hypothesis. Typically quantitative methods use a large sample and complete data analysis via statistical analysis.

Race: A group distinguishable by common physical characteristics such as skin color or facial features.

Rape myths: Prejudicial attitudes and beliefs that justify sexual violence.

Reach: The proportion of the community that will be exposed to the media message.

Reliability: The degree to which the study has accurately assessed the specific behavior that the researcher was attempting to measure.

Safeness: The extent to which the media may upset or irritate the consumer.

Salience: The extent to which a piece of information is memorable, meaningful, or readily available.

Sampling: The selection of research participants.

Sapphire: A historic stereotypical representation of the sassy, bitchy, evil, and stubborn black woman.

Scripts: Cognitive templates for guiding behavior in different situations.

Secondary audience: Those (individuals, groups, and organizations) able to influence the primary audience.

Second Life: A popular online virtual world in which members create avatars of themselves and interact with other avatars in a member-created digital community.

Segmentation: Dividing a target audience into smaller homogeneous groups based on demographics, psychographics, etc. and targeting these groups differently through their specific characteristics.

Selectivity bias: The tendency to choose to attend to information that conforms to your already existing attitudes and beliefs.

Self-disclosure: To reveal personal information about one's self. In online social communities, it is used as a means to make up for the lack of sensory cues.

Self-efficacy: The belief in one's own ability to achieve a goal or perform a behavior.

Self-esteem: Overall appraisal of one's own self-worth or value.

Self-revelatory behavior: The act of revealing or not revealing information about one's self.

Social capital: When an individual helps another, there is an expectation of assistance from that person at a later date. When one creates a large social network, one has a greater chance of obtaining needed assistance from someone in that network.

Social categorization: The construction of social groups to which people are assigned.

Social Cognitive Theory: The reformulation of Social Learning Theory (1986) that adds cognitive processes such as attention and retention to how children learn new behaviors from the media.

Social Comparison Theory: A theory that describes the propensity of individuals to compare themselves (e.g., their own body shape) with others, who may be held up as role models.

Socialization: A continuing process in which people learn about their culture, values, and behavior norms.

Social Learning Theory: A theory that uses the principles of learning (such as observation and imitation) to explain the development of behavior.

Social marketing: The use of marketing strategies for societal good.

Soft news: News that does not deal with serious topics or events.

Solipsistic introjections: In the absence of social cues, we tend to create images and identities of the person with whom we interact online, serving a psychological purpose that allows us to relate to someone according to our needs.

Sponsored programming: Corporate funding for production of a program in return for a high-profile advertisement or association with the program.

Stereotype: A generalization or simplified belief about a group of people. Stereotypes are typically shared beliefs and may be positive or negative in nature, though most often we think of stereotypes as negative.

Subliminal messages: Stimuli presented below the threshold for conscious perception.

Surveys: A research tool for gathering data on a topic by using a number of standard questions and asking participants to answer them with a series of preset responses.

Target audience: The group of people that the information is aimed at, both directly and indirectly.

Taylor Competitive Reaction Time Test: A common laboratory measure of aggressive behavior, which involves participants competing against a fictitious person to see who can respond first upon presentation of a tone. After each trial the "loser" receives a noise blast, the intensity of which is supposedly set by the opponent.

Television parental guidelines: Ratings for television shows modeled after movie ratings. TV-G: geared for all audiences; TV-Y: geared for all children; TV-Y7: geared for children seven and older; TV-Y7-FV: children seven and older plus programs contain fantasy violence; TV-PG: parental guidance suggested; TV-14: not suitable for children under fourteen years; TV-MA: mature audiences only—not suitable for those under seventeen.

Thematic analysis: A form of qualitative analysis in which the researcher identifies a number of reoccurring patterns (themes).

Triangulation: The use of multiple methodologies.

Trust formation: The process of developing trust with someone.

Uncertainty reduction: Using means, such as sensory cues, question-asking, and self-disclosure to gain information about someone until a level of trust has been achieved.

Uses and gratification perspective: The notion that audience members select media to serve predetermined purposes, such as risk assessment or confirmation beliefs.

Video games: The term "video game" is used as a generic term to include all electronic games, which can be played in arcades, on game consoles, hand-held consoles, PCs, and over the Internet.

Viral messages: The rapid exponential spread of information from person to person through digital communication mediums.

Virtual placement: The post-production addition of brands to movies or television programs.

Virtual worlds: Online places where people gather, usually through avatars, to pursue mutual interests.

Watchdog: The responsibility of the mass media and journalists to monitor the government for abuses and corruption.

Web metrics: The study of web content and usage.

Wishful identification: Wanting to be like or act like a fictional character.

Wolfenstein 3D: This is an iconic first-person shooter game, created by id Software and released in 1992. Players adopt the role of an American soldier and attempt to escape castle Wolfenstein.

References

Abernethy, A. M. (1991). "Television exposure: Programs vs advertising." *Journal of Current Issues and Research in Advertising, 13*, 61–77.

Abrams, D. & Hogg, M. (1990). "An introduction to the social identity approach." In D. Abrams and M. Hogg (eds), *Social identity theory: Constructive and critical advances* (pp. 1–9). Hertfordshire, UK: Harvester Wheatsheaf.

Agliata, D. & Tantleff-Dunn, S. (2004). "The impact of media exposure on males' body image." *Journal of Social and Clinical Psychology, 23*, 7–22.

Albert, R. S. (1996). "What the study of eminence can teach us." *Creativity Research Journal, 9*, 307–315.

Allan, K. & Coltrane, S. (1996). "Gender displaying television commercials: A comparative study of television commercials in the 1950s and 1980s." *Sex Roles, 35*, 185–203.

Allport, G. W. (1955). *Becoming: Basic considerations for a psychology of personality.* New Haven: Yale University Press.

Alperstein, N. M. (1991). "Imaginary social relationships with celebrities appearing in television commercials." *Journal of Broadcasting and Electronic Media, 35*, 43–58.

Aluja-Fabregat, A. (2000). "Personality and curiosity about TV and films violence in adolescents." *Personality and Individual Differences, 29*, 379–392.

American Heart Association (2010). "Go Red for Women: About the movement." Retrieved on October 2010 from http://www.goredforwomen.org/about_the_movement.aspx.

Ana, M. (2004). "Croatian campaign promotes lifestyle change." *Lancet, 363*, 538–539.

Anderson, C. A., Benjamin, A. J., & Bartholow, B. D. (1998). "Does the gun pull the trigger? Automatic priming effects of weapon pictures and weapon names." *Psychological Science, 9*, 308–314.

Anderson, C. A., Berkowitz, L., Donnerstein, E., Huesmann, L. R., Johnson, J., Linz, D., Malamuth, N., & Wartella, E. (2003). "The influence of media violence on youth." *Psychological Science in the Public Interest, 4*, 81–110.

Anderson, C. A. & Bushman, B. J. (2001). "Effects of violent video games on aggressive behavior, aggressive cognition, aggressive affect, physiological arousal and pro-social behavior: A meta-analytic review of the scientific literature." *Psychological Science, 12*, 353–359.

Anderson, C. A. & Bushman, B. J. (2002). "Human aggression." *Annual Review of Psychology. 53*, 27–51.

Anderson, C. A. & Carnagey, N. L. (2004). "Violent evil and the general aggression model. In A. Miller (ed.), *The social psychology of good and evil* (pp. 168–192). New York: Guilford Publications.

Anderson, C. A. & Carnagey, N. L. (2009). "Causal effects of violent sports video games on aggression: Is it competitiveness or violent content?" *Journal of Experimental Social Psychology, 45,* 731–739.

Anderson, C. A., Carnagey, N. L., & Eubanks, J. (2003). "Exposure to violent media: The effects of songs with violent lyrics on aggressive thoughts and feelings." *Journal of Personality and Social Psychology, 84,* 960–971.

Anderson, C. A., Carnagey, N. L., Flanagan, M., Benjamin, A. J., Eubanks, J., & Valentine, J. C. (2004). "Violent video games: Specific effects of violent content on aggressive thoughts and behavior." *Advances in Experimental Social Psychology, 36,* 199–249.

Anderson, C. A. & Dill, K. E. (2000). "Video games and aggressive thoughts, feelings and behavior in the laboratory and in life." *Journal of Personality and Social Psychology, 78,* 772–790.

Anderson, C. A. & Ford, C. M. (1986). "Affect of the game player: Short-term effects of highly and mildly aggressive video games." *Personality and Social Psychology Bulletin, 12,* 390–402.

Anderson, C. A., Gentile, D. A., & Buckley, K. E. (2007). *Violent video game effects on children and adolescents: Theory, research, and public policy.* New York: Oxford University Press.

Anderson, C. A. & Huesmann, L. R. (2003). "Human Aggression: A Social-Cognitive View." In M. A. Hogg & J. Cooper (2003), *The Sage handbook of social psychology* (pp. 296–323). Thousand Oaks, CA: Sage.

Anderson, C. A. & Morrow, M. (1995). "Competitive aggression without interaction effects of competitive versus cooperative instructions on aggressive behavior in video games." *Personality and Social Psychology Bulletin, 21,* 1020–1030.

Anderson, C. A. & Murphy, C. (2003). "Violent video games and aggressive behavior in young women." *Aggressive Behavior, 29,* 423–429.

Anderson, C. A., Shibuya, A., Ihori, N., Swing, E. L., Bushman, B. J., Sakamoto, A., Rothstein, H. R., & Saleem, M. (2010). "Violent video game effects on aggression, empathy, and prosocial behavior in Eastern and Western countries: A meta-analytic review." *Psychological Bulletin, 136,* 151–173.

Anderson, P., de Bruijn, A., Angus, K., Gordon R., & Hastings, G. (2009). "Impact of alcohol advertising and media exposure on adolescent alcohol use: A systematic review of longitudinal studies." *Alcohol and Alcoholism, 44,* 229–43.

Anderson, R. E., Crespo, C. J., Barlett, S. J., Cheskin, L. J., & Pratt, M. (1998). "Relationship of physical activity and television watching with body weight and level of fatness among children." *Journal of the American Medical Association, 179,* 938–942.

Andrews, J. C., Durvasala, S., & Netemeyer, R. G. (1994). "Testing the cross-national applicability of US and Russian advertising belief and attitude measures." *Journal of Advertising, 23,* 71–82.

Angell, S., Silver, L., Gail, G., Johnson, C., Deitcher, D., Frieden, T., & Bassett, M. (2009). "Cholesterol control beyond the clinic: New York City's trans fat restriction." *Annals of Internal Medicine, 151,* 129–135.

Arnett, J. J. (2001). *Adolescence and emerging adulthood: A cultural approach.* Upper Saddle River, NJ: Prentice Hall.

Arriaga, P., Esteves, F., Carneiro, P., & Monteiro, M. B. (2008). "Are the effects of unreal violent video games pronounced when playing with a Virtual Reality System? *Aggressive Behavior, 34*, 521–538.

Ashe, D. D. & McCutcheon, L. E. (2001). "Shyness, loneliness, and attitude toward celebrities." *Current Research in Psychology, 6*. Retrieved from www.uiowa.edu/~grpproc/crisp/crisp.6.9.htm.

Atkin, C., Greenberg, B., & McDermott, S. (1983). "Television and race role socialization." *Journalism Quarterly, 60*, 407–414.

Atkin, C. K. (2001). "Theory and principles of media health campaigns." In R. Rice & C. Atkin (eds), *Public communication campaigns* (3rd edn, pp. 49–68). Thousand Oaks, CA: Sage.

Atkin, D. (1991). "The evolution of television series addressing single women, 1966–1990." *Journal of Broadcasting & Electronic Media, 35*, 517–523.

Aubrey, J. S. & Harrison, K. (2004). "The gender-role content of children's favorite television programs and its links to their gender-related perceptions." *Media Psychology, 6*, 111–146.

Aucoin, D. (2010, July). "'Airbender' reopens race debate." Retrieved from http://www.boston.com/ae/movies/articles/2010/07/04/last_airbender_opens_debate_on_race/.

Augustus-Horvath, C. L. & Tylka, T. L. (2009). "A test and extension of objectification theory as it predicts disordered eating: Does women's age matter?" *Journal of Counselling Psychology, 56*, 253–65.

Axelrod, R. M. (1984). *The evolution of cooperation.* New York: Basic Books.

Bailey, J. V., Murray, E., Rait, G., Mercer, C. H., Morris, R. W., Peacock, R., Cassell, J., & Nazareth, I. (2010). "Interactive computer-based interventions for sexual health promotion." *Cochrane Database of Systematic Reviews, 9*.

Baker, L. & Gringart, E. (2009). "Body image and self-esteem in older adulthood." *Ageing & Society, 29*, 977–95.

Baker, K. & Raney, A. A. (2007). "Equally super?: Gender-role stereotyping of superheroes in children's animated programs." *Mass Communication & Society, 10*, 25–41.

Ballentine, L. W. & Ogle, J. P. (2005). "The making and unmaking of body problems in Seventeen Magazine, 1992–2003." *Family and Consumer Sciences Research Journal, 33*, 281–307.

Bandura, A. (1965). "Influence of models' reinforcement contingencies on the acquisition of imitative responses." *Journal of Personality and Social Psychology, 1*, 589–595.

Bandura, A. (1973). *Aggression: A social learning theory analysis.* Englewood Cliffs, NJ: Prentice Hall.

Bandura, A. (1977). *Social learning theory.* New York: Prentice Hall.

Bandura, A. (1986). *Social foundations of thought and action: A social cognitive theory.* Englewood Cliffs, NJ: Prentice-Hall.

Bandura, A. (2001). "Social cognitive theory of mass communication." *Media Psychology, 3*, 265–299.

Bandura, A. (2009). "Social cognitive theory of mass communication." In J. Bryant & M. B. Oliver (eds), *Media effects: Advances in theory and research*, (3rd edn, pp. 94–124). New York: Routledge.

Bandura, A., Ross, D., & Ross, S. (1963). "Imitation of film-mediated models." *Journal of Abnormal Social Psychology, 66*, 3–11.

Bandura, A. & Walters, R. H. (1963). *Social learning and personality development*. New York: Holt, Rinehart and Winston.

Bardone-Cone, A. M. & Cass, K. M. (2007). "What does viewing a pro-anorexia website do? An experimental examination of website exposure and moderating effects." *International Journal of Eating Disorders, 49*, 537–548.

Bardwell, M. D. & Choudry, I. Y. (2000). "Body dissatisfaction and eating attitudes in slimming and fitness gyms in London and Lahore: A cross-cultural study." *European Eating Disorders Review, 8*, 217–224.

Barker, M. (1997). "The Newson report: A case study in 'common sense'." In M. Barker & J. Petley (eds), *Ill effects: The media/violence debate* (pp. 12–31). London: Routledge.

Barlett, C., Harris, R., Smith, S., & Bonds-Raacke, J. (2005). "Action figures and men." *Sex Roles, 53*, 877–85.

Barner, M. R. (1999). "Sex-role stereotyping in FCC-mandated children's educational television." *Journal of Broadcasting & Electronic Media, 43*, 551–564.

Bartholow, B. D. & Anderson, C. A. (2002). "Effects of violent video games on aggressive behavior: Potential sex differences." *Journal of Experimental Social Psychology, 38*, 283–290.

Bartholow, B. D., Bushman, B. J., & Sestir, M. A. (2006). "Chronic violent video game exposure and desensitization to violence: Behavioral and event-related brain potential data." *Journal of Experimental Social Psychology, 42*, 532–539.

Bartholow, B. D., Sestir, M. A., & Davis, E. B. (2005). "Correlates and consequences of exposure to video game violence: Hostile personality, empathy and aggressive behavior." *Personality and Social Psychology Bulletin, 31*, 1573–1586.

Bartle, R. A. (2004). *Designing virtual worlds*. Berkeley, CA: New Riders.

Bartsch, R. A., Burnett, T., Diller, T. R., & Rankin-Williams, E. (2000). "Gender representation in television commercials: Updating an update." *Sex Roles, 43*, 735–743.

Basu, S. & Jones, R. (2007). "Regulating cyberstalking." *Journal of Law, Information, and Technology*. Retrieved from http://go.warwick.ac.uk/jilt/2007_2/basu_jones.

Bauman, A., Bowles, H. R., Huhman, M., Heitzler, C. D., Owen, N., Smith, B. J., & Reger-Nash, B. (2008). "Testing a Hierarchy-of-Effects Model: Pathways from Awareness to Outcomes in the VERB Campaign 2002–2003." *American Journal of Preventive Medicine, 34*, S249–S256.

Baumgartner, F. R. & Jones. B. D. (1993). *Agendas and instability in American politics*. Chicago: University of Chicago Press.

Baumgartner, J. C. & Morris, J. S. (2010). "Who wants to be my friend? Obama, youth, and social networks in the 2008 campaign." In J. A. Hendricks & R. E. Denton, Jr (eds), *Communicator-in-chief: How Barack Obama used new media technology to win the White House*. New York: Lexington.

Bazzini, D. G., McIntosh, W. D., Smith, S. M., Cook, S., & Harris, C. (1997). "The aging woman in popular film: Underrepresented, unattractive, unfriendly, and unintelligent." *Sex Roles, 36*, 531–543.

Becker, L. B. & Whitney. C. D. (1980). "Effects of media dependencies: Audience assessment of government." *Communication Research, 7*, 95–120.

Behm-Morawitz, E. & Mastro, D. E. (2008). "Mean girls? The influence of gender portrayals in teen movies on emerging adults' gender-based attitudes and beliefs." *Journalism & Mass Communication Quarterly, 85*, 131–146.

Behm-Morawitz, E. & Mastro, D. (2009). "The effects of the sexualization of female video game characters on gender stereotyping and female self-concept." *Sex Roles, 61,* 808–23.

Bennett, C. (2000). "Cassandra and the 'Sistahs': The peculiar treatment of African American women in the myth of women as liars." *Journal of Gender, Race and Justice,* 626–657.

Berelson, B., Lazerfeld, P., & McPhee, W. (1954). *Voting: A study of opinion formation in a presidential campaign.* Chicago: University of Chicago Press.

Berger, C. R. & Bradac, J. J. (1982). *Language and social knowledge.* London: Edward Arnold.

Berkowitz, L. (1989). "Frustration-aggression hypothesis: Examination and reformulation." *Psychological Bulletin, 106,* 59–73.

Berkowitz, L. (1993). *Aggression: Its causes, consequences and control.* New York: McGraw-Hill.

Berkowitz, L. & Geen, R. G. (1967). "Stimulus qualities of the target of aggression: A further study." *Journal of Personality and Social Psychology, 5,* 364–368.

Berry, G. & Mitchell-Kerman, C. (eds). (1982). *Television and the socialization of the minority child.* New York: Academic Press.

Berry, Jr, J. P. (1987). *John F. Kennedy and the media: The first television president.* Lanham: University Press of America.

Beuick, M. D. (1927). "The limited social effect of radio broadcasting." *The American Journal of Sociology, 32,* 615–622.

Billig, M. & Tajfel, H. (1973). "Social categorization and similarity in intergroup behavior." *European Journal of Social Psychology, 3,* 27–52.

Bird, S. E. (ed.). (1996). *Dressing in feathers: The construction of the Indian in popular culture.* Boulder, CO: Westview Press.

Bird, S. E. (1999). "Gendered construction of the American Indian in popular media." *Journal of Communication, 49,* 61–83.

Black, K. A., Marola, J. A., Littman, A. I., Chrisler, J. C., & Neace, W. P. (2009). "Gender and form of cereal box characters: Different medium, same disparity." *Sex Roles, 60,* 882–889.

Blond, A. (2008). "Impacts of exposure to images of ideal bodies on male body dissatisfaction: A review." *Body Image, 5,* 244–250.

Bolls, P. D. (2010). "Understanding emotion from a superordinate dimensional perspective: A productive way forward for communication processes and effects studies." *Communication Monographs, 77,* 146–152.

Bond, T. G. & Fox, C. M (2007). *Applying the Rasch model: Fundamental measurement in the human sciences* (2nd edn). Mahwah, NJ: Lawrence Erlbaum.

Boorstin, D. J. (1961). *The image.* New York: Atheneum.

Borzekowski, D., Schenk, S., Wilson, J., & Peebles, R. (2010). "e-Ana and e-Mia: A content analysis of pro-eating disorder web sites." *American Journal of Public Health, 100,* 1526–1534.

Borzekowski, D. L., Robinson, T. N., & Killen, J. D. (2000). "Does the camera add 10 pounds? Media use, perceived importance of appearance and weight concerns among teenage girls." *Journal of Adolescent Health, 26,* 36–41.

Boster, F. J. & Mongeau, P. (1984). "Fear-arousing persuasive messages." In R. N. Bostrom (ed.), *Communication yearbook 8*, (pp. 330–375). Beverly Hills, CA: Sage.

Botta, R. A. (1999). "Television images and adolescent girls' body image disturbance." *Journal of Communication, 49*, 22–41.

Botta, R. A. (2000). "The mirror of television: A comparison of black and white adolescents' body image." *Journal of Communication, 49*, 22–41.

Botta, R. A. (2003). "For your health? The relationship between magazine reading and adolescents' body image and eating disturbances." *Sex Roles, 48*, 389–99.

Bourdieu, P. & Wacquant, L. (1992). *An invitation to reflexive sociology*. Cambridge: Polity Press.

BPS code of conduct. (2009). Retrieved from http://www.bps.org.uk/sites/default/files/documents/code_of_ethics_and_conduct.pdf, Retrieved on August 4, 2011.

Braun, V. & Clarke, V. (2006). "Using thematic analysis in psychology." *Qualitative Research in Psychology, 3*, 77–101.

Brennan, I., Dubas, K. M., & Babin, L. A. (1999). "The effects of placement type and exposure time on product placement recognition." *International Journal of Advertising*, 323–38.

Bretl, D. J. & Cantor, J. (1988). "The portrayal of men and women in U.S. television commercials: A recent content analysis and trends over 15 years." *Sex-Roles, 18*, 595–609.

Broadcasters Audience Research Board. (2007). Retrieved from http//www.barb.co.uk/.

Brody, G. H., Stoneman, Z., & Sanders, A. K. (1980). "Effects of television viewing on family interactions: An observational study." *Family Relations, 29*, 216–220.

Brown, C. & Lloyd, K. (2001). "Qualitative methods in psychiatric research." *Advances in Psychiatric Treatment, 7*, 350–356.

Browne, B. A. (1998). "Gender stereotypes in advertising on children's television in the 1990s: A cross-national analysis." *Journal of Advertising, 27*, 83–96.

Browne, K. D. & Hamilton-Giachritsis, C. (2005). "The influence of violent media on children and adolescents: A public-health approach." *The Lancet, 365*, 702–710.

Brumberg, J. J. (1997). "From psychiatric syndrome to 'communicable' disease: The case of anorexia nervosa." In C. E. Rosenberg & J. Golden (eds), *Framing disease: Studies in cultural history* (pp. 134–154). Piscataway, NJ: Rutgers University Press.

Bryant, J. & Thompson, S. (2002). *Fundamentals of Media Effects*. New York: McGraw-Hill.

Bryant, Y. (2008). "Relationships between exposure to rap music videos and attitudes toward relationships among African American youth." *Journal of Black Psychology, 34*, 356–380.

Bryce, J. & Rutter, J. (2006). "Digital Games and the Violence Debate." In J. Rutter & J. Bryce (eds), *Understanding digital games* (pp. 205–222). London: Sage.

Bryman, A. (2006). "Integrating quantitative and qualitative research: How is it done?" *Qualitative Research, 6*, 97–113.

Buckley, K. E. & Anderson, C. A. (2006). "A theoretical model of the effects and consequences of playing video games." In P. Vorderer & J. Bryant (eds), *Playing video games: Motives, responses, and consequences*. Mahwah, NJ: Lawrence Erlbaum.

Buijxen, M. & Valkenburg, P. M. (2003). "The effects of television advertising on materialism, parent-child conflict, and unhappiness: A review of research." *Applied Developmental Psychology, 24*, 437–456.

Burgess, M. C. R., Stermer, S. P., & Burgess, S. R. (2007). "Sex, lies, and video games: The portrayal of male and female characters on video game covers." *Sex Roles, 57*, 419–33.

Bushman, B. J. (1995). "Moderating role of trait aggressiveness in the effects of violent media on aggression." *Journal of Personality and Social Psychology, 69*, 950–960.

Bushman, B. J. & Anderson, C. A. (2001). "Media violence and the American public: Scientific facts versus media misinformation." *American Psychologist, 56*, 477–489.

Bushman, B. J. & Anderson, C. A. (2002). "Violent video games and hostile expectations: A test of the General Aggression Model." *Personality and Social Psychology Bulletin, 28*, 1679–1686.

Bushman, B. J. & Anderson, C. A. (2009). "Comfortably numb: Desensitising effects of violent media on helping others." *Psychological Science, 20*, 273–277.

Bushman, B. J. & Huesmann, L. R. (2001). "Effects of televised violence on aggression." In D. Singer & J. Singer (eds), *Handbook of children and the media* (pp. 223–254). Thousand Oaks, CA: Sage.

Bushman, B. J. & Huesmann, L. R. (2006). "Short-term and long-term effects of violent media on aggression in children and adults." *Archives of Paediatrics and Adolescent Medicine, 160*, 348–353.

Buss, A. (1961). *The psychology of aggression*. New York: John Wiley.

Byrd-Bredbenner, C., Murray, J., & Schlussel, Y. R. (2005). "Temporal changes in anthropometric measurements of idealized females and young women in general." *Women & Health, 41*, 13–30.

Byron, T. (2008). *Safer children in a digital world: The report of the Byron Review*. Department for Children, Schools and Families, and the Department for Culture, Media and Sport: London. Available at http://www.dcsf.gov.uk/ukccis/userfiles/file/FinalReportBookmarked.pdf.

Cabiria, J. (2010). "Idle conversations: Mundane discussions that create strong social connections." (unpublished).

Cabiria, J. (2008a). "Benefits of virtual world engagement: Implications for marginalized gay and lesbian people." *The Media Psychology Review, 1*, Retrieved from http://mprcenter.org/mpr/index.php?option=com_content&view=article&id=167&Itemid=120.

Cabiria, J (2008b). "Virtual world and real world permeability: Transference of positive benefits for marginalized gay and lesbian populations." *Journal of Virtual Worlds Research, 1*, Retrieved from http://journals.tdl.org/jvwr/article/view/284.

Campbell, A., Converse, P. E., Miller, W. E., & Stokes, D. (1960). *The American voter*. New York: John Wiley.

Campbell, A., Gurin, G., & Miller, W.E. (1954). *The voter decides*. Evanston: Row, Peterson.

Campbell, R., Martin, C.R., & Fabos, B. (2009). *Media and culture: An introduction to mass communication* (6th edn). New York: Bedford/St. Martin's.

Cantor, J. (2000). "Media and children's fears, anxieties, and perceptions of danger." In D. G. Singer & J. L. Singer (eds), *Handbook of children and the media* (pp. 27–222). Thousand Oaks, California: Sage.

Cantor, J. & Nathanson, A. I. (1996). "Children's fright reactions to television news." *Journal of Communication, 46*, 139–152.

Cantor, J. & Wilson B. J. (2003). "Media and violence: Intervention strategies for reducing aggression." *Media Psychology, 5,* 363–403.

Carlson, M., Marcus-Newhall, A., & Miller, N. (1989). "Evidence for a general construct of aggression." *Personality and Social Psychology Bulletin, 15,* 377–389.

Carnagey, N. L. & Anderson, C. A. (2005). "The effects of reward and punishment in violent video games on aggressive affect, cognition and behavior." *Psychological Science, 16,* 882–889.

Carnagey, N. L., Anderson, C. A., & Bushman, B. J. (2007). "The effect of video game violence on physiological desensitisation to real-life violence." *Journal of Experimental Social Psychology, 43,* 489–496.

Cash, T. F. (1990). "The psychology of physical appearance: Aesthetics, attributes and images." In T. F. Cash & T. Pruzinsky (eds), *Body images: Development, deviance and change* (pp. 51–79). New York: Guilford Press.

Cash, T. F., Cash, D. W., & Butters, J. W. (1983). "Mirror, mirror on the wall ...? Contrast effects and self-evaluations of physical attractiveness." *Personality and Social Psychology, 9,* 359–364.

Cash, T. F. & Henry, P. E. (1995). "Women's body images: The results of a national survey in the USA." *Sex Roles, 33,* 19–28.

Cash, T. F. & Szymanski, M. L. (1995). "The development and validation of the Body-Image Ideals Questionnaire." *Journal of Personality Assessment, 64,* 466–477.

Cash, T. F., Winstead, B. A., & Janda, L. H. (1986). "The great American shape-up." *Psychology Today, 20,* 30–37.

Cattarin, J., Thompson, J. K., Thomas, C. M., & Williams, R. (2000). "Body image, mood and televised images of attractiveness: The role of social comparison." *Journal of Social and Clinical Psychology, 19,* 220–239.

Centerwall, B. S. (1989). "Exposure to television as a risk factor for violence." *American Journal of Hygiene, 129,* 643–652.

Cerf, V. G. (2010). "A Brief History of the Internet and Related Networks. Retrieved from http://www.isoc.org/internet/history/cerf.shtml. Retrieved on June 23, 2010.

Chaffee, S. H. & Frank, S. (1996). "How Americans get political information: Print versus broadcast news." *Annals of the American Academy of Political and Social Science, 546,* 48–58.

Chaffee, S. H. & Metzger, M. (2001). "The end of mass communication?" *Mass Communication and Society, 4,* 365–379.

Chaffee, S. H., Xinshu, Z., & Leshner, G. (1994). "Political knowledge and the campaign media of 1992." *Communication Research, 21,* 305–324.

Champion, H. & Furnham, A. (1999). "The effect of the media on body satisfaction in adolescent girls." *European Eating Disorders Review, 7,* 213–228.

Chappell, D., Eatough, V., Davies, M. N., & Griffiths, M. D. (2006). "EverQuest: It's just a computer game right? An interpretative phenomenological analysis of online gaming addiction" *International Journal of Mental Health Addiction, 4,* 205–216.

Chayko, M. (2002). *Connecting: How we form social bonds and communities in the internet age.* Albany, NY: SUNY Press.

Chideya, F. (1995). *Don't believe the hype: Fighting cultural misinformation about African-Americans.* New York: Plume/Penguin Books.

Children Now. (2001). *Fall colors, 2000–2001: Prime time diversity report.* Oakland, CA: Children Now.

Children Now. (2004). *Fall colors, 2003–2004: Prime time diversity report.* Oakland, CA: Children Now.

Chiles, T. H. & McMackin, J. F. (1996). "Integrating variable risk preference, trust, and transaction cost economics." *Academy of Management Review, 21,* 73–99.

Chiricos, T., Eschholz, S., & Gertz, M. (1997). "Crime, news, and fear of crime: Toward an identification of audience effects." *Social Problems, 44,* 342–357.

Choi, D. & Kim, J. (2004). "Why people continue to play online games: In search of critical design factors to increase customer loyalty to online contents." *CyberPsychology and Behavior, 7,* 11–24.

Chumbley, J. & Griffiths, M. (2006). "Affect and the computer game player: The effect of gender, personality, and game reinforcement structure on affective responses to computer game-play." *CyberPsychology and Behavior, 9,* 308–316.

Clark, C. (1969). "Television and social controls: Some observations of the portrayal of ethnic minorities." *Television Quarterly, 8,* 18–22.

Cohen, B. C. (1963). *The press and foreign policy.* Princeton: Princeton University Press.

Cole, H. & Griffiths, M. D. (2007). "Social interactions in Massively Multiplayer Online Role-Playing Gamers." *CyberPsychology and Behavior, 10,* 575–583.

Coleman, J. S. (1988). "Social capital in the creation of human capital." *The American Journal of Sociology, 94,* S95–S120.

Coleman, L. H., Paternite, C. E., & Sherman, R. C. (1999). "A reexamination of deindividuation in synchronous computer-mediated communication." *Computers in Human Behavior, 15,* 51–65.

Colwell, J. (2007). "Needs met through computer game play among adolescents. *Personality and Individual Differences, 43,* 2072–2082.

Colwell, J. & Kato, M. (2003). "Investigation of the relationship between social isolation, self-esteem, aggression and computer game play in Japanese adolescents." *Asian Journal of Social Psychology, 6,* 149–158.

Comstock, G. (1989). *The evolution of American television.* Newbury Park, CA: Sage.

Comstock, G. A. (1985). "Television and film violence." In S. Apter & A. Goldstein (eds), *Youth violence: Programs and prospects.* New York: Perhamon.

Consoli, J. (2005). "ANA Survey: 63 pct. use branded entertainment." *Brandweek,* 23 March.

Cooper, M. (1997). "Do interpretive biases maintain eating disorders?" *Behavior Research and Therapy, 35,* 619–626.

Cornell, S. & Hartmann, D. (1998). *Ethnicity and race: Making identities in a changing world.* Thousand Oaks, CA: Pine Forge.

Coyne, S. M. & Archer, J. (2004). "Indirect aggression in the media: A content analysis of British television programs." *Aggressive Behavior, 30,* 254–271.

Coyne, S. M. & Archer, J. (2005). "The relationship between indirect and physical aggression on television and in real life." *Social Development, 14,* 324–338.

Coyne, S. M., Nelson, D. A., Lawton, F., Haslam, S., Rooney, L., Titterington, I., Trainor, H., Remnant, J., & Ogunlaja, L. (2008). "The effects of viewing physical and relational aggression in the media: Evidence for a cross-over effect." *Journal of Experimental Social Psychology, 44,* 1551–1554.

Coyne, S. M. & Whitehead, E. (2008). "Indirect aggression in animated disney films." *Journal of Communication, 58,* 382–395.

Craig, C. L., Bauman, A., & Reger-Nash, B. (2009). "Testing the hierarchy of effects model: ParticipACTION's serial mass communication campaigns on physical activity in Canada. *Health Promotion International, 25,* 14–23.

Craig, R. S. (1992a). "The effect of television day part on gender portrayals in television commercials: A content analysis." *Sex Roles, 26,* 197–211.

Craig, R. S. (1992b). "Women as home caregivers: Gender portrayal in OTC drug commercials." *Journal of Drug Education, 22,* 303–312.

Crespo, C. J., Smit, E., Troiano, R. P., Bartlett, S. J., Macera, C. A., & Andersen, R. E. (2001). "Television watching, energy intake, and obesity in US children: Results from the third National Health and Nutrition Examination Survey, 1988–1994." *Archives of Pediatric & Adolescent Medicine, 155,* 360–365.

Crick, N. R. & Dodge, K. A. (1994). "A review and reformulation of social information-processing mechanisms in children's social adjustment." *Psychological Bulletin, 115,* 74–101.

Crick, N. R. & Grotpeter, J. K. (1995). "Relational aggression, gender and social-psychological adjustment." *Child Development, 66,* 710–722.

Crisp, A. H. (1992). *Anorexia nervosa: Let me be.* Hove, UK: Lawrence Erlbaum Associates.

Crisp, A. H., Palmer, R. L., & Kalucy, R. S. (1976). "How common is anorexia nervosa? A prevalence study." *British Journal of Psychiatry, 218,* 549–554.

Crook, J. (2004). "On covert communication in advertising." *Journal of Pragmatics, 36,* 715–738.

Daniel, S. & Bridges, S. K. (2010). "The drive of muscularity in men: Media influences and objectification theory." *Body Image, 7,* 32–38.

Davies, P. & Lipsey, Z. (2003). "Ana's gone surfing. *Psychologist, 16,* 424–425.

Davis, D. M. (1990). "Portrayals of women in prime-time network television: Some demographic characteristics." *Sex Roles, 23,* 325–332.

Debraganza, N. & Hausenblas, H. A. (2010). "Media exposure of the ideal physique on women's body dissatisfaction and mood: The moderating effects of ethnicity." *Journal of Black Studies, 40,* 700–16.

Delli Carpini, M. X., Keeter, S., & Webb, S. (2000). "The Impact of Presidential Debates." In P. Norris (ed.), *Politics and the press: The news media and their influences.* Boulder: Lynne Rienner.

Demare, D., Lips, H. M., & Briere, J. (1993). "Sexually violent pornography, anti-women attitudes, and sexual aggression: A structural equation model." *Journal of Research in Personality, 27,* 285–300.

De Mooij, M. (2010). *Global marketing and advertising: Understanding cultural paradoxes* (3rd edn). Thousand Oaks, CA: Sage.

Desmond, R. & Carveth, R. (2007). "The Effects of Advertising on Children and Adolescents: A Meta-Analysis." In R. W. Preiss, B. M. Gayle, N. Burrell, M. Allen, & J. Bryant. (eds), *Mass media effects research: Advances through meta-analysis* (pp. 169–180). New York: Lawrence Erlbaum.

Deutsch, M. (1993). "Educating for a peaceful world." *American Psychologist, 48*, 510–517.

Devine, P. G. & Hirt, E. R. (1989). "Message strategies for information campaigns: A social-psychological analysis." In C. Salmon (ed.), *Information campaigns: Balancing social values and social change* (pp. 229–258). Newbury Park, CA: Sage.

Dewey, J. (1899). *The school and society: being three lectures; supplemented by a statement of the University Elementary School.* Chicago: University of Chicago Press.

Dias, K. (2003). "The Ana Sanctuary: Women's pro-anorexia narratives in cyberspace." *Journal of International Women's Studies, 4*, 31–45.

Diedriche, P. C. & Lee, C. (2010). "GI Joe or Average Joe? The impact of average size and muscular male fashion models on men's and women's body image and advertisement effectiveness." *Body Image, 7*, 218–226.

Dill, K. E. & Dill, J. C. (1998). "Video game violence: A review of the empirical literature." *Aggression and Violent Behavior, 3*, 407–428.

Dill, K. E. & Thill, K. P. (2007). "Video game characters and the socialization of gender roles: Young people's perceptions mirror sexist media depictions." *Sex Roles, 57*, 851–64.

Disordered Eating (2010). "Anorexia Nervosa Statistics (UK)." Available at http://www.disordered-eating.co.uk/eating-disorders-statistics/anorexia-nervosa.

Dittmar, H., Halliwell, E., & Ive, S. (2006). "Does Barbie make girls want to be thin? The effect of experimental exposure to images of dolls on the body image of 5- to 8-year old girls." *Developmental Psychology, 42*, 283–92.

Dixon, T. L. (2006a). "Psychological reactions to crime news portrayals of Black criminals: Understanding the moderating roles of prior news viewing and stereotype endorsement." *Communication Monographs, 73*, 162–187.

Dixon, T. L. (2006b). "Schemas as average conceptions: Skin tone, television news exposure, and culpability judgments." *Journalism & Mass Communication Quarterly, 83*, 131–149.

Dixon, T. L. (2008). "Network news and racial beliefs: Exploring the connection between national television news exposure and stereotypical perceptions of African Americans." *Journal of Communication, 58*, 321–337.

Dixon, T. L., Azocar, C. L., & Casas, M. (2003). "The portrayal of race and crime on television network news." *Journal of Broadcasting & Electronic Media, 47*, 498–523.

Dixon, T. L. & Linz, D. (2000). "Overrepresentation and underrepresentation of African Americans and Latinos as lawbreakers on television news." *Journal of Communication, 50*, 131–154.

Dixon, T. L. & Linz, D. (2002). "Television news, prejudicial pretrial publicity, and the depiction of race." *Journal of Broadcasting & Electronic Media, 46*, 112–136.

Dixon, T. L. & Maddox, K. (2005). "Skin tone, crime news, and social reality judgments: Priming the stereotype of the dark and dangerous Black criminal." *Journal of Applied Social Psychology, 35*, 1555–1570.

Dixon, M., Scully, M., Wakefield, V., White, D., & Crawford, H. (2007). "The effects of television advertisements for junk food versus nutritious food on children's food attitudes and preferences." *Social Science & Medicine, 65*, 1311–1323.

Dohnt, H. & Tiggemann, M. (2006). "The contribution of peer and media influences to the development of body satisfaction and self-esteem in young girls." *Developmental Psychology, 42*, 929–936.

Dolan, B. (1989). "Cross-cultural aspects of anorexia nervosa and bulimia: A review." *International Journal of Eating Disorders, 10*, 67–78.

Dolan, D. (2003). "Learning to love anorexia? 'Pro-Ana' web sites flourish." *The New York Observer*, 2 February. Available at www.observer.com/node/47063.

Dominick, J. R. (1990). *The Dynamics of Mass Communication*. New York: McGraw Hill.

Donath, J. (1999). "Identity and deception in the virtual community." In M. Smith & P. Kollock (eds), *Communities in cyberspace* (pp. 29–59). London: Routledge.

Doob, A. & McDonald, G. E. (1979). "Viewing and the fear of victimization: Is the relationship causal?" *Journal of Personality and Social Psychology, 37*, 170–179.

Douglas, W. (1994). "The acquaintanceship process: An examination of uncertainty, information seeking, and social attraction during initial conversation." *Communication Research, 21*, 154–176.

Downing, J. & Husband, C. (2005). *Representing race: Racism, ethnicities and media.* Thousand Oaks, CA: Sage.

Downs, A. C. & Harrison, S. K. (1985). "Embarrassing age spots or just plain ugly? Physical attractiveness stereotyping as an instrument of sexism on American television commercials." *Sex Roles, 13*, 9–19.

Drabman, R. S. & Thomas, M. H. (1974). "Does media violence breed indifference?" *Journal of Communication, 25*, 86–89.

Dreze, X. & Zufryden, F. (1997). "Is internet advertising ready for prime time?" *Journal of Advertising Research, 38*, 7–18.

Druckman, J. (2001). "The implications of framing effects for citizen competence." *Political Behavior, 23*, 225–256.

Duffy, M. & Thorson, E. (2009). "Emerging trends in the new media landscape." In J. C. Parker & E. Thorson (eds), *Health communication in the new media landscape* (pp. 93–116). New York: Springer Publishing Company.

Dundes, L. (2001). "Disney's modern heroine Pocahontas: Revealing age-old gender stereotypes and role discontinuity under a facade of liberation." *The Social Science Journal, 38*, 353–365.

Durkin, K. & Aisbett, K. (1999). *Computer games and Australians today.* Sydney: Office of Film and Literature Classification.

Durkin, K. & Nugent, B. (1998). "Kindergarten children's gender-role expectations for television actors." *Sex Roles, 38*, 387–402.

Dworkin, A. & MacKinnon, C. (1988). "Pornography and civil rights: A new day for women's equality." Retrieved from www.nostatusquo.com/ACLU/dworkin/other/ordinance/newday/TOC.htm Retrieved on August 15, 2010.

Eddy, K. T., Hennessey, M., & Thompson-Brenner, H. (2007). "Eating pathology in East African women: The role of media exposure and globalization." *Journal of Nervous & Mental Disease, 195*, 196–202.

Ellison, N., Steinfield, C., & Lampe, C. (2007). "The benefits of Facebook 'friends': Social capital and college students' use of online social network sites." *Journal of Computer-Mediated Communication, 12*, 1143–1168.

Ellsworth, J. W. (1965). "Rationality and campaigning: A content analysis of the 1960 presidential campaign debates." *Western Political Quarterly, 18*, 794–802.

Entertainment and Leisure Software Publishers Association (2008). *Facts and Figures.* Retrieved from http://www.askaboutgames.com/?c=/pages/factsFigures.jsp.

Entertainment Software Association (2010). *Essential facts about the computer and video game industry.* ESA, 2010. Available at http://www.theesa.com/facts/pdfs/ESA_EF_2011.pdf.

Entman, R. (2004). *Projections of power: Framing news, public opinion, and U.S. foreign policy.* Chicago: University of Chicago Press.

Erikson, E. (1968). *Identity: Youth and crisis.* New York: Norton.

Eschholz, S., Bufkin, J., & Long, J. (2002). "Symbolic reality bites: Women & racial/ethnic minorities in modern film." *Sociological Spectrum, 22,* 299–334.

Eysenck, H. J. & Eysenck, M. W. (1985). *Personality and individual differences: A natural science approach.* New York: Plenum.

Fabrianesi, B., Jones, S. C., & Reid, A. (2008). "Are pre-adolescent girls' magazines providing age-appropriate role models?" *Health Education, 108,* 437–49.

Fallon, A. & Rozin, P. (1985). "Sex differences in perceptions of desirable body shape. *Journal of Personality and Social Psychology, 94,* 102–105.

Feick, L. & Gierl, H. (1996). "Scepticism about advertising: A comparison of East and West German consumers." *International Journal of Research in Marketing, 13,* 227–235.

Feighery, E. C., Henriksen, L., Wang, Y., Schleicher, N. C., & Fortmann, S. P. (2006). "An evaluation of four measures of adolescents' exposure to cigarette marketing in stores." *Nicotine & Tobacco Research, 8,* 751–759.

Ferguson, C. J. (2002). "Media violence: Miscast causality." *American Psychologist, 57,* 446–447.

Ferguson, C. J. (2007). "Evidence of publication bias in video game violence effects literature: A meta-analytic review." *Aggression and Violent Behavior, 12,* 470–482.

Ferguson, C. J. (2008). "The school shooting/violent game link: Causal relationship or moral panic?" *Journal of Investigative Psychology and Offender Profiling, 5,* 25–37.

Ferguson, C. J. & Kilburn, J. (2009). "The public health risks of media violence: A meta-analytic review." *The Journal of Pediatrics, 154,* 759–763.

Ferguson, C. J. & Kilburn, J. (2010). "Much ado about nothing: The misestimation and over-interpretation of violent video game effects in Eastern and Western nations: Comment on Anderson et al. (2010)." *Psychological Bulletin, 136,* 174–178.

Ferguson, C. J. & Rueda, S. M. (2009). "Examining the validity of the modified Taylor competitive reaction time test of aggression." *Journal of Experimental Criminology, 5,* 121–137.

Ferguson, C. J., Rueda, S. M., Cruz, A. M., Ferguson, D. E., Fritz, S., & Smith, S. M. (2008a). "Violent video games and aggression: Causal relationships or by-product of family violence and intrinsic violence motivation?" *Criminal Justice and Behavior, 35,* 311–332.

Ferguson, C. J., Smith, S., Miller-Stratton, H., Fritz, S., & Heinrich, E. (2008b). "Aggression in the laboratory: Problems with the validity of the Modified Taylor Competitive Reaction Time test as a measure of aggression in media violence studies." *Journal of Aggression, Maltreatment and Trauma, 17,* 118–132.

Feshbach, N. D. (2005). "Gender and the portrayal of direct and indirect aggression on television." In E. Cole & J. H. Daniel (eds), *Featuring females: Feminist analyses of media* (pp. 155–165). Washington, DC: American Psychological Association.

Festinger, L. (1954). "A theory of social comparison processes." *Human Relations, 7,* 117–140.

Festinger, L., Pepitone, A., & Newcomb, T. (1952). "Some consequences of de-individuation in a group." *Journal of Abnormal and Social Psychology, 47,* 382–389.

Fiorina, M. P. (2004). *Culture war? The myth of a polarized America.* New York: Longman.

Fischer, E. & Halpenny, K. (1993). "The nature of influence of idealised images of men in advertising." In J. A. Costa (ed.), Gender and Consumer Behavior: Proceedings of the Second Conference (p. 196). Salt Lake City, UT: University of Utah Printing Services.

Fischer, P., Kastenmuller, A., & Greitemeyer, T. (2010). "Media violence and the self: The impact of personalized gaming characters in aggressive video games on aggressive behavior." *Journal of Experimental Social Psychology, 46,* 192–195.

Fischoff, S. (2005). "Media Psychology: A Personal Essay in Definition and Purview." Retrieved from http://www.apa.org/divisions/div46/images/MEDIADEF.pdf.

Fishbein, M. & Ajzen, I. (2010). *Predicting and changing behavior: The reasoned action approach.* New York: Taylor & Francis.

Fishman, M. (1978). "Crime waves as ideology." *Social Problems, 25,* 531–543.

Fleming, K., Thorson, E., & Atkin, C. K. (2004). "Alcohol advertising exposure and perceptions: Links with alcohol expectancies and intentions to drink or drinking in underaged youth and young adults." *Journal of Health Communication, 9,* 3–29.

Folta, S. C., Goldberg, J. P., Economos, C., Bell, R., & Meltzer, R. (2006). "Food advertising targeted at school-age children: A content analysis." *Journal of Nutrition Education and Behavior, 38,* 244–248.

Food Standards Agency (2003). "Does Food Promotion Influence Children? A Systematic Review of the Evidence." Available from: http://www.food.gov.uk/multimedia/pdfs/promofoodchildrenexec.pdf.

Ford, T. (1997). "Effects of stereotypical television portrayals of African-Americans on person perception." *Social Psychology Quarterly, 11,* 155–169.

Francis, L. A., Lee, Y., & Birch, L. L. (2003). "Parental weight status and girls' television viewing, snacking and body mass indexes." *Obesity Research, 11,* 143–152.

Frankovic, K.A. (1998). "Public Opinion and Polling." In D. A. Graber, D. McQuail, & P. Norris (eds), *The politics of news, the news of politics.* Washington, DC: CQ Press.

Fujioka, Y., Ryan, E., Agle, M., Legaspi, M., & Toohey, R. (2009). "The role of racial identity in responses to thin media ideals: Differences between White and Black college women." *Communication Research, 36,* 451–74.

Furnham, A. & Mak, T. (1999). "Sex-role stereotyping in television commercials: A review and comparison of fourteen studies done on five continents over 25 years." *Sex Roles, 41,* 413–437.

Furnham, A., Mak, T., & Tanidjojo, L. (2000). "An Asian perspective on the portrayal of men and women in television advertisements: Studies from Hong Kong and Indonesian television." *Journal of Applied Social Psychology, 30,* 2341–2364.

Furnham, A. & Paltzer, S. (2010). "The portrayal of men and women in television advertisements: An updated review of 30 studies published since 2000." *Scandinavian Journal of Psychology, 51,* 216–236.

Galen, B. R. & Underwood, M. K. (1997). "A developmental investigation of social aggression among children." *Developmental Psychology, 33,* 589–600.

Ganahl, D. J., Prinsen, T. J., & Netzley, S. B. (2003). "A content analysis of prime time commercials: A contextual framework of gender representation." *Sex Roles, 49,* 546–551.

Garvin, A. W. & Damson, C. (2008). "The effects of idealized fitness images on anxiety, depression and global mood states in college age males and females." *Journal of Health Psychology, 13,* 433–37.

Gauntlett, D. (1995). *Moving experiences: Understanding television's influences and effects.* London: John Libbey.

Gentile, D. A. (2003). *Media violence and children.* Westport, CT: Praeger.

Gentile, D. A. (2009). "Pathological video-game use among youth ages 8 to 18: A National Study." *Psychological Science, 20,* 594–602.

Gentile, D. A., Lynch, P. J., Linder, J. R., & Walsh, D. A. (2004). "The effects of violent video game habits on adolescent hostility, aggressive behaviors, and school performance." *Journal of Adolescence, 27,* 5–22.

Gerber, A. S., Karlan, D., & Bergan, D. (2007). "Does the media matter? A field experiment measuring the effect of newspapers on voting behavior and political opinions." *Applied Economics, 1,* 35–52.

Gerbner, G. (1990). "Epilogue: Advancing in the path of righteousness (maybe)." In N. Signorielli & M. Morgan, (eds), *Cultivation analysis: New directions in media effects research* (pp. 249–262). Newbury Park, CA: Sage.

Gerbner, G. (1993). *Violence in cable-originated television programs.* Philadelphia, PA: The Annenberg School for Communication.

Gerbner, G. (1994). "Growing up with television: The cultivation perspective." In J. Bryant & D. Zillmann (eds), *Media effects: Advances in theory and research* (pp. 17–41). Hillsdale, NJ: Lawrence Erlbaum.

Gerbner, G. & Gross, L. (1980). "The violent face of television and its lessons." In E. L. Palmer & A. Dorr (eds), *Children and the faces of television: Teaching, violence, selling* (pp. 149–162). New York: Academic Press.

Gerbner, G., Gross, L. K., Morgan, M., & Signorielli, N. (1980). "The 'mainstreaming' of America: Violence profile No. 11." *Journal of Communication, 30,* 10–29.

Gerbner, G., Morgan, M., Gross, L., Signorielli, N., & Shanahan, J. (2002). "Growing up with television: Cultivation processes." In J. Bryant & D. Zillmann (eds), *Media Effects: Advances in theory and research* (2nd edn). Hillsdale, NJ: Lawrence Erlbaum.

Gerbner, G. & Signorielli, N. (1979). *Women and minorities in television drama, 1969–1978.* Philadelphia, PA: University of Pennsylvania, The Annenberg School of Communication.

Geuens, M., De Pelsmacker, P., & Faseur, T. (2011). "Emotional advertising: Revisiting the role of product category." *Journal of Business Research, 64,* 418–426.

Giles, D. (2006). "Constructing identities in cyberspace: The case of eating disorders." *British Journal of Social Psychology, 45,* 463–477.

Giles, D. C. (2000). *Illusions of immortality: A psychology of fame and celebrity.* London: Macmillan.

Gitlin, T. (1980). *The Whole World is Watching.* Berkeley: University of California Press.

Glascock, J. (2003). "Gender, race, and aggression in newer TV networks' primetime programming." *Communication Quarterly, 51,* 90–100.

Goffman, E. (1959). *The presentation of self in everyday life.* Garden City, NY: Doubleday Anchor.

Golman, D. (2007, February). "Flame First, Think Later: New Clues to E-Mail Misbehavior." *The New York Times,* Retrieved from http://www.nytimes.com/2007/02/20/health/psychology/20essa.html Retrieved on May 31, 2010.

Golombok, S. & Fivush, R. (1994). *Gender development.* New York: Cambridge University Press.

Gong, W. & Maddox, L. (2003). "Measuring Web advertising effectiveness in China." *Journal of Advertising Research, 43,* 34–49.

Gonzalez-Levin, A. & Smolak, L. (1995). *Relationships between television and eating problems in middle school girls.* Paper presented at the meeting of the Society for Research in Child Development, Indianapolis, IN.

Gordon, M. T. & Heath, L. (1981). "The news business, crime, and fear." In D. Lewis (ed.), *Reactions to crime* (pp. 227–250). Beverly Hills, CA: Sage.

Gorsky, M., Krajewski-Siuda, K., Dutka, W., & Verridge, V. (2010). "Anti-alcohol posters in Poland, 1945–1989: Diverse meanings, uncertain effects." *American Journal of Public Health, 100,* 2059–2069.

Grabe, M. E. & Kamhawi, R. (2006). "Hard wired for negative news? Gender differences in processing broadcast news." *Communication Research, 33,* 346–369.

Graber, D. A. (2010). *Mass media and American politics* (8th edn). Washington, DC: CQ Press.

Graber, D. A. & Holyk, G. G. (2011). "The News Industry." In R. Y. Shapiro, L. R. Jacobs, & G. C. Edwards (eds), *The Oxford handbook of American public opinion and the media.* New York: Oxford University Press.

Graber, D. A. & Holyk, G. G. Holyk. (forthcoming). "Civic Knowledge and Audiovisual Learning." In Holli Semetko (ed.), *The Sage handbook of visual learning.* Thousand Oaks, CA: Sage.

Graber, D. A., McQuail, D., & Norris, P. (eds). (1998). *The politics of news, the news of politics.* Washington, DC: CQ Press.

Granovetter, M. (1973). "The strength of weak ties." *American Journal of Sociology, 78,* 1360–1380.

Granovetter, M. S. (1983). "The strength of weak ties: A network theory revisited." *Sociological Theory, 1,* 201–233.

Green, C. S. & Bavelier, D. (2003). "Action video game modifies visual selective attention." *Nature, 423,* 534–537.

Greenberg, B. S. & Brand, J. E. (1993). "Television news and advertising in schools: The 'Channel One' controversy." *Journal of Communication, 43,* 143–151.

Greenberg, B. S., Mastro, D., & Brand, J. E. (2002). "Minorities and the mass media: Television into the 21st century." In J. Bryant & D. Zillmann (eds), *Media effects: Advances in theory and research* (2nd edn, pp. 333–351). Mahwah, NJ: Lawrence Erlbaum.

Greenberg, B. S. & Worrell, T. R. (2007). "New faces on television: A 12-season replication." *The Howard Journal of Communications, 18,* 277–290.

Greene, A. L. & Adams-Price, C. (1990). "Adolescents' secondary attachment to celebrity figures." *Sex Roles, 23,* 335–347.

Greene, K., Krcmar, M., Rubin, D. I., Walters, L. H., & Hale, J. L. (2002). "Elaboration in processing adolescent health messages: The impact of egocentrism and sensation seeking on message processing." *Journal of Communication, 52*, 812–831.

Greenwald, A. G., Banaji, M. R., Rudman, L. A., Farnham, S. D., Nosek, B. A., & Mellott, D. S. (2002). "A unified theory of implicit attitudes, stereotypes, self-esteem, and self-concept." *Psychological Review, 109*, 3–25.

Greenwood, D. N. (2007). "Are female action heroes risky role models: Character identification, idealization and viewer aggression." *Sex Roles, 57*, 725–732.

Greitemeyer, T. (2011). "Exposure to music with prosocial lyrics reduces aggression: First evidence and test of the underlying mechanism." *Journal of Experimental Social Psychology, 47*, 28–36.

Griffiths, J. A. & McCabe, M. P. (2000). "The influence of significant others on disordered eating and body dissatisfaction among early adolescent girls." *European Eating Disorders Review, 8*, 301–314.

Griffiths, M. D. (2008). "Video game addiction: Further thoughts and observations." *International Journal of Mental Health Addiction, 6*, 182–185.

Griffiths, M. D., Davies, M. N. O., & Chappell, D. (2003). "Breaking the stereotype: The case of online gaming." *CyberPsychology and Behavior, 6*, 81–91.

Groebel, J. (1998). "Media violence and children." *Educational Media International, 35*, 216–227.

Groebel, J. (2001). "Media violence in cross-cultural perspective: A global study on children's media behavior and some educational implications." In D. G. Singer & J. L. Singer (eds), *Handbook of children and the media* (pp. 255–268). Thousand Oaks, CA: Sage.

Grogan, S. (1999). *Body image: Understanding body dissatisfaction in men, women and children.* London: Routledge.

Grogan, S. (2008). *Body image: Understanding body dissatisfaction in men, women and children* (2nd edn). London: Routledge.

Grogan, S. & Richards, H. (2002). "Body image: Focus groups with boys and men." *Men and Masculinities, 4*, 219–292.

Grube, J. & Waiters, E. (2005). "Alcohol in the media: Content and effects on drinking beliefs and behaviors among youth." *Adolescent Medicine Clinics, 16*, 327–43.

Guillen, T. (2002). "Serial killer communiqués: Helpful or hurtful?" *Journal of Criminal Justice & Popular Culture, 9*, 2.

Gulati, G. J. (2010). "No Laughing Matter: The Role of the New Media in the 2008 Election." In L. J. Sabato (ed.), *The year of Obama: How Barack Obama won the White House* (pp. 187–204). New York: Longman.

Gunter, B. (1987). *Poor reception: Misunderstanding and forgetting broadcast news.* Hillsdale: Lawrence Erlbaum.

Gunter, B. & Furnham, A. (1998). *Children as consumers: A psychological analysis of the young people's market.* London: Routledge.

Gupta, P. B. & Gould, S. J. (1997). "Consumers' perceptions of the ethics and acceptability of product placements in movies: Product category and individual differences." *Journal of Current Issues and Research in Advertising, 19*, 42.

Habermas, J. (1989). *The structural transformation of the public sphere: An inquiry into a category of bourgeois society*. Translated by Thomas Burger. Cambridge: MIT Press.

Halford, J. C. G., Gillespie, J., Brown, V., Pontin, E. E., & Dovey, T. M. (2004). "Effect of television advertisements for foods on food consumption in children." *Appetite, 42,* 221–225.

Halimi, S. (1998). "Blood and celebrity." *Le Monde Diplomatique*. Reprinted in *World Press Review*, 1998, 30–31.

Hamilton, K. & Waller, G. (1993). "Media influences on body size estimation in anorexia and bulimia: An experimental study." *British Journal of Psychiatry, 162,* 837–840.

Hancox, R. J., Milne, B. J., & Poulton, R. (2004). "Association between child and adolescent television viewing and adult health: A longitudinal birth cohort study." *Lancet. 364,* 257–62.

"Hands-Only CPR" (2009). Ad Council. Retrieved from http://www.adcouncil.org/default. aspx?id=618 Retrieved on August 4, 2011.

Harmatz, M. G., Gronendyke, J., & Thomas, T. (1985). "The underweight male: The unrecognised problem group in body image research." *Journal of Obesity and Weight Regulation, 4,* 258–267.

Harris, R. J. (1999). *A cognitive psychology of mass communication* (3rd edn). Mahwah, NJ: Lawrence Erlbaum.

Harris , R. J. (2004). *A cognitive psychology of mass communication* (4th edn). Mahwah, NJ: Lawrence Erlbaum.

Harrison, K. (1997). "Does interpersonal attraction to thin media personalities promote eating disorders?" *Journal of Broadcasting and Electronic Media, 41,* 478–500.

Harrison, K. (2000a). "Television viewing, fat stereotyping, body shape standards, and eating disorder symptomatology in grade school children." *Communication Research, 27,* 617–640.

Harrison, K. (2000b). "The body electric: Thin-ideal media and eating disorders in adolescents." *Journal of Communication, 50,* 119–143.

Harrison, K. & Cantor, J. (1997). "The relationship between media consumption and eating disorders." *Journal of Communication, 47,* 40–67.

Harrison, K. & Cantor, J. (1999). "Tales from the screen: Enduring fright reactions to scary media." *Media Psychology, 1,* 97–116.

Head, S. (1954). "Content analysis of television drama programs." *Quarterly of Film, Radio, and Television, 9,* 175–194.

Hearold, S. (1986). "A synthesis of 1043 effects of television on social behavior." In G. Comstock (ed.), *Public Communication and Behavior, 1* (pp. 65–133). Orlando, FL: Academic Press.

Heath, L. (1984). "Impact of newspaper crime reports on fear of crime: Multi-methodological investigation." *Journal of Personality and Social Psychology, 47,* 263–276.

Heath, L., Gordon, M. T., & LeBailly, R. (1981). "What newspapers tell us (and don't tell us) about rape." *Newspaper Research Journal, 2,* 48–55.

Heath, L., Kavanagh, J., & Thompson, R. (2001). "Perceived vulnerability and fear of crime: Why fear stays high when crime rates drop." *Journal of Offender Rehabilitation, 33,* 1–14.

Heath, L. & Petraitis, J. (1987). "Television viewing and fear of crime: Where is the scary world?" *Basic and Applied Social Psychology, 8,* 97–123.

Heinberg, L. J. & Thompson, J. K. (1992a). "The effects of figure size feedback (positive vs negative) and target comparison group (particularistic vs universalistic) on body image disturbance." *International Journal of Eating Disorders, 12*, 441–448.

Heinberg, L. J. & Thompson, J. K. (1992b). "Social comparison: Gender, target importance ratings and relation to body image disturbance." *Journal of Social Behavior and Personality, 7*, 335–344.

Heinberg, L. J. & Thompson, J. K. (1995). "Body image and televised images of thinness and attractiveness: A controlled laboratory investigation." *Journal of Social and Clinical Psychology, 14*, 325–338.

Helliwell, J. F. K. & Putnam, R. D. K. (2004). "The social context of well-being. *Philosophical Transactions of the Royal Society. Biological Sciences, 359*, 1435–1446.

Hendricks, J. A. & Denton, R. E. Jr. (eds). (2010). *Communicator-in-chief: How Barack Obama used new media technology to win the White House.* Lanham: Lexington Books.

Hennigan, K., del Rosario, M., Heath, L., Cook, T., Wharton, J., & Calder, B. (1982). "Impact of the introduction of crime in the United States: Empirical findings and theoretical implications." *Journal of Personality and Social Psychology, 42*, 461–477.

Henwood, K., Gill, R., & McLean, C. (1999). "Masculinities and the body: Mapping men's psychologies." End of grant report to Unilever Research. Norwich, University of East Anglia, School of Medicine, Health Policy and Practice.

Henwood, K., Gill, R., & McLean, C. (2002). "The changing man." *The Psychologist, 15*, 182–186.

Herr, P. M., Kardes, F. R., & Kim, J. (1991). "Effects of word-of-mouth and product-attribute information on persuasion: An accessibility-diagnosticity perspective." *The Journal of Consumer Research, 17*, 454–462.

Herrett-Skjellum, J. & Allen, M. (1996). "Television programming and sex stereotyping: A meta-analysis." In B. R. Burleson (ed.), *Communication yearbook 19* (pp. 157–185), Thousand Oaks, CA: Sage.

Hill, K. A. & Hughes, J. E. (1998). *Cyberpolitics: Citizen activism in the age of the Internet.* Lanham: Rowan & Littlefield.

Ho, S. M. Y. & Lee, T. M. C. (2001). "Computer usage and its relationship with adolescent lifestyle in Hong Kong". *Journal of Adolescent Health, 29*, 258–266.

Hoekstra, S. J., Harris, R. J., & Helmick, A. L. (1999). "Autobiographical memories about the experience of seeing frightening movies in childhood." *Media Psychology, 1*, 117–140.

Hoffner, C. (1996). "Children's wishful identification and parasocial interaction with favorite television characters." *Journal of Broadcasting & Electronic Media, 40*, 389–402.

Hoffner, C. A., Levine, K. J., & Toohey, R. A., (2008). "Socialization to work in late adolescence: The role of television and family." *Journal of Broadcasting & Electronic Media, 52*, 282–302.

Hogben, M. (1998). "Factors moderating the effect of television aggression on viewer behavior." *Communication Research, 25*, 220–247.

Hopf, W. H., Huber, G. L., & Weiß, R. H. (2008). "Media violence and youth violence: A two-year longitudinal study." *Journal of Media Psychology, 20*, 79–96.

Hornik, R. (2002a). "Public health communication: Making sense of contradictory evidence." In R. Hornik (ed.), *Public health communication: Evidence for behavior change* (pp. 1–19). Mahwah, NJ: Lawrence Erlbaum.

Hornik, R. (2002b). "Epilogue: Evaluation design for public health communication programs." In R. Hornik (ed.), *Public health communication: Evidence for behavior change* (pp. 385–405). Mahwah, NJ: Lawrence Erlbaum.

Houck, M. M. (2006). "CSI: Reality." *Scientific American, 295,* 84–89.

Hoving, C., Visser, A., Mullen, P. D., & van den Borne, B. (2010). "A history of patient education by health professionals in Europe and North America: From authority to shared decision making education." *Patient Education and Counseling, 78,* 275–281.

Howard, P. N. (2006). *New media campaigns and the managed citizen.* New York: Cambridge University Press.

Hudson, S. V. (1998). "Re-creational television: The paradox of change and continuity within stereotypical iconography." *Sociological Inquiry, 68,* 242–257.

Huesmann, L. R. (1986). "Psychological processes promoting the relation between exposure to media violence and aggressive behavior by the viewer." *Journal of Social Issues, 42,* 125–139.

Huesmann, L. R. (1998). "The role of social information processing and cognitive schema in the acquisition and maintenance of habitual aggressive behavior." In R. G. Geen & E. Donnerstein (eds), *Human Aggression: Theories, research and implication for social policy* (pp. 73–109). San Diego, CA: Academic Press.

Huesmann, L. R. & Eron, L. D. (eds). (1986). *Television and the aggressive child: A cross-national comparison.* Hillsdale, NJ: Lawrence Erlbaum.

Huesmann, L. R., Moise-Titus, J., Podolski, C., & Eron, L. D. (2003). "Longitudinal relations between children's exposure to TV violence and their aggressive and violent behavior in young adulthood: 1977–1992." *Developmental Psychology, 39,* 201–221.

Ihori, N., Sakamoto, A., Shibuya, A., & Yukawa, S. (2007). *Effect of video games on children's aggressive behavior and pro-social behavior: A panel study with elementary school students.* Situated Play, Proceedings of DiGRA 2007 Conference.

Iiyama, P. & Kitano, H. H. L. (1982). "Asian-Americans and the media." In G. L. Berry & C. Kitchell-Kernas (eds), *Television and the socialization of the minority child* (pp. 151–186). New York: Academic Press.

IMHI (1997). "Women's work: Will it ever be done?" *Dialogue, 5,* 1–4.

Institute of Medicine. (1989). *Speaking of health: Assessing health communication strategies for diverse populations.* Washington, DC: The National Academies Press.

Irving, L. (1990). "Mirror images: Effects of the standard of beauty on the self and body esteem of women exhibiting varying levels of bulimic symptoms." *Journal of Social and Clinical Psychology, 9,* 230–242.

Iyengar, S. (1991). *Is anyone responsible? How television frames political issues.* Chicago: University of Chicago Press.

Iyengar, S. & Kinder, D. R. (1987). *News that matters: Television and American opinion.* Chicago: University of Chicago Press.

Jackman, L. P., Williamson, D. A., Netemeyer, R. G., & Anderson, D. A. (1995). "Do weight preoccupied women misinterpret ambiguous stimuli related to body size?" *Cognitive Therapy and Research, 19,* 341–355.

Jackson-Beeck, M. (1977). "The non-viewers: Who are they?" *Journal of Communication, 27,* 65–72.

Jacobs, L. & Shapiro, R. (2000). *Politicians don't pander: Political manipulation and the loss of democratic responsiveness.* Chicago: University of Chicago Press.

Jamieson, K. H. & Campbell, K. K. (1992). *The interplay of influence: News, advertising, politics, and the mass media* (3rd edn). Belmont, CA: Wadsworth.

Jansz, J. & Tanis, M. (2007). "Appeal of playing online First Person Shooter games." *CyberPsychology and Behavior, 10,* 133–136.

Jeon, J. O. & Beatty, S. E. (2002). "Comparative advertising effectiveness in different national cultures." *Journal of Business Research, 55,* 907–913.

Jewell, S. K. (1993). *From mammy to Miss America and beyond: Cultural images and the shaping of US social policy.* London: Routledge.

Jhally, S. & Lewis, J. (2007). "Enlightened racism: The Cosby Show, audiences and the myth of the American dream." In W. Brooker & D. Jermyn (eds), *The audience studies reader* (pp. 279–286). New York: Routledge.

Johnson, C. & Connors, M. E. (1987). *The etiology and treatment of bulimia nervosa: A biopsychosocial perspective.* New York: Basic Books.

Johnson, J. G., Cohen, P., Smailes, E. M., Kasen, S., & Brook, J. S. (2002). "Television viewing and aggressive behavior during adolescence and adulthood. *Science, 295,* 2468–2472.

Joinson, A. (1998). "Causes and implications of disinhibited behavior on the Internet." In J. Gackenbach (ed.), *Psychology and the Internet* (pp. 43–60). San Diego, CA: Academic Press.

Joinson, A. (2003). *Understanding the psychology of internet behavior: Virtual worlds, real lives.* Basingstoke: Palgrave Macmillan.

Joinson, A. N. (1999). "Anonymity, disinhibition, and social desirability on the Internet." *Behavior Research Methods, Instruments and Computers, 31,* 433–438.

Joinson, A. N. (2001a). "Self-disclosure in computer-mediated communication: The role of self-awareness and visual anonymity." *European Journal of Social Psychology, 31,* 177–192.

Joinson, A. N. (2001b). "Knowing me, knowing you: Reciprocal self-disclosure on the Internet." *CyberPsychology and Behavior, 4,* 587–591.

Joinson, A. N. & Paine, C. B. (2007). "Self-disclosure, privacy and the Internet." In A. N. Joinson, K. Y. A. McKenna, T. Postmes, & U-D. Reips (eds), *Oxford handbook of internet psychology* (pp. 237–252). Oxford: Oxford University Press.

Joint Statement. (2000). "Joint statement on the impact on entertainment violence on children." Retrieved from http://www.aap.org/advocacy/releases/jstmtevc.htm Retrieved on August 4, 2011.

Joy, L. A., Kimball, M. M., & Zabrack, M. L. (1986). "Television and children's aggressive behavior." In T. Williams (ed.), *The impact of television* (pp. 303–360). Orlando, FL: Academic Press.

Jung, C. G. (1946). *Psychological types or the psychology of individuation.* New York: Harcourt, Brace.

Jung, C. G. (1948). *The undiscovered self.* London: Routledge & Kegan Paul.

Kafia, Y. B. (1996). "Gender differences in children's constructions of video games." In P. M. Greenfield & R. R. Cocking (eds), *Interacting with video* (pp. 39–66). Norwood, NJ: Ablex.

Kaiser, U. & Song, M. (2009). "Do media consumers really dislike advertising? An empirical assessment of the role of advertising in print media markets." *International Journal of Industrial Organization, 27*, 292–301.

Kaplan, E. A. (2008, June 24). *Who's afraid of Michelle Obama?* Retrieved from http://www.salon.com/life/feature/2008/06/24/michelle_obama/index.html Retrieved on August 4, 2011.

Karremans, J. C., Stroebe, W., & Claus, J. (2006). "Beyond Vicary's fantasies: The impact of subliminal priming and brand choice." *Journal of Experimental Social Psychology, 42*, 792–798.

Karrh, J. A. (1998). "Brand placement: A review." *Journal of Current Issues and Research in Advertising, 20*, 31–49.

Karrh, J. A., Brittain McKee, K., & Pardun, C. J. (2003). "Practitioners' evolving views on product placement effectiveness." *Journal of Advertising Research, 43*, 138–49.

Katz, E. (1957). "The two-step flow of communication: An up-to-date report on a hypothesis." *Public Opinion Quarterly, 21*, 61–78.

Katz, J. & Aspden, P. (1997). "A nation of strangers?" *Communications of the Association for Computing Machinery, 40*, 81–86.

Kaye, L. K. & Bryce, J. (under review). Putting the "fun factor" into gaming: The influence of social contexts on experiences of playing videogames."

Keck, K. (2010). "Latinos not flexing political muscle – yet." Retrieved from http://articles.cnn.com/2010-07-05/politics/latino.vote_1_latino-turnout-latino-politics-william-c-velasquez-instititute?_s=PM:POLITICS Retrieved on August 4, 2011.

Kelly, J., St. Lawrence, J. S., Diaz, Y. E., Stevenson, L. Y., Hauth, A. C., Brasfield, T. L., Kalichman, S. S., Smith, J. E., & Andrew, M. E. (1991). "HIV risk behavior reduction following intervention with key opinion leaders of population: An experimental analysis." *American Journal of Public Health, 81*, 168–171.

Kenski, K., Hardy, B. W., & Jamieson, K. H. (2010). *The Obama victory: How media, money, and message shaped the 2008 election.* New York: Oxford University Press.

Key, B. W. (1994). *Subliminal seduction.* New York: New American Library.

Kiewitz, C. & Weaver, J. B. (2001). "Trait aggressiveness, media violence, and perceptions of interpersonal conflict." *Personality and Individual Differences, 31*, 821–835.

Kim, Y. & Ross, S. D. (2006). "An exploration of motives in sport video gaming." *International Journal of Sports Marketing and Sponsorship, 8*, 34–46.

Kimball, M. M. (1986). "Television and sex-role attitudes." In T. M. Williams (ed.), *The impact of television: A natural experiment in three communities* (pp. 265–301). New York: Academic Press.

King, C. (2000). "Effects of humorous heroes and villains in violent action films." *Journal of Communication, 7*, 33–47.

King, D. & Delfabbro, P. (2009). "Understanding and assisting excessive players of video games." *The Australian Community Psychologist, 21*, 62–74.

Kitzinger, J. (1995). "Qualitative Research: Introducing focus groups." *British Medicine Journal, 311*, 299–302.

Klapp, O. E. (1962). *Heroes, villains, and fools.* Englewood Cliffs, NJ: Prentice-Hall.

Klapper, J. T. (1960). *The effects of mass communication.* New York: Free Press.

Kleinnijenhuis, J. (1991). "Newspaper complexity and the knowledge gap." *European Journal of Communication, 6*, 499–522.

Klimmt, C., Hartmann, T., & Frey, A. (2007). "Effectance and control as determinants of video game enjoyment." *CyberPsychology and Behavior, 10*, 845–848.

Ko, D. M. & Kim, H. S. (2010). "Message framing and defensive processing: A cultural examination." *Health Communication, 25*, 61–68.

Koo, D. (2009). "The moderating role of locus of control on the links between experiential motives and intention to play online games." *Computers in Human Behavior, 25*, 466–474.

Korgaonkar, P. & Wolin, L. (2002). "Web usage, advertising, and shopping: Relationship patterns." *Internet Research: Electronic Networking Applications and Policy, 12*, 191–204.

Kotler, P. & Lee, N. (2008). *Social marketing: Influencing behaviors for good* (3rd edn). Thousand Oaks, CA: Sage.

Krahé, B. & Möller, I. (2004). "Playing violent electronic games, hostile attribution style, and aggressive-related norms in German adolescents." *Journal of Adolescence, 27*, 53–69.

Krahé, B. & Möller, I. (2011). "Links between self-reported media violence exposure and teacher ratings of aggression and prosocial behavior among German adolescents." *Journal of Adolescence, 34*, 279–87.

Kraut, R., Kiesler, S., Boneva, B., Cummings, J., Helgeson, V., & Crawford, A. (2002). "Internet paradox revisited." *Journal of Social Issues, 58*, 49–74.

Kraut, R., Patterson, M., Landmark, V., Kiesler, S., Mukophadhyay, T., & Scherlis, W. (1998). "Internet paradox: a social technology that reduces social involvement and psychological well being?" *American Psychologist, 53*, 1017–1031.

Kreps, G. & Thornton, B. (1992). *Health Communication: Theory & Practice* (2nd edn). Long Grove, IL: Waveland Press.

Kreuter, D., Farell, D., Olevitch, L., & Brennan, L. (2000). *Tailoring health messages: Customizing communication with computer technology.* Mahwah, NJ: Lawrence Erlbaum.

Krippendorff, K. (2004). *Content analysis: An introduction to its methodology.* Thousand Oaks, CA: Sage.

Kubey, R. (1998). "Obstacles to the development of media education in the United States." *Journal of Communication, 48*, 58–70.

Kubey, R., Shifflet, M., Weerakkody, N., & Ukeiley, S. (1995). "Demographic diversity on cable: Have the new cable channels made a difference in the representation of gender race and age?" *Journal of Broadcasting & Electronic Media, 39*, 459–471.

Lagerspetz, K., Bjorkqvist, K., & Peltonen, T. (1988). "Is indirect aggression typical of females? Gender differences in aggressiveness in 11- to 12-year-old children." *Aggressive Behavior, 14*, 403–414.

Lancendorfer, K. M., Atkin, J. L., & Reece, B. B. (2008). "Animals in advertising: Love dogs? Love the ad!" *Journal of Business Research, 61*, 384–391.

Lang, A. (1990). "Involuntary attention and physiological arousal evoked by structural features and emotional content in TV commercials." *Communication Research, 17*, 275–299.

Lang, A. (2006). "Using the limited capacity model of motivated mediated message processing to design effective cancer communication messages." *Journal of Communication, 56*, S57–S80.

Lang, A., Yongkuk, C., Seungwhan, L., Schwartz, N., & Mija, S. (2005). "It's an arousing, fast-paced kind of world: The effects of age and sensation seeking on the information processing of substance-abuse PSAs" *Media Psychology, 7*, 421–454.

Langman, P. (2009). "Rampage school shooters: A typology." *Aggression and Violent Behavior, 14*, 79–86.

Lapinski, M. K. & Witte, K. (1998). "Health communication campaigns." In L. D. Jackson & B. K. Duffy (eds), *Health communication research: A guide to developments and directions* (pp. 139–161). Westport, CT: Greenwood Press.

Lauzen, M. M. & Dozier, D. M. (2005). "Recognition and respect revisited: Portrayals of age and gender in prime-time television." *Mass Communication & Society, 8*, 241–256.

Lavidge, R. C. & Steiner, G. A. (1961). "A model for predictive measurements of advertising effectiveness." *Journal of Marketing, 25*, 59–62.

Lavine, H., Sweeney, D., & Wagner, S. H. (1999). "Depicting women as sex objects in television advertising: Effects on body dissatisfaction." *Personality and Social Psychology Bulletin, 25*, 1049–1058.

Lazerfeld, P., Berelson, B., & Gaudet, H. (1944). *The people's choice.* New York: Columbia University Press.

Leaper, C., Breed, L., Hoffman, L., & Perlman, C. A. (2002). "Variations in the gender-stereotyped content of children's television cartoons across genres." *Journal of Applied Social Psychology, 32*, 1653–1662.

Lederman, L., Stewart, L, Goodhart, F., & Laitman, L. (2008). "A case against 'binge' as the term of choice: Convincing college students to personalize messages about dangerous drinking." In L. C. Lederman (ed.), *Beyond these walls* (pp. 292–303). New York: Oxford University Press.

Lee, M. J., Bichard, S. L., Irey, M. S., Walt, H. M., & Carlson, A. J. (2009). "Television viewing and ethnic stereotypes: Do college students form stereotypical perceptions of ethnic groups as a result of heavy television viewing?" *The Howard Journal of Communication, 20*, 95–110.

Lefkowitz, M. M., Eron, L. D., Walder, L. O., & Huesmann, L. R. (1977). "Effects of movie violence on aggression in a field setting as a function of group dominance and cohesion." *Journal of Personality and Social Psychology, 32*, 346–360.

Lefkowitz, M. M. & Huesmann, L. R. (1980). "Concomitants of television violence viewing in children." In E. L. Palmer & A. Dorr (eds), *Children and the faces of television: Teaching, violence, selling* (pp. 163–181). New York: Academic Press.

Lehu, J-M. & Bressoud, E. (2008). "Effectiveness of brand placement: New insights about viewers." *Journal of Business Research, 61*, 1083–1090.

Leiner, B. M., Cerf, V. G., Clark, D. D., Kahn, R. E., Kleinrock, L., Lynch, D. C., Postel, J., Roberts, L. G., and Wolff, S. (2010). "A Brief History of the Internet." Retrieved from http://www.isoc.org/internet/history/brief.shtml Retrieved June 23, 2010.

Lenhart, A., Kahne, J., Middaugh, E., Macgill, A. R., Evans, C., & Vitak, J. (2008). "Teens, video games, and civics." *Pew Internet & America Life Project.* Please amend to Retrieved from http://www.pewinternet.org/~/media//Files/Reports/2008/PIP_Teens_Games_and_Civics_Report_FINAL.pdf.pdf Retrieved on August 4, 2011.

Lenhart, A., Purcell, K., Smith, A., & Zikuhr, K. (2010). "Social Media and Mobile Internet Use Among Teens and Young Adults." *Pew internet and American Life Project.*

Lepore, L. & Brown, R. (1999). "Exploring automatic stereotype activation: A challenge to the inevitability of prejudice." In D. Abrams and M. A. Hogg (eds), *Social identity and social cognition* (pp. 141–163). Malden, MA: Blackwell.

Leshner, G., Bolls, P., & Thomas, E. (2009). "Scare 'em or disgust 'em: The effects of graphic health promotion messages." *Health Communication, 24,* 447–458.

Leshner, G., Vultee, F., Bolls, P. D., & Moore, J. (2010). "When a fear appeal isn't just a fear appeal: The effects of graphic anti-tobacco messages." *Journal of Broadcasting & Electronic Media, 54,* 485–507.

Levine, M. A. (1995). *Presidential Campaigns and Elections: Issues and Images in the Media Age* (2nd edn). Itasea: F. E. Peacock.

Levine, M. P., Smolak, L., & Hayden, H. (1994). "The relation of sociocultural factors to eating attitudes and behaviors among middle school girls." *Journal of Early Adolescence, 14,* 471–490.

Lichter, S. R. & Amundson, D. (1994). *A day of TV violence: 1992 vs 1994.* Washington DC: Center for Media and Public Affairs.

Lim, S. & Lee, J. R. (2009). "When playing together feels different: Effects of task types and social contexts on physiological arousal in multiplayer online gaming contexts." *CyberPsychology and Behavior, 12,* 59–61.

Lim, S. & Reeves, B. (2010). "Computer agents versus avatars: Responses to interactive game characters controlled by a computer or other player." *International Journal of Human-Computer Studies, 68,* 57–68.

Lin, C. A. (1997). "Beefcake versus cheesecake in the 1990s: Sexist portrayals of both genders in television commercials." *Howard Journal of Communications, 8,* 237–249.

Lin, N. (1999). "Building a network theory of social capital." *Connections, 22,* 28–51.

Linder, J. R. & Gentile, D. A. (2009). "Is the television rating system valid? Indirect, verbal and physical aggression in programs viewed by fifth grade girls and associations with behavior." *Journal of Applied Developmental Psychology, 30,* 286–297.

Linz, D. (1988). "The methods and merits of pornography research." *Journal of Communication, 38,* 180–184.

Liska, A. E. & Baccaglini, W. (1990). "Feeling safe by comparison: Crime in the newspapers." *Social Problems, 37,* 360–374.

Livingstone, S. (2008). "Taking risky opportunities in youthful content creation: Teenagers' use of social networking sites for intimacy, privacy and self-expression." *New Media & Society, 10,* 393–411.

Long, T., Taubenheim, A., Wayman, J., Temple, S., Ruoff, B. (2009). "'The Heart Truth': Using the power of branding and social marketing to increase awareness of heart disease in women." *Social Marketing Quarterly, 14,* 3–29.

Lorber, J. & Moore, L. (2002). "If a situation is defined as real: Premenstrual syndrome and menopause." In J. Lorber & L. Moore (eds), *Gender and the social construction of illness* (2nd edn, pp. 71–91). Walnut Creek, CA: Altamira Press.

Lorenzen, L. A., Grieve, F. G., & Thomas, A. (2004). "Exposure to muscular media models decreases men's body satisfaction." *Sex Roles, 51,* 743–48.

Lovdal, L. T. (1989). "Sex role messages in television commercials: An update." *Sex Roles, 21,* 715–724.

Low, G. S. (2000). "Correlates of integrated marketing communications." *Journal of Advertising Research, 40,* 27–39.

Lowry, D. T., Nio, T. C., & Leitner, D. W. (2003). "Setting the public fear agenda: A longitudinal analysis of network TV crime reporting, public perceptions of crime, and FBI statistics." *Journal of Communication, 53,* 61–73.

Luhmann, N. (1979). *Trust and power.* Toronto: John Wiley.

Luhmann, N. (1988). "Familiarity, confidence, trust: Problems and alternatives." In D. Gambetta (ed.), *Trust: Making and breaking cooperative relations* (pp. 94–107). New York: Basil Blackwell.

Maddison, R., Mhurchu, C. N., Jull, A., Jiang, Y., Prapavessis, H., & Rodgers, A. (2007). "Energy expended playing video console games: An opportunity to increase children's physical activity?" *Pediatric Exercise Science, 19,* 334–343.

Maiman, L. A. & Becker, M. H. (1974). "The Health Belief Model: Origins and correlates in psychological theory." *Health Education Monographs, 2,* 336–353.

Maltby, J., Day, L., McCutcheon, L. E., Gillett, R., Houran, J., & Ashe, D. (2004). "Personality and coping: A context for examining celebrity worship and mental health." *British Journal of Psychology, 95,* 411–428.

Maltby, J., Day, L., McCutcheon, L. E., Houran, J. & Ashe, D. (2006). "Extreme celebrity worship, fantasy proneness and dissociation: Developing the measurement and understanding of celebrity worship within a clinical personality context." *Personality and Individual Differences, 40,* 273–283.

Maltby, J., Giles, D. C., Barber, L., & McCutcheon, L. E. (2005). "Intense-personal celebrity worship and body image: Evidence of a link among female adolescents." *British Journal of Health Psychology, 10,* 17–32.

Maltby, J., Houran, J., Lange, R., Ashe, D. D., & McCutcheon, L. E. (2002). "Thou shalt worship no other gods—unless they are celebrities: The relationship between celebrity worship and religious orientation." *Personality and Individual Differences, 32,* 1157–1172.

Maltby, J., Houran, J., & McCutcheon, L. E. (2003). "A clinical interpretation of attitudes and behaviors associated with celebrity worship." *The Journal of Nervous and Mental Disease, 191,* 25–29.

Maltby, J., McCutcheon, L., Ashe, D. D., & Houran, J. (2001). "The self-reported psychological well-being of celebrity worshippers." *North American Journal of Psychology, 3,* 441–452.

Markey, P. M. & Scherer, K. (2009). "An examination of psychoticism and motion capture as moderators of the effects of violent video games." *Computers in Human Behavior, 25,* 407–411.

Martin, M. C., Gentry, J. W., & Hill, R. P. (1999). "The beauty myth and the persuasiveness of advertising: A look at adolescent girls and boys." In M. C. Macklin and L. Carlson (eds), *Advertising to Children: Concepts and Controversies* (pp. 165–187). Thousand Oaks, CA: Sage.

Martinez, K. Z. (2007). "Monolingualism, biculturalism, and cable TV: HBO Latino and the promise of the multiplex." In S. Banet-Weiser, C. Chris, & A. Freitas (eds), *Cable visions: Television beyond broadcasting* (pp. 194–214). New York: New York University Press.

Maslow, A. H. (1968). *Toward a psychology of being.* New York: Van Nostrand Reinhold.

Massar, K. & Buunk, A. P. (2009). "The effect of a subliminally primed context on intra-sexual competition depends on individual differences in sex drive." *Journal of Research in Personality, 43,* 691–694.

Massar, K., Buunk, A. P., & Dechesne, M. (2009). "Jealousy in the blink of an eye: Jealous reactions following subliminal exposure to rival characteristics." *European Journal of Social Psychology, 39,* 768–779.

Mastro, D. (2003). "A social identity approach to understanding the impact of television messages." *Communication Monographs, 70,* 98–113.

Mastro, D. (2009). "Effects of racial and ethnic stereotyping." In J. Bryant & M. B. Oliver (eds), *Media effects: Advances in theory and research* (3rd edn, pp. 325–341). New York: Routledge.

Mastro, D. & Behm-Morawitz, E. (2005). "Latino representation on primetime television." *Journalism & Mass Communication Quarterly, 70,* 98–113.

Mastro, D., Behm-Morawitz, E., & Ortiz, M. (2007). "The cultivation of social perceptions of Latinos: A mental models approach." *Media Psychology, 9,* 1–19.

Mastro, D. & Greenberg, B. (2000). "The portrayal of racial minorities on prime time television." *Journal of Broadcasting & Electronic Media, 44,* 690–703.

Mastro, D., Lapinski, M. K., Kopacz, M. A., & Behm-Morawitz, E. (2009). "The influence of exposure to depictions of race and crime in TV news on viewer's social judgments." *Journal of Broadcasting & Electronic Media, 53,* 615–635.

Mastro, D., Tamborini, R., & Hullett, C. (2005). "Linking media to prototype activation and subsequent celebrity attraction: An application of self-categorization theory." *Communication Research, 32,* 323–348.

Mastro, D. E. & Stern, S. R. (2003). "Representations of race in television commercials: A content analysis of prime-time advertising." *Journal of Broadcasting & Electronic Media, 47,* 638–647.

McArdle, K.A. & Hill, M. S. (2009). "Understanding body dissatisfaction in gay and hetero-sexual men: The roles of self-esteem, media, and peer influence." *Men and Masculinities, 11,* 511–32.

McClelland, D. C. & Cheriff, A. D. (1997). "The immunoenhancing effects of humor on secre-tory IgA and resistance to respiratory infections." *Psychology & Health, 12,* 329–344.

McClure, A., Dal Cin, S., Gibson, J., & Sargent, J. D. (2006). "Ownership of alcohol-branded merchandise and initiation of teen drinking." *American Journal of Preventive Medicine, 30,* 277–283.

McClure, E. B., Parrish, J. M., Nelson, E. E., Easter, J., Thorne, J. F., Rilling, J. K., Ernst, M., & Pine, D. S. (2007). "Responses to conflict and cooperation in adolescents with anxiety and mood disorders." *Journal of Abnormal Child Psychology, 35,* 567–577.

McCombs, M. E. & Shaw, D. L. (1972). "The agenda-setting function of mass media." *Public Opinion Quarterly, 36,* 176–187.

McCombs, M. E. & Shaw, D. L. (1993). "The evolution of agenda-setting research: Twenty-five years in the marketplace of ideas." *Journal of Communication, 43,* 58–67.

McConnell, H. A. (2003). "The terror: An examination of the emerging discourse on terrorism and its media representations." Master's thesis. University of Toronto: Canada.

McCutcheon, L. E. (2002). "Are parasocial relationship styles reflected in love styles?" *Current Research in Social Psychology, 7.* 82–94, Retrieved from www.uiowa.edu/~grpproc/crisp/crisp.7.6.htm.

McCutcheon, L. E. (2003). "Machiavellianism, belief in a just world, and the tendency to worship celebrities." *Current Research in Social Psychology, 8,* 131–138. Retrieved from http://www.uiowa.edu/~grpproc/crisp.

McCutcheon, L. E., Aruguete, M., Scott, V. B., Parker, J. S., & Calicchia, J. (2006). "The development and validation of an indirect measure of celebrity stalking." *North American Journal of Psychology, 8,* 503–516.

McCutcheon, L. E., Ashe, D. D., Houran, J., & Maltby, J. (2003). "A cognitive profile of individuals who tend to worship celebrities. *Journal of Psychology, 137,* 309–322.

McCutcheon, L. E., Lange, R., & Houran, J. (2002). "Conceptualization and measurement of celebrity worship." *British Journal of Psychology, 93,* 67–87.

McCutcheon, L. E. & Maltby, J. (2002). "Personality attributions about individuals high and low in the tendency to worship celebrities." *Current Research in Social Psychology, 7,* 325–338. Retrieved from http://www.uiowa.edu/~grpproc/crisp/crisp.7.19.html.

McCutcheon, L. E., Maltby, J., Houran, J., & Ashe, D. D. (2004). *Celebrity worshippers: Inside the minds of stargazers.* Frederick, MD: PublishAmerica.

McCutcheon, L. E., Scott, V. B., Aruguete, M., & Parker, J. S. (2006). "Exploring the link between attachment and the inclination to obsess about or stalk celebrities." *North American Journal of Psychology, 8,* 289–300.

McGraw, P. (2007). *Virginia Tech Massacre: Interview with Larry King Live.* Retrieved from http://transcripts.cnn.com/TRANSCRIPTS/0704/16/lkl.01.html Retrieved on September 10, 2010.

McIver, T. (2010). *Social Webinar presentation media: The collision of MySpace, your space, and our space.*

McLuhan, M. (1964). *Understanding media: The extensions of man.* Cambridge: MIT Press.

Medved, M. (1995). "Hollywood's 3 big lies." *Reader's Digest,* 155–159.

Mehta, A. (2000). "Advertising attitudes and advertising effectiveness." *Journal of Advertising Research, 40,* 67–72.

Mehta, K., Coveney, J., Ward, P., Magarey, A., Spurrier, N., & Udell, T. (2010). "Australian children's views about food advertising on television." *Appetite, 55,* 49–55.

Melzoff, A. N. (1988). "Imitation of televised models by infants." *Child Development, 59,* 1221–1229.

Merskin, D. (1998). "Sending up signals: A survey of Native American media use and representation in the mass media." *Howard Journal of Communication, 9,* 333–345.

Messaris, P. (1994). *Visual literacy: Image, mind, and reality.* Boulder: Westview Press.

Messner, S. (1986). "Television violence and violent crime: An aggregate analysis." *Social Problems, 33,* 218–235.

Metcalfe, J. & Mischel, W. (1999). "A hot/cool system analysis of delay of gratification: Dynamics of willpower." *Psychological Review, 106,* 3–19.

Mideast consumers "top in smart phone use." (2010, October 17). *TradeArabia.*

Minow, N. (1996). *Abandoned in the wasteland: Children, television and the first amendment.* New York: Hill and Wang.

Mintz, L. B. & Betz, N. E. (1988). "Prevalence and correlates of eating disordered behaviors among undergraduate women." *Journal of Counseling Psychology, 35*, 463–471.

Mittell, J. (2010). *Television and American culture.* New York: Oxford University Press.

Möller, I. & Krahé, B. (2009). "Exposure to violent video games and aggression in German adolescents: A longitudinal analysis." *Aggressive Behavior, 35*, 75–89.

Monahan, J. L. (1995). "Thinking positively: Using positive affect when designing health messages." In E. Maibach & R. L. Parrott (eds), *Designing health messages* (pp. 81–98). Thousand Oaks, CA: Sage.

Mongeau, P. (1998). "Another look at fear-arousing persuasive appeals." In M. Allen & R. W. Preiss (eds), *Persuasion: Advances through meta-analysis* (pp. 53–68). Cresskill, NJ: Hampton Press.

Montaner, M., Lopez, B., & de la Rosa, J. L. (2003). "A taxonomy of recommender agents on the Internet." *Artificial Intelligence Review, 19*, 285–330.

Moore, D. J., Harris, W. D., & Chen, H. C. (1995). "Affect intensity: An individual difference response to advertising appeals." *Journal of Consumer Research, 22*, 154–164.

Morahan-Martin, J. (1999). "The relationship between loneliness and Internet use and abuse. *CyberPsychology and Behavior, 2*, 431–440.

Morgan, M. (1982). "Television and adolescent's sex-role stereotypes: A longitudinal study." *Journal of Personality and Social Psychology, 43*, 947–955.

Morgan, M. (1987). "Television, sex-role attitudes, and sex-role behavior." *The Journal of Early Adolescence, 7*, 269–282.

Morgan, M. & Shanahan, J. (1997). "Two decades of cultivation research: An appraisal and meta-analysis." In B. R. Burleson (ed.), *Communication yearbook 20* (pp. 1–46). Thousand Oaks, CA; Sage.

Morgan, M., Shanahan, J., & Signorielli, N. (2009). "Growing up with television: Cultivation Processes." In J. Bryant & M. B. Oliver (eds), *Media effects: Advances in theory and research* (3rd edn, pp. 34–49). New York: Routledge.

Morris, J. S. (1982). "Television portrayal and the socialization of the American Indian child." In J. Lull (ed.), *World families watch television* (pp. 22–48). Newbury Park, CA: Sage.

Morrow, V. (1999). "Conceptualizing social capital in relation to the well-being of children and young people: A critical review." *Sociological Review, 47*, 744–765.

Mundorf, N., Allen, M., D'Alessio, D., & Emmers-Sommer, T. (2007). "Effects of Sexually Explicit Media." In R. W. Preiss, B. M. Gayle, N. Burrell, M. Allen, & J. Bryant (eds), *Mass Media Effects Research: Advances Through Meta-Analysis.* (2007). New York: Lawrence Erlbaum.

Myers, P. N. & Biocca, F. (1992). "The elastic body image: The effect of television advertising and programming on body image distortion in young women." *Journal of Communication, 42*, 108–133.

Nabi, R. L. (2010). "The case for emphasizing discrete emotions in communication research." *Communication Monographs, 77*, 153–159.

National Asian American Pacific Islander Mental Health Association. (2010). *Fact Sheet.* Retrieved from http://www.naapimha.org/issues/Fact%20Sheet.pdf.

National Heart Lung and Blood Institute (2010). About The Heart Truth®. Retrieved from the US Department of Health & Human Services web site http://www.nhlbi.nih.gov/educational/hearttruth/about/index.htm Retrieved on October 30, 2010.

National Television Violence Study (1998). Thousand Oaks, CA: Sage Publications.

Nelson T. E., Clawson, R. A., & Oxley, Z. M. (1997). "Media framing of a civil liberties conflict and its effects on tolerance." *American Political Science Review, 93*, 567–583.

Newhagen, J. E. (1998). "TV news images that induce anger, fear, and disgust: Effects on approach-avoidance and memory." *Journal of Broadcasting and Electronic Media, 42*, 265–276.

Newman, B. I. (1999). *The mass marketing of politics: Democracy in an age of manufactured images*. Thousand Oaks, CA: Sage.

Nie, N. (2001). "Sociability, interpersonal relations, and the Internet: Reconciling conflicting findings." *American Behavioral Scientist, 45*, 420–435.

Nielson. (2009, September 4). *Hispanic homes in U.S. show largest growth for 2009-2010 TV season*. Retrieved from http://blog.nielsen.com/nielsenwire/media_entertainment/hispanic-homes-in-u-s-show-largest-growth-for-2009-2010-tv-season/ Retrieved on August 4, 2011.

Norris, P. (ed.). (2000a). *Politics and the press*. Boulder: Lynne Rienner Publishers.

Norris, P. (2000b). *A virtuous circle: Political communication in postindustrial societies*. Cambridge: Cambridge University Press.

Nylander, I. (1971). "The feeling of being fat and dieting in a school population." *Acta Socio-Medica Scandinavia, 1*, 17–26.

Oddone-Paolucci, E. Genuis, M., & Violato, C. (2000). "A meta-analysis of the published research on the effects of pornography." In C. Violato, E. Oddone-Paolucci, M. Genuis (eds), *The changing family and child development* (pp. 48–59). Aldershot, UK: Ashgate Publishing.

Ogden, J. & Mundray, K. (1996). "The effect of the media on body satisfaction: The role of gender and size." *European Eating Disorders Review, 4*, 171–181.

Ogletree, S. M., Mason, D. V., Grahmann, T., & Raffeld, P. (2001). "Perceptions of two television cartoons: Powerpuff Girls and Johnny Bravo." *Communication Research Reports, 18*, 307–313.

Ogunnaike, L. (2003, October 13). "The perks and pitfalls of a ruthless-killer role." *The New York Times*, E1.

Oliver, M. B., Jackson, R., Moses, N., & Dangerfield, C. (2004). "The face of crime: Viewers' memory of race-related facial features of individuals pictured in the news." *Journal of Communication, 54*, 88–104.

Oppliger, P. A. (2007). "Effects of gender stereotyping on socialization." In R. W. Preiss, B. M. Gayle, N. Burrell, M. Allen, & J. Bryant (eds), *Mass media effects research: Advances through meta-analysis* (pp. 199–214). Mahwah, NJ: Lawrence Erlbaum.

Ortiz, M. & Harwood, J. (2007). "A social cognitive theory approach to the effects of mediated intergroup contact on intergroup attitudes." *Journal of Broadcasting & Electronic Media, 51*, 615–631.

Orvalho, V., Miranda, J., & Sousa, A. A. (2009). "Facial synthesis of 3D avatars for therapeutic applications." *Annual Review of Cybertherapy and Telemedicine, 7*.

Oser, K. (2005). "Marketers fume over click fraud." *Advertising Age, 76*, 34.

O'Toole, K. (2000, 16 February). "Study offers early look at how Internet is changing daily life." *Stanford News*. Retrieved from http://www.stanford.edu/dept/news/pr/00/000216internet.html Retrieved on February 21, 2000.

Overbeke, G. (2008). "Pro-anorexia websites: Content, impact and explanations of popularity." *Mind Matters: The Wesleyan Journal of Psychology, 3*, 49–62.

Owens, T. J., Stryker, S., & Goodman, N. (2006). *Extending self-esteem theory and research.* NY: Cambridge University Press.

Page, B. I., Shapiro, R. Y., & Dempsey, G. R. (2000). "What Moves Public Opinion?" In D. A. Graber (ed.), *Media Power in Politics.* Washington, DC: CQ Press.

Paik, H. & Comstock, G. (1994). "The effects of television violence on antisocial behavior: A meta-analysis." *Communication Research, 21*, 516–546.

Paisley, W. J. (2001). "Public communication campaigns: The American experience." In R. Rice & C. Atkin (eds), *Public communication campaigns* (3rd edn, pp. 3–21). Thousand Oaks, CA: Sage.

Paluck, E. L. (2009). "Reducing intergroup prejudice and conflict using the media: A field experiment in Rwanda." *Journal of Personality and Social Psychology, 96*, 574–587.

Panagopoulos, C. (ed.). (2007). *Rewiring Politics: Presidential Nominating Conventions in the Media Age.* Baton Rouge: Louisiana State University Press.

Paquette, M. (2002). "Bad company: Internet sites with dangerous information." *Perspectives in Psychiatric Care, 38*, 39–41.

Park, J. H., Gabbadon, N. G., & Chernin, A. R. (2006). "Naturalizing racial differences through comedy: Asian, black, and white views on racial stereotypes in Rush Hour 2." *Journal of Communication, 56*, 157–177.

Passel, J. S. (2006, March 7). *The size and characteristics of the unauthorized migrant population in the U.S.* Retrieved from http://pewhispanic.org/files/reports/61.pdf Retrieved on August 4, 2011.

Patterson, T. E. (1976). *The mass media election: How Americans choose their president.* New York: Praeger.

Pavlik, J. V. (2001). *Journalism and new media.* New York: Columbia University Press.

Peitz, M. & Valetti, T. (2008). "Advertising and content in media: Pay TV versus free-to-air." *International Journal of Industrial Organization, 26*, 949–965.

Pempek, T. A., Yevdokiya, A., Yermolayeva, S., & Calvert, C. (2009). "College students' social networking experiences on Facebook." *Journal of Applied Developmental Psychology, 30*, 227–238.

Petty, R. E. & Cacioppo, J. T. (1981). *Attitudes and persuasion: Classic and contemporary approaches.* Dubuque, IA: W.C. Brown.

Petty, R. E. & Cacioppo, J. T. (1983). "Central and Peripheral routes to persuasion: Application to advertising." In L. Percy and A. G. Woodside (eds), *Advertising and consumer psychology* (pp. 3–23). Lexington, MA: Lexington Books.

Petty, R. E. & Cacioppo, J. T. (1986). "The elaboration likelihood model of persuasion. *Advances in Experimental Social Psychology, 19*, 123–205.

Petty, R. E., Cacioppo, J. T., & Shumann, D. (1983). "Does playing violent video games induce aggression? Empirical evidence of Functional Magnetic Resonance Imaging study." *Journal of Consumer Research, 10*, 135–146.

Pew Internet & American Life Project (2009). "Tracking surveys." Retrieved from http://www.pewinternet.org Retrieved on June 4, 2010.

Pew Research Center Biennial News Consumption Survey. (2008). "Key News Audiences Now Blend Online And Traditional Sources: Audience Segments in a Changing News Environment." The Pew Research Center For The People & The Press.

Pfau, M., Houston, J. B., & Semmler, S. M. (2007). *Mediating the vote: The changing media landscape in U.S. presidential campaigns.* Lanham: Rowan and Littlefield.

Philo, G. (1990). *Seeing and believing: The influence of television.* London: Routledge.

Pike, J. J. & Jennings, N. A. (2005). "The effects of commercials on children's perceptions of gender appropriate toy use." *Sex Roles, 52,* 83–91.

Pine, K. & Nash, A. (2001). "The effects of television advertising on young children." Paper presented at the British Psychology Centenary Conference, SECC, Glasgow.

Planalp, S. & Fitness, J. (1999). "Thinking/feeling about social and personal relationships." *Journal of Social and Personal Relationships, 16,* 731–750.

Polivy, J. & Herman, C. P. (1985). "Dieting and binging: A causal analysis." *American Psychologist, 40,* 193–201.

Pollack, D. (2003). "Pro-eating disorder websites: What should be the feminist response?" *Feminism and Psychology, 13,* 246–251.

Poniewozik, J. (2001, May). "What's wrong with this picture?" *Time,* 80–82.

Posavec, N. D., Posavec, S. S., & Posavec, E. J. (1993). "Exposure to media images of female attractiveness and concern with body weight among young women." *Sex Roles, 38,* 187–209.

Postman, N. (1986). *Amusing ourselves to death: Public discourse in the age of show business.* New York: Penguin.

Potter, W. J. & Warren, R. (1998). "Humor as a camouflage of televised violence." *Journal of Communication, 48,* 40–57.

Powell, L. (2010). "Obama and Obama Girl: YouTube, Viral Videos, and the 2008 Presidential Campaign." In J. A. Hendricks & R. E. Denton, Jr (eds), *Communicator-in-chief: How Barack Obama used new media technology to win the White House.* Lanham: Lexington Books.

Pratkanis, A. R. & Aronson, E. (1992). *Age of propaganda: The everyday use and abuse of persuasion.* New York: W. H. Freeman and Company.

Prochaska, J., DiClemente, C., & Norcross, J. (1992). "In search of how people change: Applications to addictive behaviors." *American Psychologist, 47,* 1102–1114.

Proctor, M. H., Moore, L. L., Cupples, L. A., Bradlee, Hood, M. Y., & Ellison, R. C. (2003). "Television viewing and change in body fat from preschool to early adolescence: The Framingham Children's Study." *International Journal of Obesity, 27,* 287–833.

Pure intimacy. "Fatal addiction: Ted Bundy's final interview." Retrieved on June 2011 from http://www.pureintimacy.org/piarticles/A000000433.cfm.

Putnam, R. (2000). *Bowling alone: The collapse and revival of American community.* New York: Simon and Schuster.

Radvansky, G. A. & Zacks, R. T. (1997). "The retrieval of situation-specific information." In M. A. Conway (ed.), *Cognitive models of memory* (pp. 173–213). Cambridge, MA: MIT Press.

Ramasubramanian, S. (2010). "Television viewing, racial attitudes, and policy preferences: Exploring the role of social identity and intergroup emotions in influencing support for affirmative action." *Communication Monographs, 77,* 102–120.

Ramirez Berg, C. (1990). "Stereotyping in films in general and of the Hispanic in particular." *Howard Journal of Communication, 2,* 286–300.

Rasch, G. (1960/1980). *Probabilistic models for some intelligence and attainment tests.* Chicago, IL: Mesa Press.

Raviv, A., Bar-Tal, D., Raviv, A., & Ben-Horin, A. (1996). "Adolescent idolization of pop singers: Causes, expressions, and reliance." *Journal of Youth and Adolescence, 25,* 631–650.

Redondo, I. (2006). "Product-placement planning: How is the industry placing brands in relation to moviegoer consumption?" *Journal of International Consumer Marketing, 18,* 33–55.

Reep, D. C. & Dambrot, F. H. (1987). "Television's professional women: Working with men in the 1980s." *Journalism Quarterly, 64,* 376–381.

Reeves, B., Lang, A., Kim, E. Y., & Tatar, D. (1999). "The effects of screen size and message content on attention arousal." *Media Psychology, 1,* 49–67.

Reid, C. (1999). "AAP, ABA hail Hill's rejection of media violence bill." *Publishers Weekly, 246,* 11.

Reinsch, J. L. (1998). *Getting elected: From radio and Roosevelt to television and Reagan.* New York: Hippocrene Books.

Reiss, R. & Wiltz, J. (2004). "Why People watch reality TV." *Media Psychology, 6,* 363–378.

Rheingold, H. (1993). *The virtual community: Homesteading on the electronic frontier.* Reading, MA: Addison-Wesley.

Richins, M. (1991). "Social comparison and the idealised images of advertising." *Journal of Consumer Research, 18,* 71–83.

Riedel, S. (2005). "Edward Jenner and the history of smallpox and vaccination." *Baylor University Medical Center Proceedings, 18,* 21–25.

Riley, S., Rodham, K., & Gavin, J. (2009). "Doing weight: Pro-ana and recovery identities in cyberspace." *Journal of Community and Applied Social Psychology, 19,* 348–359.

Ritter, D. & Eslea, M. (2005). "Hot sauce, toy guns and graffiti: A critical account of current laboratory aggression paradigms." *Aggressive Behavior, 31,* 407–419.

Rivadeneyra, R. (2006). "Do You See What I See? Latino Adolescents' Perceptions of the Images on Television." *Journal of Adolescent Research, 21,* 393–414.

Roberts, D. F. (2000). "Media and youth: Access, exposure, and privatization." *Journal of Adolescent Health, 27S,* 8–14.

Roberts, D. F. & Bachen, C. M. (1981). "Mass communication effects." *American Review of Psychology, 32,* 307–356.

Roberts, D. F. & Maccoby, N. (1985). "Effects of mass communication." In G. Lindzey & E. Aronson (eds), *Handbook of social psychology* (3rd edn) (pp. 539–598). New York: Random House.

Robinson, T. & Anderson, C. (2006). "Older characters in children's animated television programs: A content analysis of their portrayal." *Journal of Broadcasting & Electronic Media, 50,* 287–304.

Rodgers, S. & Thorson, E. (2000). "The Interactive Advertising Model: How users perceive and process online ads." *Journal of Interactive Advertising, 1.* Retrieved from http://jiad.org/article5. Retrieved on August 4, 2011.

Rogers, C. (1954). *Psychotherapy and personality and change.* Chicago: University of Chicago Press.

Rogers, E. (2003). *Diffusion of innovations* (5th edn). New York: Free Press.

Rojas-Mendez, J. I. & Davies, G. (2005). "Avoiding television advertising: Some expectations from time allocation theory." *Journal of Advertising Research, 38,* 7–22.

Romer, D., Jamieson, K. H., & Aday, S. (2003). "Television news and the cultivation of fear of crime." *Journal of Communication, 53,* 88–104.

Romer, D., Jamieson, K., & DeCoteau, N. (1998). "The treatment of persons of color in local television news: Ethnic blame discourse or realistic group conflict." *Communication Research, 25,* 286–305.

Rosen, C. (2007). "Virtual friendship and the new narcissism." *The New Atlantis, 17,* 15–31.

Rosenberg, M. (1965). *Society and the adolescent self-image.* Princeton, NJ: Princeton University Press.

Rosenberg, M. (1989). *Society and the adolescent self-image* (2nd edn). Princeton, NJ: Princeton University Press.

Ross, M. W. (2005). "Typing, doing and being: Sexuality and the Internet." *Journal of Sex Research. 42,* 342–352.

Rousseau, D., Sitkin, S., Burt, R., & Camerer, C. (1998). "Not so different after all: A cross-discipline view of trust." *Academy of Management Review, 23,* 393–404.

Rubin, A. M. (2002). "The uses-and-gratifications perspective of media effects." In J. Bryant & D. Zillman (eds), *Media effects: Advances in theory and research* (2nd edn, pp. 525–548). Mahwah NJ: Lawrence Erlbaum.

Rubin, A. M., Perse, E. M., & Powell, R. A. (1985). "Loneliness, parasocial interaction, and local television news viewing." *Human Communication Research, 12,* 155–180.

Rubin, R. B. & McHugh, M. P. (1987). "Development of parasocial interaction relationships." *Journal of Broadcasting & Electronic Media, 31,* 279–292.

Rudofsky, B. (1972). *The unfashionable human body.* New York: Doubleday.

Ruiz, S. & Sicilia, M. (2004). "The impact of cognitive and/or affective processing styles on consumer response to advertising appeals." *Journal of Business Research, 57,* 657–664.

Said. E. (1979). *Orientalism.* New York: Vintage Books.

Saito, S. (2007). "Television and the cultivation of gender-role attitudes in Japan: Does television contribute to the maintenance of the status quo?" *Journal of Communication, 57,* 511–531.

Salmon, C. & Atkin, C. (2003). "Using media campaigns for health promotion." In T. L. Thompson, A. Dorsey, K. I. Miller, & R. Parrott (eds), *Handbook of health communication* (pp. 449–472). New York: Lawrence Erlbaum.

Salmon, C. T. & Murray-Johnson, L. (2001). "Communication campaign effectiveness." In R. Rice & C. Atkin (eds), *Public communication campaigns* (3rd edn, pp. 168–180) Thousand Oaks, CA: Sage.

Sanders, C., Field, T., Diego, M., & Kaplan, M. (2000). "The relationship of Internet use to depression and social isolation among adolescents." *Adolescence, 35,* 237–242.

Sanders, K. (2009). *Communicating politics in the twenty-first century.* New York: Palgrave Macmillan.

Savage, J. (2004). "Does viewing violent media really cause criminal violence? A methodological review." *Aggression and Violent Behavior, 10,* 99–128.

Schaller, M. (1997). "The psychological consequences of fame: Three tests of the self-consciousness hypothesis." *Journal of Personality, 65*, 291–309.

Scharrer, E., Kim, D. D., Lin, K., & Liu, Z. (2006). "Working hard or hardly working? Gender, humor, and the performance of domestic chores in television commercials." *Mass Media & Society, 9*, 215–238.

Scheufele, D. A. (2000). "Agenda-setting, priming and framing revisited: Another look at cognitive effects of political communication." *Mass Communication & Society, 3*, 297–316.

Schiavo, R. (2007). *Health communication: From theory to practice.* San Francisco: Jossey-Boss.

Schudson, M. (1998). *The good citizen: A history of American civic life.* New York: Free Press.

Seddon, L. & Berry, N. (1996). "Media-induced disinhibition or dietary restraint." *British Journal of Health Psychology, 1*, 27–33.

Shaheen, J. G. (1984). *The TV Arab.* Bowling Green, OH: Bowling Green State University Press.

Shaheen, J. G. (1997). *Arab and Muslim stereotyping in American popular culture.* Washington, DC: Georgetown University Center for Muslim-Christian Understanding.

Shaheen, J. G. (2001). *Reel bad Arabs: How Hollywood vilifies a people.* New York: Olive Branch Press.

Shanahan, J., Signorielli, N., & Morgan, M. (2008). "Television and sex roles 30 years hence: A retrospective and current look from a Cultural Indicators perspective." Paper presented at the annual conference of the International Communication Association Montreal, Canada.

Shaw, B. & Gant, L. (2002). "In defense of the Internet: The relationship between Internet communication and depression, loneliness, self-esteem, and perceived social support." *CyberPsychology & Behavior, 5*, 157–171.

Shen, L., Monahan, J. L., Rhodes, N., & Roskos-Ewoldsen, D. R. (2009). "The impact of attitude accessibility and decision style on adolescents' biased processing of health-related public service announcements." *Communication Research, 36*, 104–128.

Sherry, J. & Lucas, K. (2003). "Video game uses and gratifications as predictors of use and game preference." Paper presented at the annual conference of the International Communication Association, San Diego, CA.

Shomaker, L. B. & Furman, W. (2010). "A prospective investigation of interpersonal influences on the pursuit of muscularity in late adolescent boys and girls." *Journal of Health Psychology, 15*, 391–404.

Siegal, J., Dubrovsky, V., Kiesler, S., & McGuire, T. (1986). "Group processes in computer-mediated communication." *Organizational Behavior and Human Decision Processes, 37*, 157–187.

Siegel, M., Albers, A., Cheng, D., Hamilton, W., & Biener, L. (2008). "Local restaurant smoking regulations and the adolescent smoking initiation process." *Archives of Pediatrics and Adolescent Medicine, 162*, 477–483.

Signorielli, N. (1985). *Role Portrayal and Stereotyping on Television: An annotated bibliography of studies relating to women, minorities, aging, sexual behavior, health, and handicaps.* Westport, CT: Greenwood Press.

Signorielli, N. (1989). "Television and conceptions about sex-roles: Maintaining conventionality and the status quo." *Sex Roles, 21*, 341–360.

Signorielli, N. (1993). "Television and adolescents' perceptions about work." *Youth & Society, 24*, 314–341.

Signorielli, N. (2004). "Aging on television: Messages relating to gender, race, and occupation in prime time." *Journal of Broadcasting & Electronic Media, 48,* 279–301.

Signorielli, N. (2008). "Children's programs 2007: Basic demography and violence." Paper presented at the annual conference of the National Communication Association. San Diego CA.

Signorielli, N. (2009). "Race and sex in prime time: A look at occupations and occupational prestige." *Mass Communication & Society, 12,* 332–353.

Signorielli, N. & Bacue, A. (1999). "Recognition and respect: A content analysis of prime-time television characters across three decades." *Sex Roles, 40,* 527–544.

Signorielli, N., Gerbner, G., & Morgan, M. (1995). "Violence on television: The cultural indicators project." *Journal of Broadcasting and Electronic Media, 39,* 278–283.

Signorielli, N. & Kahlenberg, S. (2001). "Television's world of work in the nineties." *Journal of Broadcasting & Electronic Media, 45,* 1–19.

Signorielli, N. & Lears, M. (1992). "Children, television and conceptions about chores: Attitudes and behaviors." *Sex Roles, 27,* 157–170.

Signorielli, N. & Morgan, M. (1990). *Cultivation Analysis: New Directions in Media Effects Research.* Newbury Park, CA: Sage.

Simons, D. & Silveira, W. R. (1994). "Post-traumatic stress disorder in children after television programmes." *British Medical Journal, 308,* 308–389.

Simonton, D. K. (1999). "Significant samples: The psychological study of eminent individuals." *Psychological Methods, 4,* 425–451.

Skowronski, J. J. & Carlston, D. E. (1987). "Social judgment and social memory: The role of cue diagnosticity in negativity, positivity, and extremity biases." *Journal of Personality and Social Psychology, 52,* 689–699.

Skowronski, J. J. & Carlston, D. E. (1989). "Negativity and extremity biases in impression formation: A review of explanations." *Psychological Bulletin, 105,* 131–142.

Slater, M. D. (1995). "Choosing audience segmentation strategies and methods for health communication." In E. Maibach & R. L. Parrott (eds), *Designing health messages* (pp. 186–198). Thousand Oaks, CA: Sage.

Slovic, P., Fischoff, B., & Lictenstein, S. (1982). "Facts versus fears: Understanding perceived risk." In D. Kahneman, P. Slovic, & A. Tversky (eds), *Judgment under uncertainty: Heuristics and biases* (pp. 463–489). New York: Cambridge University Press.

Smith, B. P. (2007). *Flow and the enjoyment of video games.* Dissertation Abstracts. International Section A: Humanities and Social Sciences. pp. 2374.

Smith, M., Mak, D., Watson, J., Bastian, L., Smith, A., & Pitts, M. (2008). "Conversant or clueless? Chlamydia-related knowledge and practice of general practitioners in Western Australia." *BMC Family Practice, 9,* 1–6.

Smith, S. L. & Cook C. A. (2008). "Gender stereotypes: An analysis of popular films and TV." CA: The Geena Davis Institute on Gender and Media.

Smith Maguire, J. (2002). "Body lessons: Fitness publishing and the cultural production of the fitness consumer." *International Review for the Sociology of Sport, 37,* 449–64.

Smolak, L., Levine, M. P., & Gralen, S. (1993). "The impact of puberty and dating on eating problems among middle school girls." *Journal of Youth and Adolescence, 22,* 355–368.

Smythe, D. W. (1954). "Reality as presented by television." *Public Opinion Quarterly*, *18*, 143–154.

Snyder, L. B. (2007). "Health communication campaigns and their impact on behavior." *Journal of Nutrition Education and Behavior*, *39*, S32–S40.

Solop, F. I. (2010). "'RT @BarackObama We just made history': Twitter and the 2008 Presidential Election." In J. A. Hendricks & R. E. Denton, Jr (eds), *Communicator-in-chief: How Barack Obama used new media technology to win the White House*. Lanham: Lexington Books.

Sotirovic, M. & McLeod, J. M. (2004). "Knowledge as understanding: The information processing approach to political learning." In L. L. Kaid (ed.), *Handbook of political communication research*." Mahwah, NJ: Lawrence Erlbaum.

Sparks, G. G. (2006). *Media effects research: A basic overview* (2nd edn). Belmont, CA: Thomson Wadsworth.

Speck, P. S. & Elliot, M. T. (1997). "Predictors of advertising avoidance in print and broadcast media." *The Journal of Advertising*, *26*, 61–76.

Spitzer, B. L., Henderson, K. A., & Zivian, M. T. (1999). "Gender differences in population versus media sizes: A comparison over four decades." *Sex Roles*, *40*, 545–65.

Stangor, C. & Schallor, M. (1996). "Stereotypes as individual and collective representations." In C. N. Macrae, C. Stangor, & M. Hewstone (eds), *Stereotypes and stereotyping* (pp. 3–27). New York: Guilford.

Staude-Müller, F., Bliesener, T., & Luthman, S. (2008). "Hostile and hardened? An experimental study on (de-)sensitization to violence and suffering through playing video games." *Swiss Journal of Psychology*, *67*, 41–50.

Steet, L. (2000). *Veils and daggers: A century of National Geographic's representation of the Arab world*. Philadelphia: Temple University Press.

Steiner, P. (1993). "On the internet, nobody knows you're a dog [Cartoon caption]." *The New Yorker*, *69*, 61.

Steinfeld, J. (1972). "Statement in hearings before Subcommittee on Communications of Committee on Commerce" (U.S. Senate, Serial No. 92-52, pp. 25–27). Washington, DC: U.S. Government Printing Office.

Stern, S. R. & Mastro, D. E. (2004). "Gender portrayals across the life span: A content analytic look at broadcast commercials." *Mass Communication & Society*, *7*, 215—236.

Stephenson, M. T. & Southwell, B. G. (2006). "Sensation seeking, the Activation Model, and mass media health campaigns: Current findings and future directions for Cancer communication." *Journal of Communication*, *56*, S38–S56.

Stever, G. S. (1991). "The Celebrity Appeal Questionnaire." *Psychological Reports*, *68*, 859–866.

Stice, E. & Shaw, H. E. (1994). "Adverse effects of the media portrayed thin-ideal on women and linkages to bulimic symptoms." *Journal of Social and Clinical Psychology*, *13*, 288–308.

Stice, E., Schupak-Neuberg, E., Shaw, H. E., & Stein, R. (1994). "Relation of media exposure to eating disorder symptomatology: An examination of mediating mechanisms." *Journal of Abnormal Psychology*, *103*, 836–840.

Stoutjesdyk, D. & Jevne, R. (1993). "Eating disorders among high performance athletes. *Journal of Youth and Adolescence*, *22*, 271–282.

Strasburger, V. C. & Wilson, B. J. (2002). *Children, adolescents and the media.* Thousand Oaks, CA: Sage.

Straubhaar, J. & LaRose, R. (2006). *Media now: Understanding media, culture, and technology* (5th edn). Belmont, CA: Thomson Wadsworth.

Strauman, T. J., Vookles, J., Berenstein, V., Chaiken, S., & Higgins, E. T. (1991). "Self-discrepancies and vulnerability to body dissatisfaction and disordered eating." *Journal of Personality and Social Psychology, 61,* 946–956.

Striegel-Moore, R. H., Silverstein, L. R., & Rodin, J. (1986). "Toward an understanding of risk factors for bulimia." *American Psychologist, 41,* 246–263.

Striegel-Moore, R. H., Wilfley, D. E., Caldwell, M. B., Needham, M.L., & Brownell, K. D. (1996). "Weight-related attitudes and behaviors of women who diet to lose weight: A comparison of black dieters and white dieters." *Obesity Research, 4,* 109–116.

Stroud, D. (2008). "Social networking: An age-neutral commodity." *Journal of Direct, Data and Digital Marketing Practice, 9,* 278–292.

Suleiman, M. W. (1988). *The Arab in the mid of America.* Brattleboro, VT: Amana Books.

Suler, J. (2004). "The online disinhibition effect." *CyberPsychology & Behavior, 7,* 321–326.

Sullivan, D. G. & Masters, R. D. (1993). "Nonverbal behavior, emotions, and democratic leadership." In G. E. Marcus & R. L. Hanson (eds), *Reconsidering the Democratic Public.* University Park: Pennsylvania State University Press.

Sullivan, H. (1953). *The interpersonal theory of psychiatry.* New York: Norton.

Swami, V. *et al.* (2010). "The attractive female body weight and female body dissatisfaction in 26 countries across 10 world regions: Results of the International Body Project I." *Personality and Social Psychology Bulletin, 36,* 309–25.

Sweetser, K. D., Golan, G. J., & Wanta, W. (2008). "Intermedia agenda setting in television, advertising, and blogs during the 2004 election." *Mass Communication & Society, 11,* 197–216.

Swing, E. L., Gentile, D. A., & Anderson, C. A. (2009). "Violent video games: Learning processes and outcomes." In R. E. Ferdig (ed.), *Handbook of research on effective electronic gaming in education* (pp. 876–892). Hershey, PA: Information Science Reference.

Tajfel, H. & Turner, J. C. (1986). "The social identity theory of intergroup behavior." In S. Worchel & W. G. Austin (eds), *The psychology of intergroup relations* (2nd edn, pp. 7–24), Chicago: Nelson-Hall.

Tanner, L. R., Haddock, S. A., Zimmerman, T. S., & Lund, L. K. (2003). "Images of couples and families in Disney feature-length animated films." *The American Journal of Family Therapy, 31,* 355–373.

Tantleff-Dunn, S. & Thompson, J. K. (1998). "Body image and appearance-related feedback: Recall, judgement, and affective response." *Journal of Social and Clinical Psychology, 17,* 319–340.

Tedeschi, J. T. & Quigley, B. M. (1996). "Limitations of laboratory paradigms for studying aggression." *Aggression and Violent Behavior, 1,* 163–177.

Thomas, R. (2006). *Health communication.* New York: Springer Science+Business Media.

Thompson, J. (2007). *Massacre at Virginia Tech: Interview with MSNBC.* Retrieved from http://www.msnbc.msn.com/id/18220228/ Retrieved on September 10, 2010.

Thompson, J. K. (1990). *Body image disturbance: Assessment and treatment*. New York: Pergamon Press.

Thompson, J. K. (1992). "Body image: Extent of disturbance, associated features, theoretical models, assessment methodologies, intervention strategies and a proposal for a new DSM-IV diagnostic category – Body image disorder." In M. Hersen, R. M. Eisler, & P. M. Miller (eds), *Progress in behavior modification* (pp. 3–54). Sycamore, IL: Sycamore.

Thompson, J. K., Heinberg, L. J., & Tantleff, F. (1991). "The Physical Appearance Comparison Scale (PACS)." *The behavior Therapist, 14*, 174.

Thompson, T. L. & Zerbinos, E. (1995). "Gender roles in animated cartoons: Has the picture changed in 20 years?" *Sex Roles, 32*, 651–673.

Thompson, T. L. & Zerbinos, E. (1997). "Television cartoons: Do children notice it's a boy's world?" *Sex Roles, 37*, 415–432.

Thomsen, S. R., McCoy, J. K., & Williams, M. (2001). "Internalizing the impossible: Anorexic outpatients' experiences with women's beauty and fashion magazines." *Eating Disorders, 9*, 49–64.

Thomsen, S. R., Weber, M. M., & Brown, L. B. (2001). "The relationship between health and fitness magazine reading and eating-disordered weight-loss methods among high school girls." *American Journal of Health Education, 32*, 133–38.

Thornton, B. & Maurice, J. (1997). "Physique contrast effects: Adverse impact of idealised body images for women." *Sex Roles, 37*, 433–439.

Tidwell, L. C. & Walther, J. B. (2002). "Computer-mediated communication effects on disclosure, impressions and interpersonal evaluations: Getting to know one another a bit at a time." *Human Communication Research, 28*, 317–348.

Tiggemann, M. & Pickering, A. S. (1996). "Role of television in adolescent women's body dissatisfaction and drive for thinness." *International Journal of Eating Disorders, 20*, 199–203.

Till, B. D. & Shimp, T. A. (1998). "Endorsers in advertising: The case of negative celebrity information." *Journal of Advertising, 27*, 67–82.

Todorov, A. & Bargh J. A. (2002). "Automatic sources of aggression." *Aggression and Violent Behavior, 7*, 53–68.

Tourangeau, R. (2004). "Survey research and societal change." *Annual Review of Psychology, 55*, 775–801.

Tripp, C., Jensen, T. D., & Carlson, L. (1994). "The effects of multiple product endorsement on consumers' attitudes and intentions." *Journal of Consumer Research, 20*, 535–547.

Tse, A. B. C. & Lee, R. P. W. (2001). "Zapping behavior during commercial breaks." *Journal of Advertising Research, 41*, 25–29.

Turkle, S. (1995). *Life on the screen: Identity in the age of the Internet*. New York: Simon & Schuster.

Turnock, B. J. (2004). *Public health: What it is and how it works*. Boston: Jones and Bartlett Publishers.

Uhlmann, E. & Swanson, J. (2004). "Exposure to violent video games increases automatic aggressiveness." *Journal of Adolescence, 27*, 41–52.

United States Department of Health and Human Services. (2000a). "Chapter 11: Health communication." *Healthy People 2010* (2nd edn). Washington, DC: U.S. Government Printing Office.

United States Department of Health and Human Services. (2000b). "A systematic approach to health improvement." *Healthy People 2010* (2nd edn). Washington, DC: U.S. Government Printing Office.

Unsworth, G., Devilly, G. J., & Ward, T. (2007). "The effect of playing violent video games on adolescents: Should parents be quaking in their boots?" *Psychology, Crime and Law, 13*, 383–394.

U.S. Census (2008). "Census fact finder." Retrieved from http://factfinder.census.gov/servlet/ACSSAFFFacts?_event=&geo_id=01000US&_geoContext=01000US&_street=&_county=&_cityTown=&_state=&_zip=&_lang=en&_sse=on&ActiveGeoDiv=&_useEV=&pctxt=fph&pgsl=010&_submenuId=factsheet_1&ds_name=null&_ci_nbr=null&qr_name=null&reg=null%3Anull&_keyword=&_industry= Retrieved on August 4, 2011.

U.S. Commission on Civil Rights (1979). *Window dressing on the set: An update.* Washington DC. Retrieved from http://www.eric.ed.gov/PDFS/ED166336.pdf Retrieved on August 4, 2011.

Valente, T. W. (2001). "Evaluating communication campaigns." In R. Rice & C. Atkin (eds), *Public communication campaigns* (3rd edn, pp. 105–124). Thousand Oaks, CA: Sage.

Valkenburg, P. M., Cantor, J., & Peeters, A. L. (2000). "Fright reactions to television: A child Survey." *Communication Research, 27*, 82–99.

Valkenburg, P. M. & Peter, J. (2007). "Preadolescents' and adolescents' online communication and their closeness to friends." *Developmental Psychology, 43*, 267–277.

Valkenburg, P. M., Peter, J., & Schouten, A. P. (2006). "Friend networking sites and their relationship to adolescents' well being and social self-esteem." *CyberPsychology & Behavior, 9*, 584–590.

Van den Bulck, J. (2000). "Is television bad for your health? behavior and body image of the adolescent 'couch potato'." *Journal of Youth and Adolescence, 219*, 273–288.

Vliegenthart, R. & Walgrave, S. (2008). "The contingency of intermedia agenda setting: A longitudinal study in Belgium." *Journalism & Mass Communication Quarterly, 85*, 860–877.

Vincent, M. A. & McCabe, M. P. (2000). "Gender differences among adolescents in family and peer influences on body dissatisfaction, weight loss, and binge eating behaviors." *Journal of Youth and Adolescence, 29*, 205–211.

Vollmers, S. & Mizerski, R. (1994). "A review and investigation into the effectiveness of product placements in films." *Proceedings of the American Academy of Advertising*, 97–102.

Vorderer, P. & Ritterfield, U. (2003). "Children's future programming and media use between entertainment and education." In E. L. Palmer & B. Young (eds), *The faces of televisual media: Teaching, violence, selling to children* (pp. 241–262). Mahwah, NJ: Lawrence Erlbaum.

Vorhaus, M. (2008). "Internet and TV lead list of ways men pass the time." *Advertising Age, 79*, 17.

Waite, B. C. (2010). "E-mail and Electoral Fortunes: Obama's Campaign Internet Insurgency." In J. A. Hendricks & R. E. Denton, Jr (eds), *Communicator-in-chief: How Barack Obama used new media technology to win the White House.* Lanham: Lexington Books.

Wakefield, K. L. (1995). "The pervasive effects of social influence on sporting event attendance." *Journal of Sport and Social Issues, 19*, 335–351.

Walker, M., Langmeyer, L., & Langmeyer, D. (1992). "Celebrity endorsers: Do you get what you pay for?" *Journal of Consumer Marketing, 9*, 69–76.

Wallack, L. & Dorfman, L. (2004). "Putting policy into health communication: The role of media advocacy." In R. Rice & C. Atkin (eds), *Public communication campaigns* (3rd edn, pp. 389–401). Thousand Oaks, CA: Sage.

Waller, D. S. (1999). "Attitudes towards offensive advertising: An Australian study." *Journal of Consumer Marketing, 16*, 288–294.

Waller, D. S. (2004). "What factors make controversial advertising offensive? A preliminary study." Paper presented at ANZAC Conference, Sydney.

Waller, G., Hamilton, K., & Shaw, J. (1992). "Media influences on body size estimation in eating disordered and comparison subjects." *British Review of Bulimia and Anorexia Nervosa, 6*, 81–87.

Walma van der Molen, J. H. & Bushman, B. J. (2008). "Children's direct fright and worry reactions to violence in fiction and news television programs." *The Journal of Pediatrics, 153*, 420–424.

Wang, Y. & Sun, S. (2010). "Assessing beliefs, attitudes, and behavioral responses toward online advertising in three countries." *International Business Review, 19*, 333–344.

Wann, D. L. (1995). "Preliminary validation of the Sport Fan Motivation Scale." *Journal of Sport and Social Issues, 19*, 377–396.

Want, S. C. (2009). "Meta-analytic moderators of experimental exposure to media portrayals of women on female appearance satisfaction: Social comparisons as automatic processes." *Body Image, 6*, 257–269.

Want, S. C., Vickers, K., & Amos, J. (2009). "The influence of television programs on appearance satisfaction: Making and mitigating social comparisons to 'Friends'." *Sex Roles, 60*, 642–655.

Wartella, E. A. & Stout, P. A. (2002). "The evolution of mass media and health persuasion models." In W. Crano & M. Burgoon (eds), *Mass media and drug prevention: Classic and contemporary theories and research* (pp. 19–34). Mahwah, NJ: Lawrence Earlbaum.

Wason, S. D. (2004). *Grant writing handbook.* Hoboken, NJ: John Wiley.

Wassenaar, D., Le Grange, D., & Winship, J. (2000). "The prevalence of eating disorder pathology in a cross-ethnic population of female students in South Africa." *European Eating Disorders Review, 8*, 225–236.

Watkins, N. (2010). "I set up a 'pro-ana' site and dropped to 6st. Now I know this destroys lives." *The Sun*, 23 March. Retrieved from www.thesun.co.uk/sol/homepage/woman/2903057.

Weaver, D. H. & Drew, D. (2006). "Voter learning in the 2004 presidential election: Did the media matter?" *Journalism and Mass Communication Quarterly, 83*, 25–42.

Weber, R., Ritterfeld, U., & Mathiak, K. (2006). "Does playing violent video games induce Aggression? Empirical Evidence of Functional Magnetic Resonance Imaging Study." *Media Psychology, 8*, 39–60.

Weisband S. & Atwater L. (1999). "Evaluating self and others in electronic and face-to-face groups." *Journal of Applied Psychology, 84*, 632–639.

Weisband, S. & Kiesler, S. (1996). "Self disclosure on computer forms: Meta analysis and implications." CHI '96. Retrieved from http://www.sigchi.org/chi96/proceedings/papers/Weisband/sw_txt.htm Retrieved on August 4, 2011.

Weston, M. A. (1996). *Native Americans in the news: Images of Indians in the twentieth century press*. Wesport, CT: Greenwood.

What Americans Do Online: Social Media and Games Dominate Activity. New York: The Nielsen Company web site. Retrieved from http://blog.nielsen.com/nielsenwire/online_mobile/what-americans-doonline-social-media-and-games-dominate-activity/ Retrieved on August 4, 2011.

White, D. G. (1985). *Ar'n't I a woman? Female slaves in the plantation south*. New York: W. W. Norton and Company.

Whittaker, A., Davis, M., Shaffer, D., & Johnson, J. (1989). "The struggle to be thin: A survey of anorexic and bulimic symptoms in a non-referred adolescent population." *Psychological Medicine, 19*, 143–163.

Wike, T. L. & Fraser, M. W. (2009). "School shootings: Making sense of the senseless." *Aggression and Violent Behavior, 14*, 162–169.

Wilcox, D. L., Cameron, G. T., Ault, P. H., & Agee, W. K. (2003). *Public Relations: Strategies and Tactics*. Boston, MS: Pearson Education.

Wilkins, K. (1995). "Middle Eastern Women in Western Eyes: A Study of US Press Photographs of Middle Eastern Women." In Y. Kamalipour (ed.), *The US Media and the Middle East: Image and Perception* (pp. 50–61). Westport CT: Greenwood Press.

Williams, D., Yee, N., & Caplan, S. (2008). "Who plays, how much and why? Debunking the stereotypical gamer profile." *Journal of Computer Mediated Communication, 13*, 993–1018.

Williams, J. M. & Currie, C. (2000). "Self-esteem and physical development in early adolescence: Pubertal timing and body image." *Journal of Early Adolescence, 20*, 129–149.

Williams, T. M. (1986). *The impact of television: A natural experiment in three communities*. New York: Academic Press.

Wilson, B. J., Kunkel, D., Linz, D. Potter, W. J., Donnerstein, E., Smith, S. L., Blumenthal, E., & Berry, M. (1997). "Violence in television programming overall: University of California, Santa Barbara study." In M. Seawall (ed.), *National Television Study* (pp. 3–268). Thousand Oaks, CA: Sage.

Wilson, J., Peebles, R., Hardy, K. K., & Litt, I. F. (2006). "Surfing for thinness: A pilot study of pro-eating disorder web site usage in adolescents with eating disorders." *Pediatrics, 118*, 1635–1643.

Wilson, N. (2010). "Civilized vampires versus savage werewolves: Race and ethnicity in the Twilight series." In M. Click, J. S. Aubrey, & E. Behm-Morawitz, *Bitten by Twilight: Youth culture, media, & the vampire franchise*. New York: Peter Lang.

Witte, K. & Allen, M. (2000). "A meta-analysis of fear appeals: Implications for effective public health campaigns." *Health Education & Behavior, 27*, 591–615.

Witte, K., Meyer, G., & Martell, D. (2001). *Effective health risk messages: A step-by-step guide*. Thousand Oaks, CA: Sage.

Wood, R. T. A., Gupta, R., Derevensky, J. L., & Griffiths, M. (2004). "Video game playing and gambling in adolescents: Common risk factors." *Journal of Child and Adolescent Abuse, 14*, 77–100.

Wood, S. (2010, May 5). "Around the Bloc: Shifting 'divide' in CV mortality haunts former Soviet states. Retrieved from The Heart.org web site http://www.theheart.org/article/1074755.do Retrieved on October 26, 2010.

Woolf, M. (2010). "Minister demands airbrush health warning." *The Sunday Times*, 25 July, p. 7.

World Health Organization. "About WHO: Definition of Health." Retrieved from https://apps.who.int/aboutwho/en/definition.html Retrieved on August 4, 2011.

World Health Organization. (2006a). "Gaining health: The European strategy for the prevention and control of noncommunicable diseases." Copenhagen, Denmark: World Health Organization Regional Office for Europe. Retrieved from: http://www.euro.who.int/__data/assets/pdf_file/0008/76526/E89306.pdf Retrieved on August 4, 2011.

World Health Organization (2006b). "Marketing of food and non-alcoholic beverages to children: Report of a WHO forum and technical meeting." Oslo, Norway.

Wright, C. W. (1986). *Mass communication: A sociological perspective* (3rd edn). New York: Random House.

Wykes, M. & Gunter, B. (2005). *The media and body image: If looks could kill.* London: Sage.

Xu, J. Q., Kochanek, K. D., Murphy, S. L., & Tejada-Vera, B. (2010). "Deaths: Final Data for 2007." *National Vital Statistics Report, 58*(19).

Yates, S. (2007). "Worldwide PC Adoption Forecast, 2007 To 2015." Retrieved from http://www.forrester.com/rb/research Retrieved on May 28, 2010.

Yee, N. (2006). "The demographics, motivations and derived experiences of users of Massively Multi-user Online Graphical Environments." *Presence: Teleoperators and Virtual Environments, 15*, 309–329.

Yee, N. (2007). "Motivations of play in online games." *CyberPsychology & Behavior, 9*, 772–775.

Yue, X. D. & Cheung, C-K. (2000). "Selection of favourite idols and models among Chinese young people: A comparative study in Hong Kong and Nanjing." *International Journal of Behavioral Development, 24*, 91–98.

Zhang, Y., Dixon, T. L., & Conrad, K. (2009). "Rap music videos and African American women's body image: The moderating role of ethnic identity." *Journal of Communication, 59*, 262–278.

Zillmann, D. (1983). "Arousal and aggression." In R. G. Geen & E. Donnerstein (eds). *Aggression: Theoretical and empirical reviews* (pp. 75–102). New York: Academic Press.

Zillmann, D. & Bryant, J. (1984). "Effects of massive exposure to pornography." In N. M. Malamuth & E. Donnerstein (eds), *Pornography and sexual aggression* (pp. 115–138). New York: Academic Press.

Zillmann, D., Bryant, J., Comisky, P., & Medoff, N. (1981). "Sexual material, anger, and aggression." *European Journal of Social Psychology, 11*, 233–252.

Zillmann, D., Lei, C., Knobloch, S., & Callison, C. (2004). "Effects of lead framing on selective exposure to Internet news reports." *Communication Research, 31*, 58–81.

Zimbardo, P.G. (1969). "The human choice: Individuation, reason, and order vs. deindividuation, impulse and chaos." In W. J. Arnold & D. Levine (eds), *Nebraska symposium on motivation* (pp. 237–307). Lincoln, NB: University of Nebraska Press.

Zorbough, H. (1949). "What adults think of comics as reading for children." *Journal of Educational Sociology*, 23, 225–235.

Zuckerman, D., Singer, C., & Singer, J. (1980). "Children's television viewing, racial and sex role attitudes." *Journal of Applied Social Psychology*, *10*, 281–294.

Zwier, S. (2009). "Medicalisation of food advertising: Nutrition and health claims in magazine food advertisements." *Appetite*, *53*, 109–113.

Index